Praise for Clare Rewcastle Brown's previous boo'-
from which this book is

'A monument to public-interest
Peter Alford, *Australia.*

'A triumph'
Andrew Leci, *Unreserved*

'A cracking read on an important financial scandal'
Andrew Swan, Head of Global Emerging Markets Equities, Blackrock

'Deserves to be read as a lesson to us all in our attempts to construct a more
humane and caring world.'
Victor T King, *Mekong Review*

'[The 1MDB scandal] would probably still be percolating if it hadn't been for Clare
Rewcastle Brown... She never stopped digging. What she dug up would form the
basis for stories in the *Wall Street Journal*, the *New York Times* and a long list of
other publications... required reading.'
John Berthelsen, *Asia Sentinel*

'Rewcastle Brown's indefatigable attention to detail and exhaustive quest to expose
the wrongdoing are a testimony to first-class investigative journalism... essential
reading.'
Sean Smith, *East Review*

'Clare embarked on what can only be described as a brilliant 10-year journey of
investigative journalism... essential reading for all government officers in authority,
to show them how sheer greed and colossal theft can deprive a country's entire
population of their economic rights and benefits as a developing nation.'
Howard Henshaw, *Interlib*

'Clare's dogged (and, to some, more than a little annoying) persistence, and an
incredible nose for the fishy stuff, uncovered the heist of the century. The explosive
exposés rocked the nation, and precipitated the fall of the Malaysian government for
the first time in 60 years.'
The Right Honourable Tony Pua, Member of Parliament for Damansara, Malaysia

'I cannot overstate Clare's role in the changes that Malaysia is seeing today.
Were it not for her dogged perseverance in digging for the truth, Malaysia would
probably still be under the BN/UMNO regime, and fast rotting into a bankrupt
kleptocracy.'
The Right Honourable Baru Bian, Member of Parliament for Selangau, Malaysia

Clare Rewcastle Brown is an investigative journalist who focuses on environmental destruction in Malaysia and global financial corruption. She is the founder of the website sarawakreport.org, the radio stations Radio Free Sarawak and Radio Nyawa Sarawak, and the reforestation organisation ForestSEA. She was born in Sarawak and lives in London.

Eddie Barnes is a political advisor and a former journalist, living in Scotland. He was political editor of *The Scotsman* and *Scotland on Sunday* between 2004 and 2013. His interest in Malaysia stems from his wife, Geeta, who comes from Malaysian Borneo and is an activist in the Global Bersih movement. They live in Glasgow and have three children.

THE WOLF CATCHER

*The true story of how one woman exposed
the world's biggest heist*

Clare Rewcastle Brown
with Eddie Barnes

Lost World Press

Published in the UK in 2019 by Lost World Press
an imprint of Lost World Productions

A CIP catalogue record for this book is available from the British Library.

ISBN 978-1-5272-4475-7

This book is adapted from *The Sarawak Report* by Clare Rewcastle Brown

Cover design by Colin Foo, Colinslab

Book design by LTD Design Consultants, www.ltddesign.co.uk

Printed in the UK by TJ International
Trecerus Industrial Estate
Padstow, Cornwall, PL28 8RW, UK

To the brave people who faced great danger
to bring this story to light

CONTENTS

PART THREE: THE BACKLASH

PART FOUR: DOWNFALL

ACKNOWLEDGEMENTS

The adage two heads are better than one is never truer than in the world of journalism and particularly in this case, where Eddie's head has been added to the telling of my story. This was an assignment we both jumped at not with an advance in mind but because it mattered. Eddie has family from Malaysia and his many hours spent adding such a page-turning quality to the narrative has also been a tribute to the invaluable advice and support of his wife Geeta, and their children Ishan, Anya and Kiran. We owe a big debt also to Naomi Roth for guiding the publication, See See Leong for her wonderful support and encouragement, Colin Foo for his fantastic cover design, Patricia Kuckelmann for her skilful editing and Sam Warshaw for his help in so many ways in bringing the story to print. My thanks also to so many friends and colleagues from the media world who have generously supported me in this project – Yasmin Pasha and Michelle Bramley particularly for their added work at ForestSEA. And again to my father John, my husband Andrew, sons Alexander and Patrick, my brother Patrick and dog Jake for patiently sticking by the wandering female in the family through so many years of unexpected adventure.

INTRODUCTION

I'M a journalist, a working mum, based in London. A decade ago, I started digging around dirty money and corruption in Malaysia, the country where I was born. I ended up facing an international arrest warrant (since rescinded), death threats, an assassination plot, and I nearly lost my home. I joined up with some incredibly courageous people from around the world who were in danger themselves, but who were prepared to face it down in pursuit of the truth. Together, we ended up kick-starting the largest kleptocracy investigation in US judicial history, humbled one of Wall Street's mightiest banking institutions, and helped a democracy movement on the other side of the world change the course of a nation.

We discovered that, without checks, balances and a free press, authoritarian politicians can end up thinking they can get away with murder, literally. We found out how uncomfortable truths and facts can be quashed by those in power, and how they are using social media to slander and defame their opponents. And we saw how crime and corruption is aided and abetted across the world by so-called respectable financial institutions, PR firms and legal practices, all willing to add a varnish of credibility to the actions of petty thieves and turn a blind eye in pursuit of an easy pay day.

We had to take them on. And in my case, do so while juggling the needs of one increasingly bemused husband, two teenage boys, and a deeply under-walked dog.

People like us aren't supposed to be able to take on powerful interests, are they? By that, I mean people who work on their own, with little or no money, armed only with an internet connection and a sense that the world is an unfair place and needs correcting sometimes. We're helpless against powerful political and commercial interests, aren't we? Add to all that the fact that most of us are usually too busy just trying to cope with the normal stuff of life. I mean, challenging corporates and powerful politicians, *as well* as getting the weekly shop sorted? Where are you supposed to find the time?

It turns out that you can find it, and that – with a lot of persistence – yes, you can bring the powerful to heel. This story shows how a coalition of ordinary people – from opposition politicians, radio DJs, pro-democracy campaigners, human rights lawyers, whistle-blowing bankers, and campaigning journalists – managed to do so.

Time and time again, people who were to play a part in this bizarre story would remark that it was all so outlandish and unbelievable that it was like being part of a movie. Certainly the plot is too contorted ever to be fictional. So, in a way, it's highly appropriate that I begin this story with an actual film.

It was called *The Wolf of Wall Street*, and the night is 12th January 2014, the evening of the 71st Golden Globes ceremony at the Beverly Hilton, Hollywood.

PART ONE

SARAWAK REPORT

1. WOLVES

January 2014, Hollywood

THE ballroom at the Beverly Hilton shimmered in the glare of TV lights, stage decorations, and the gleaming white smiles of hundreds of Hollywood's beautiful people. The 71st Golden Globes ceremony, the annual precursor to the Oscars, was celebrating the best of film from the previous year and, around the room, seated at round tables, tanned star after tanned star was awaiting their moment, grins fixed, preparing for the appropriate look: modesty and bashfulness should they win, well-disguised jealousy should they lose. The evening had reached one of its many climaxes: best actor in a motion picture. A-lister Jennifer Lawrence, dressed in a full length white ball gown, opened the envelope to announce the winner. Nominated were Christian Bale, Bruce Dern, Oscar Isaac and Joaquin Phoenix but "the winner is", Lawrence declared, pausing theatrically, "Leonardo DiCaprio".

In the well of the auditorium, the immaculately turned out figure of DiCaprio rose from his table to accept the applause around him. The award was for his role as Jordan Belfort in the controversial movie *The Wolf of Wall Street*, released the previous year. The film was adapted from Belfort's autobiography, charting his near deranged hedonistic lifestyle as a gambler on the international stock exchange in New York. DiCaprio had lobbied for years to make the film, and persuaded director Martin Scorsese to make it. Here was justification of his work: the appreciation and recognition of his peers.

Seated at DiCaprio's table, Scorsese led the applause. But first to get a hug from the man himself, however, was a young Asian man seated next to DiCaprio called Riza Aziz. Riza could barely contain his joy, grinning like a Cheshire Cat. DiCaprio unlocked himself from the man's embrace, ascended to the stage, kissed Lawrence, took hold of his golden award, and turned to the audience around him to commence the obligatory list of thankyous.

Scorsese was first: with all the humility he could muster, DiCaprio declared how honoured he had been to work beside him. Then DiCaprio moved to the others at his table. "So, thanks to Joey, Jho and Riz for not only being collaborators on this movie but for taking a risk on the movie," he added.

The applause continued. But around the auditorium and in living rooms across America, people would have been forgiven for asking: who? They weren't exactly household names. Joey was at the table sitting near Scorsese – he was Joey McFarland, one of the co-producers of the movie. 'Jho' was absent – that was Jho Low, a Chinese Malaysian businessman who had stumped up the cash to fund the film. We will hear a lot more of him in this story. And 'Riz'? Riz – or Riza Aziz – was the other producer of the movie. He also happened to be the step-son of Najib Razak, the then Prime Minister of Malaysia.

Riz was still applauding and now looked so happy he might burst. Not just a hug but a hug *and* a special mention. From Leonardo DiCaprio. It was a long way from his roots back in Malaysia. Now, here he was being lauded by the world's most glamorous film star at one of Hollywood's biggest nights of the year. This was quite a night for him and the absent Jho. Across Tinseltown, the award that night put fresh focus back on these two enigmatic Malaysians and their remarkably deep pockets.

Jho and Riz had first emerged into the Hollywood scene three years earlier, in 2011. This was a lean period in LA, with the financial crash having sucked out much of the investment in town. Yet Jho in particular seemed to have cash to burn. He and Riza launched their company, Red Granite, with a party of unprecedented extravagance in Cannes in 2011. Jho immediately began spending money for fun. Celebrities, in particular, benefitted from his largesse: he paid agencies millions of dollars to get them to attend his parties, including Jamie Foxx, Alicia Keys and – a particular favourite – Paris Hilton. In 2012, Jho took her to the football world cup in

South Africa (where, infamously, she was stopped for possession of cannabis). It was subsequently reported that, just to attend one of his parties, he had paid her a cool $1 million.

Most of all, Jho lavished attention, and cash, on DiCaprio. There were trips to Las Vegas, with DiCaprio reputedly paid $500,000 a time. There was a holiday on board the world's fifth largest yacht, the *Topaz*, with helicopters on stand-by to ferry DiCaprio and friends to the World Cup (this time, in Brazil). And there were donations of an original Mark Rothko painting and valuable Roy Epstein statue for some of DiCaprio's fundraisers. When, later that season, DiCaprio missed out on an Oscar for his role, Jho decided to intervene, and splashed out $600,000 to buy one of Marlon Brando's Oscars which he then presented to DiCaprio as a 40th birthday present.

The spending and the ostentation was nuts. At Jho's parties, ubiquitous magnums of the most expensive Cristal champagne became a signature feature. Jho would spend tens of thousands of pounds a night, making sure everybody got their fill. On one occasion at the exclusive Les Caves du Roy nightclub in St Tropez, in early 2010, it was reported that Jho had got involved in a bidding war with fellow tycoon Wynton Fisher, to see who could waste the most money on champagne. Fisher gave in first. It was then announced that, in just one night, Jho had bought champagne in the club worth a staggering 2 million euros.

It culminated in his funding *The Wolf of Wall Street*. DiCaprio had been desperate to get the story on film – with him in the lead role. Scorsese was lined up. But, with cash tight and nobody taking risks, even mega-firms like Sony were shrugging their shoulders and saying no. Jho and Riza, however, saw no such problems. Eyebrows soon were raised around town. Jho and Riza were still relatively unknown. And Joey McFarland wasn't even a producer: he was little more than a party planner who managed celebrity appearances at LA events and who had met Jho and Riz through his work with Paris Hilton. Yet now it appeared that this trio were able to pretty much do as they pleased.

More than $100 million was handed over. The irony was exquisite.

The Wolf of Wall Street was being made to expose the insanely excessive behaviour of those at the top of New York's financial world. Yet the self-same movie was only being made thanks to the extravagant spending habits of Jho and Riza, the new champagne kings of America.

In the background, the question grew: who were these guys? Naturally, people wanted to know their story. In an interview with the *Hollywood Reporter* in 2012, Riza was asked how he got to go from Malaysia to Hollywood. Insouciantly, he declared that he had been an investment banker in London before going on a "sabbatical" during the financial crash in 2008. "I came to the US and was offered the opportunity to get involved in a lot of different things business-wise," he added. "And one of them was to be involved in a film with some friends." From that, "we decided to have a company… I brought Joey in at an early stage," he went on.

It all sounded so reassuring and authoritative – and given his well-known political connections back home in Malaysia, plausible too. If anyone had dug a little, however, they would have discovered that the truth was rather different. His career in finance had involved jobs working in the banking section of KPMG, and as a customer and investment adviser at HSBC. So much for taking on the world of finance. And while he came from political royalty in Malaysia, there wasn't a huge amount of money in the family. Likewise, the lanky and bespectacled McFarland, who described himself as a "private equity cowboy from Kentucky", had actually left his home state with a trail of mundane jobs and little cash.

And Jho? Yes, he came from a comfortable background, having attended the top British boarding school of Harrow before studying at Wharton business school in Pennsylvania (alma mater to Donald Trump). But his family weren't super-rich. He didn't have Lamborghini money. Yet now, still in his late 20s, he was throwing dollars all over town like a latter day Rockefeller. Fortunately, nobody dug too deep. There's only one record of them being asked about their funds, when the *Hollywood Reporter* interviewed Riza and McFarland about their rapid rise to fame. "How much money are you backed by?" the reporter asked.

"We do not talk about that," McFarland replied tersely.

Riz then interjected: "I will say that I have money invested in the company. It shows that I have skin in the game."

"We also," he declared, "have a group of investors mainly from the Middle East and Asia."

It was, oddly enough, a pretty truthful answer. Within Red Granite, Riza's company, the word was that the money came from Jho's connections back home in Malaysia. That was true too. But nobody was allowed to say – or perhaps nobody knew – who those connections were.

◆ ◆ ◆

This story of those connections and where Jho and his friends got his money from is the story of this book. In total, it's the story of the theft of an estimated $7 billion, at least. Yes, you heard that right: $7 billion.

DiCaprio's award in 2014 marked a significant moment when people began to look more deeply into this theft, turning this obscure story into a global scandal. But the money trail really begins some time earlier, five years before.

And if it can be said to begin anywhere in particular, it starts in August 2009 off the coast of Monte Carlo, on board an enormous mega-yacht called the *Alfa Nero*. VIP guest that day was the "Big Boss" behind Jho and his friends, and the man I would hunt down for the coming decade: the Prime Minister of Malaysia, a man called Najib Razak.

2. ALFA MALE

20th August 2009, the French Riviera

PRIME Minister Najib Razak and his wife Rosmah Mansor looked out onto the distant coast of the French Riviera and smiled. This – the luxury, the sheer exclusivity, the smell of wealth all around them – *this* was what they had always yearned for. They'd spent years working up the greasy pole to get to this place. Now, they had made it.

The couple were on board one of the Mediterranean's most outlandish examples of ostentation and super-wealth, the 269-foot super-yacht, the *Alfa Nero*. Launched two years earlier in 2007, the yacht came complete with a 26-strong crew, six cabins, an extended main deck, and swimming pool. Today, it was Najib and Rosmah's plaything. They were the yacht's VIP guests for the day, and guests, no less of a member of the Saudi royal family. A few months earlier, in spring 2009, Najib had finally achieved his lifelong ambition, when he had been sworn in as prime minister of the Southeast Asian nation of Malaysia. Power gained, now it was time to enjoy it.

It came easily to him. A suave 57-year-old with fair skin and silver moustache, he was the son of Malaysia's second prime minister, Abdul Razak Hussein, and had long considered the top post to be his personal birthright. He had been sent to public school in England to learn the ways of Malaysia's former colonial master. He had inherited his father's seat at just 23. And he had quickly been picked out by Dr Mahathir Mohamad, Malaysia's longest serving prime minister and the country's dominant political figure, as a potential successor. All that breeding had brought with it an instinctive and confident understanding of how to gain power and exploit it. Like Mahathir, he had given himself the title of finance minister as well as the top post, which put numerous state-owned conglomerates under his authority. At a stroke, he had gained control over about half the value of the 35th largest economy in the world. "Cash is king," he liked to tell Mahathir at the time, referring to the practice of Malaysian money politics: the doling out of contracts, party patronage and bribes to keep and win votes. The practice had been going on for decades. Najib had grander ambitions.

As did his wife. Rosmah, the self-styled First Lady of Malaysian politics was already a notorious figure in Southeast Asia. She, many Malaysians believed, was the dominant force in her marriage with Najib, conducting her own kitchen cabinet and known to insist on decisions being made one way or the other. She sent an agent each week to her husband's office to pick up copies of all the paperwork to make sure she knew exactly what was going on. As well as enjoying political power, she was known widely for her addiction to material excess. Like the Philippines' Imelda Marcos, Rosmah was hooked on everything from oversized jewellery, eye-wateringly expensive Hermès and Birkin handbags, as well as gold and fancy diamond bling of every description.

The *Alfa Nero* was the stuff of her dreams. And she and Najib's host that day, Turki bin Abdullah, only added to the sense of exclusivity. Turki was the seventh son of the then king of Saudi Arabia. And while he may not have actually owned the yacht (it had been rented out for the occasion (at a reputed cost of a million dollars a week), nor had the cash to pay for the rent himself (the cost was met from family funds), his position as a member of the Saudi royalty gave him superstar status. Turki was building a career trading on the vast prestige that came from being a scion to the wealthiest dynasty on earth. He knew that his status would give him access to governments, leaders and money men the world over. He also knew that access to a yacht like the *Alfa Nero* would shine even more stardust in their eyes.

That day, Turki was joined by his business partner and childhood friend, Tarek Obaid. The pair had already set up a number of companies which picked up business exploiting the prince's family connections. The group was completed by the same Malaysian businessman who, five years later, would be thanked so effusively by

DiCaprio: Jho Low. Given the exalted status of the rest of the group, Low looks in the photographs like the odd one out that day: as if he is a bystander who has somehow managed to blag his way into an aristocrat's party. Yet he was, in fact, the crucial fixer behind the day's events.

Hailing from the Malaysian city of Penang, the former colonial outpost in the northwest of the country, Jho had, from a young age, been steeped in the art of a fast buck. His father, Larry, became a millionaire and one of the city's wealthier residents. He wasn't shy of showing it either.

Jho would turn out to be very much his father's son. At Wharton, before he even graduated, he had set up his first company, the British Virgin Islands-based Wynton group. In his early 20s, he began to make contacts in the Middle East, in particular, Abu Dhabi. His business plan was simply to act as an influential dealmaker; somebody who could connect wealth to power. To begin with, he did not actually have these contacts: he was just an over-confident young man hoping that he could wing it. But, through sheer persistence and brass neck, he elbowed his way into elite circles, and then span like hell – claiming to everybody he met that he was a lynchpin operator. By the late 2000s, he had managed to ingratiate himself with Najib's wife Rosmah at a prestigious yacht race in Malaysia. From this contact, he had netted himself an advisory role at a newly set up sovereign wealth fund in Malaysia, designed to invest oil revenues in state development. In his first coup, he convinced Abu Dhabi's sovereign wealth fund Mubadala to invest in a major infrastructure project in Malaysia, and gave much of the credit to Najib, now deputy prime minister. So, when Najib ascended to the top job, Jho was well positioned to act as the new PM's Mr Fix-It. After all, so trusted had he become by the first lady, he was said to be the one man allowed into her private bedroom, where he would perch on the bed and scheme with her.

It was Jho who had conceived of the day on the *Alfa Nero* with Turki. The idea was to use the luxurious outing to get Najib involved in what later would be described as a "joint venture" between Malaysia and Saudi Arabia. The reality was rather different – to cream off hundreds of millions of dollars into their own back pockets. Not for nothing, in coming years, would Jho earn his nickname "Jay Low", in honour of F Scott Fitzgerald's legendary fictional millionaire, Jay Gatsby. And not for nothing would Najib and Rosmah soon become a byword for kleptocracy.

The scale of their con would, in time, make the Marcos clan look like petty crooks. The weird thing, however, was that it would end up being me – at that time a freelance journalist from London, on the other side of the world, with no cash and no proper job – who would help expose the whole thing.

3. IN THE BLOOD

I AM a born journalist and learnt on the job. I'm somewhat dyslexic and my shorthand's lapsed. But I have the only real quality you need: I live for the story.

A few years ago, when I was working for a TV news programme, I took my two boys, Alex and Patrick, to McDonald's. It was a rare visit – I don't approve. So, when I got to the counter, I told the server I didn't want my boys drinking some sugary gloop and I asked instead for two glasses of water. It transpired that McDonald's, at the time, wouldn't oblige: you could get Coke, Fanta, Sprite, you name it, but basic H_2O was not on the menu. Angered, I walked out and ran a story on McDonald's the following week on their refusal to serve water. I fronted them up and asked them why. And I got them to change their policy. That's why, if you go to McDonald's today (and I still don't approve, by the way), you can get water for free if you want.

For me, reporting is less a job than a way of life. You don't stop seeing news stories when you leave work in the evening; you don't suddenly take off your reporter's hat because you happen to be with your kids. There are wrongs being perpetrated everywhere, just waiting to be exposed and reported on, even when you're buying a Big Mac.

I started out in the BBC World Service back in the eighties. I just wanted in at the door at the time, so I took a job as a secretary. I couldn't type and, thanks to my dyslexia, I couldn't spell either. After about a year, my boss, a decent old chap, declared I was the worst secretary he had ever come across and that this had to end.

That was my ticket into journalism. In order to spare more people my appalling secretarial skills, I was transferred to become a researcher with BBC news in their West London studios in Lime

Grove, where all the current affairs programmes were made in the 1980s. I soon graduated to assistant producer status, broadcasting the occasional voiceover on TV. Four years later, when Sky News was being set up in 1988, I was offered a job on their new flagship investigations programme. I left.

Sky sent me to work on their *Newsline* show, based heavily on Australia's *60 Minutes* programme. There were six of us in total and our orders were to go out and make a mark. That was fine by me.

Perhaps it comes from the Rewcastle gene. I was reared on stories of my grandmother, Attacta Genevieve Rewcastle, an Irishwoman who, after coming to England, became the first commissioned female officer in the British armed forces. She died young just as she was about to become one of the country's first female MPs too. It was expected that we, her grandchildren, would follow her example. Then there was the fact that my dad was a policeman and my mum a highly motivated nurse. I was never going to just let things go by. Journalism was the outlet for my moral indignation at the world. I didn't fear confrontation. I loved the feeling of getting a big story. And nothing could beat exposing some crook or another, and bringing them to book.

And I loved standing up for the little guy or woman. Some of my best stories came from just talking to people, like the woman at the check-out of my local supermarket. The essence of a good story for me was finding people who were being ripped off or mistreated by powerful interests, persuading them to tell their stories, treating them honestly and with dignity, and then holding whoever was to blame to account.

Looking back, that era feels like the Wild West. Journalism in those days was well resourced, and there were few limits. We were able to go wherever we wanted, and front up people as we chose. We worked all hours and I loved it.

When crack cocaine hit the UK in the early nineties, we exposed the drug-runners in South London. One night, after having noised up some particularly unpleasant gangsters, we had to run for it. The cameraman said he had served in Vietnam and had been less scared.

I followed it up with an *exposé* of a British con man who had set up shop in an orphanage in Romania where he was testing bogus AIDS drugs on sick babies, and restricting their access to milk because he wanted to push a new brand of 'medicinal' carrot juice. I was very good at lying when I met people like him. And, in order to get them in front of a camera, I played on the sexism of powerful men and their common assumption that, as a female journalist, I could be easily talked over. Then the tape began to run, and I slaughtered them with my research.

Another feature about women who kill their husbands following domestic abuse made such an impact that Carlton TV came calling and said they wanted our team to come and work for them. Off we went, working for a new show called *London Tonight*, and continued where we had left off. We toured the capital and made what you might call plain sight stories. At the time, there was a plethora of Romanian beggars on the streets, all carrying listless babies, the better to prick people's sympathy. We discovered the babies were being doped. We tracked down the ring leaders and exposed the lot of them. Within a week, the beggars disappeared. So-called "squeegee merchants" who would aggressively demand cash from motorists got the same treatment. Once, while driving in Westminster, I got an entirely unjustified parking ticket and decided to go to town. I proved that the local council was behind a scheme giving incentives to wardens in order to increase the number of tickets being issued. We got the system changed. That story was typical of me at the time: quite often, I would pick up on things happening in my own life. When I got a nanny to look after my newborn son Alex, I ended up running an investigation into the exploitation of child carers.

In the late nineties, I was briefly transferred to the House of Commons to report on the political village. I wasn't cut out for it and I hated the press release culture. Indeed the only political story I did cover wasn't in Westminster but in Hackney where, I discovered, the Conservatives and Liberal Democrats were taking advantage of proxy voting to cheat Labour voters and the system with it – four charged, two jailed. After a year or so I was let out and was sent back out on the streets. That was where I belonged.

But by the early 2000s, I was finding all the juggling impossible to manage. By now I had two boys, Alex and Patrick, who needed more attention than ever. So, like thousands of mothers, I decided to pack in the full-time job and try and fit work around home life. I didn't stop investigating. Indeed, it was as a freelance that I broke some of my best stories, such as a lengthy *exposé* of crooked developers in Spain who were grabbing land off British families who had bought up properties there.

However, I realised I wanted to start prioritising my time a bit more. I had enjoyed an unrelenting 20 years in TV journalism, always just going for the story and whatever was ahead of me. Now, with my time more limited, I guess I wanted to devote more of it to things close to my heart. The degrading state of our natural environment was at the top of my list. There were numerous places I wanted to highlight. But I knew which one had to come first: the Borneo state of Sarawak.

4. GOING HOME

IT was obvious that I would turn my attention to Sarawak; it was where my life began.

In the late fifties, my mother, Karis Hutchings, had followed her adventurous spirit and decided to emigrate to Borneo to work as a nurse. On her first day, she had been walking along the riverfront and noticed a local Englishman driving in his open-top sports car along one of the few tarmacked roads in the state. "Who's that?" she asked a colleague. "Don't bother," came the reply. "That's Rewcastle, but nobody has managed to nab him in years." 'Rewcastle' was at the time running the intelligence section of the colonial police force. They married in Brunei in 1958 and a year later I was born in Kuching, the state capital of Sarawak. My brother arrived four years later, after we had moved north to the neighbouring state of Sabah. By that time the former British colonies of Borneo had been absorbed into the newly independent Malaysia and became known as East Malaysia. Our family stayed on until 1968 with my father continuing to manage the police Special Branch there.

My earliest memories come from Sarekei, a town in the middle of Sarawak, where my parents were posted when I was aged two. The mental snapshots are of the classic wooden colonial house on stilts where we lived, with an open veranda and a grassy lawn that disappeared into surrounding jungle. I remember small children, belonging to the families of the *amahs*, who lived on the premises, and with whom I would play. I remember the family at the end of our garden who kept pigs underneath the tiny living space which made their home. At the end of the garden, my father and I would walk down to a river swamp where we would look for huge black crabs and the occasional crocodile. Pineapples and papayas were plentiful for anyone who wanted to pick. And everywhere, the jungle. Always the jungle.

One of the few family entertainments at that time was our gramophone – I had some children's records including an album of Christmas songs decorated with a picture of a lady dressed in a fur-lined red cloak, standing in snow. The picture fascinated me as a child in the tropics and I used to ask my mother what snow and the cold were like and she would tell me there was lots of both where she had been a girl. She would show me the ice-compartment of the fridge, which was always frosted up. "Snow is exactly like that but everywhere around in England in the winter – feel how cold it is!" she told me and I would be amazed.

As a child, of course, I didn't grasp the world around me. But this was a time of enormous change and disruption within the newly formed state of Malaysia. Following the Second World War, Japanese occupation had given way to the return of British rule. There then followed the years of the Emergency, when Chinese Communists took up arms against the British. Two years before my birth, in 1957, as the British divested themselves of an empire, Malaya had been granted independence. Six years later, British North Borneo – comprising Sarawak and Sabah – and the port of Singapore then joined too, to form the new state of Malaysia. Malaysians celebrated the birth of their new nation but the ethnic tension and political violence of the post war years was to continue. In 1965, Singapore was expelled from the new state. Malaysia, at the same time, had to deal with the 'confrontation' with Indonesia. The end of the sixties was then marked by race riots between the dominant Chinese and Malay groups that led to the deaths of hundreds of people, mostly Chinese, and the imposition of emergency rule.

It was a scary, turbulent period for the new nation and the entire region but by the time my parents decided to leave Malaysia to return to Britain, things began to settle down. The confrontation with Indonesia had ended following the fall of Sukarno. Singapore began to boom. And the wider Southeast Asian region went about the task of establishing itself as an economic force. Malaysia expanded rapidly. Money poured in, keen to exploit its rich natural reserves of oil and timber. And, at the centre of it, the dominant figure of post-independence Malaysian politics, Mahathir Mohamed, had begun to carve out a vision for his new country.

At its heart, his plan had been to raise up the status of the majority Malay population. Following independence, much of the wealth in the country lay in the hands of the large Chinese minority population; this was one of the explanations behind the sudden explosion in race related violence in 1969 when Malays had attacked their Chinese neighbours. But with the post-colonial settlement having handed political power to the Muslim Malay elites, Mahathir set about using that power to correct what he saw as an imbalance in the relationship. In his seminal book *The Malay Dilemma*, written in the wake of the race riots, he had proposed a program of affirmative action to correct the Malaysian Chinese hegemony in business. The 'dilemma' of the book's title was whether Malays should accept government aid to do so – Mahathir concluded that they should. His ideas were adopted quickly and, in 1981, elected as prime minister, Mahathir was able to implement them himself. Malays (officially called *bumiputera*, or sons of the soil) were given reserved senior positions in the civil services. Special schools were granted for their exclusive use. A target to ensure they controlled 30 percent of all corporate equity by 1990 was established. Malay home buyers were even granted a discount of up to 15 percent on new housing.

By the 2000s, Mahathir's policies had transformed the country. Huge investment in the country, along with the leg up given to Malays, had done much of what he wanted. But with government in charge of allocating contracts on everything from infrastructure to oil to subsidies, it also led to rampant cronyism and corruption. Major projects were awarded to Malay companies with ties to UMNO, the ruling party. Kickbacks to government ministers and officials were the norm. And politicians got rich. They didn't see it as corruption, of course. All they were doing in taking their cut and handing some of it out to UMNO's network of supporters, officials and clients, was promoting the poor, downtrodden Malay people. Handily for their consciences, they numbered themselves among this category.

In the mid 2000s, one contract above all came to symbolise the state of affairs. Between 2000 and 2008, the Malaysian government oversaw a deal worth nearly a billion euros to buy two Scorpene-class submarines and one Agosta-class sub from French naval dockyard unit DCNS. Not long after, anti-corruption groups discovered that, as part of the deal, a local company named Perimekar had been handed an eye-watering $130 million to handle "administrative" matters locally. The affair then turned into one of the biggest scandals to hit Malaysia in years. A female Mongolian translator called Altantuya Shaariibuu, who was having an affair with the man in charge of the scam, had threatened to put the whole scandal into the open. Before she could tell the story, however, she was murdered in cold blood. Gruesomely, her body was blown to pieces by C4 explosives in a forested area near Kuala Lumpur. It isn't known whether she was already dead at the time.

And the man massively implicated in the affair was Najib Razak. He had overseen the purchase of the Scorpene subs earlier that decade. The man in charge of Perimekar, and who was having an affair with Altantuya, was his aide, Razak Baginda, And it was claimed by many – thought never proven – that it had been Rosmah, Najib's controversial wife, who had organised Altantuya's brutal murder, peeved by allegations – also unproven – that Altantuya's previous boyfriend had been her own husband (and that she may even have been carrying his child).

As the case wound through the courts in 2008 and 2009, the plot darkened further. Baginda had hired a private detective called PI Bala to try to deal with Altantuya. Bala later testified that, on the night she was killed, Altantuya had been forced into a car outside Baginda's house in KL by a man called Sirul Azhar Umar, a member of the elite bodyguard group who protected Najib. He was accompanied by a woman who was the girlfriend of Sirul's immediate superior, Azila Hadri. Sirul, Azila and Baginda were soon arrested and charged with her murder. Yet Baginda was let off (when the news came through, he received a text from Najib declaring: "Don't worry, I will have it sorted"). The two bodyguards were then found guilty, all the while insisting they were being made scapegoats by those in power who had ordered them to murder. In a sensational press conference, Bala then spilled all: claiming Altantuya had been Najib's mistress, suggesting Najib had 'recommended' her to Baginda because she was willing to have anal intercourse, and revealing that she had demanded cash from Najib as her share of the Scorpene deal, only to have been told where to go. A day later, however, he recanted – presumably under pressure – and promptly disappeared.

All this had happened in the wake of elections in 2008 when the ruling Barisan Nasional Alliance (led by Najib's party UMNO) had, for the first time since 1969, failed to win two-thirds of the public vote. The grotesque Altantuya case only added to growing public outrage across Malaysia at the way ordinary people were being treated. Backed by his party's traditional support, however, he simply steamrollered on. He was elected the new leader of UMNO in March 2009 and promptly sworn in as prime minister a few days later.

Malaysia had, over fifty difficult, tumultuous years, gone from being a sleepy colonial outpost, to a country of violence and insecurity, to a tiger nation of high growth and development and, now, to a country with a leadership mired in corruption, sleaze and murder. Something had to give.

◆ ◆ ◆

It was at this point that I was getting back on the scene.

I had always followed Malaysia and my Borneo homeland from afar. In the early eighties, I had watched on aghast at the coverage of the forests being burnt. As a young woman, when I still felt an outsider in the UK, the things that mattered to me were still back in Malaysia, not what was happening in Britain. The environmental ruin being inflicted on my birthplace Sarawak had become something of an obsession. I had followed the case of Bruno Manser, the Swiss environmentalist who disappeared in Borneo, presumed killed. One day, I thought, I'd get back there.

But life had kept me in Britain. In 1992, I married my Scottish-born husband, Andrew, a fellow journalist (who just happened to be brother to the then shadow chancellor, Gordon Brown). Our lives quickly took over: we had our two boys to look after and our parallel careers: me eventually working freelance, Andrew working for the BBC and Channel 4 news programmes before moving into communications in the private sector. We were stupidly busy, running to keep still, charging from work appointments to parenting.

Then Andrew accidentally got me my ticket back home. In 2006, he received an invitation to attend an environmental conference in Kuching, the city of my birth. It was a classic 'greenwash' event held by the local Sarawakian government designed to show their faux concern for the Borneo rainforest, and dampen international criticism about illegal logging. Andrew remarked that it was really his Sarawakian-born wife who should attend. Hence, that November, I found myself arriving back home. How ironic, given what followed, that my flight back was paid for by the same government I would, in time, expose for their gross corruption.

I breathed in the tropical air for the first time in 40 years. And, inevitably, I was constitutionally unable not to cause a ruckus. At the conference, I was mobbed afterwards by journalists wanting to know more. I set out my concerns about what was going on there, and how land was being snatched away from local people. I left wanting more. The shadow of Sarawak in the back of my mind had now come front and centre. The state had been good to my mother and father and me. Now it was at the forefront of a global environmental war. I was not going to let a war go by without getting involved. I got in touch with the Bruno Manser Foundation. I could see there was this massive corruption going on and that nobody was exposing it.

That was why, three years later, in August 2009 – on the same weekend Najib, Rosmah and Jho were plotting their financial fun and games off the coast of Monte Carlo – I found myself in Sarawak.

While there, I was to make a decision that would change all our lives.

5. A ROAD BLOCK

August 2009, Sarawak rainforest

STANDING at a road block, in the middle of the drenched Sarawak rainforest, the men and women from the local Penan tribe who had made their way here cast off their second-hand modern clothing. Cameras rolling, they posed semi-naked, clasping their traditional spears and blowpipes. Suddenly they were transported from modern times: they could have come from any decade or any century. This, here, was how they lived; how they had always lived. The Penan are nomadic people. The jungle is their home. For centuries they had thrived in this beautiful part of the world, hunting and gathering, a part of the very eco-system. Nowadays, however, only a handful still lived in the traditional way. Their lives, in the last two decades, had been uprooted along with the trees in whose shadow they lived.

Logging had seen to that. Millions of acres of the rainforest had been plundered and sold, literally, down the river. The Penan had been shunted into settlements by politicians who saw dollar signs hanging from every tree, and viewed the Penan as annoying obstacles to their enrichment. The Penan were now living off what they could find in the ecologically depreciated secondary growth around us. It was a desperate life. That day, the tropical rain slammed down onto the road, turning it into a river of mud. The people we met at the road block were extremely poor and very desperate. But determined too. The road block had been set up to prevent loggers moving further into the jungle. A group of nomadic cousins, almost naked, had come to join them, soaked and shivering, but proud and free. They were not going to give in without a fight.

This was my element: reporting on a forgotten injustice. It had taken hours to get here and I had brought provisions for ourselves and basic foodstuffs, all welcome presents. But I knew that the really valuable gift I could offer was less material: it was to shine a light on their desperation. I have my own picture of that day. I am squatting in front of a little crowd in the muddy road, in front of one of these road blocks, surrounded by eager little children and towered over by men carrying spears with their womenfolk crowded between them, beaming at the excitement of the occasion.

I was back where I belonged.

This was the third trip that I had made back to Borneo following the Kuching conference three years earlier, and my mind was already made up: a terrible injustice was being perpetrated, and somebody needed to expose it. One day stuck in my head: on one of the trips, I had gone upriver to visit some of the most remote parts of the state. Half way up, we encountered a sad group of tribespeople travelling down the other way. With them was a sick baby, listless in the arms of its mother – they were trying to get the child to hospital and were still several hours away. It was heart-rending. My own mother had devoted so many years to trying to improve maternal health services for these distant communities and yet, half a century later, after billions had been made from the rape of their lands, even the most basic healthcare was still lacking. Not for the first time, as I watched the baby wilting in the heat, my blood boiled at the injustice. 'Modernisation' and 'progress' had meant vast wealth, jets, cars and marbled mansions for the Sarawakian political leaders, but the condition of the indigenous people was now worse than it had been in the 'primitive' pre-industrial age. My conscience wouldn't let me sleep.

That day in August 2009, I and three Australian journalists who, like me, had gone out to cover the plight of the Penan people, were to discover the odds that they were facing. As I was filming one of those blockades, which was successfully turning back the logging lorries, a group of luxury four-wheel-drive vehicles screeched up, as we had been expecting. Inside were a bevy of angry Chinese Malaysian logging company officials, who told me to stop filming and answer their questions. Instead, I and my companions questioned them back and kept filming, and eventually they drove away.

It was clear we were not welcome – and the following day we discovered just how dirty the authorities would play. As we made the eight-hour journey back to the timber town of Miri, in Northern Sarawak, we were stopped by police with submachine guns. I had already swapped my tapes and footage just in case they were confiscated. We were marched to a local police station and asked to explain ourselves. "We're reporters," we said. "You had no permission," we were told. "Isn't this a democracy?" we replied. There was a stand-off for a few hours before I demanded to speak to a local politician who I had arranged to interview the following day. We were allowed on our way. A few hours later we arrived in Miri hoping to get our story out. But we discovered the local government had got there first.

News stands already had their version of events of the previous day: "Foreign Hands in Blockades", declared the front page of the *Borneo Post*. It continued:

> It's confirmed! Foreigners are behind many of the blockades set up by Penans in timber camps in the state. It has long been suspected that many foreign environmentalists and so-called conservationists had been instigating and encouraging the natives to erect blockades and disrupt logging activities, though they had always denied their involvement. But yesterday four foreigners, including two women, were seen among protesters manning blockades in Ulu Baram.

We had come up against the reality of a so-called free press in Malaysia. The *Post* was controlled by the logging company KTS. It had therefore been told what to write – and a story about the clearing of Sarawak's rainforests had been rewritten as a tale of foreign interference in a sovereign state.

It was deeply frustrating. I pondered over what to do. In Malaysia, there was no way of getting real news into the print media: in Sarawak, as elsewhere, news outlets need a licence from the authorities to operate – a power which effectively muzzled the press with the knowledge they'd be closed down at the first hint of independence. So, I wondered, what about the web? Back then, in 2009, the power of internet news had not yet been fully understood. What I did know was that, not that long ago, Malaysia, as part of its efforts to appear democratic, and be part of the new global technology race, had pledged to allow the web to be free of interference.

So I made a decision. I would start a blog. Anyone could just start one, couldn't they? So why not me? I would call it *Sarawak Report*. And I would use this blog to get stories out to anyone who wanted to read them. Of course, that might only be a couple of dozen people. It wasn't as if there were thousands of people out there demanding news, was there?

I remember wondering how much of a fool I was going to make of myself but I just decided: stick it up and see what happens. But that decision would take me to billionaires row in Los Angeles, to the fleshpots of Las Vegas, to the financial centres of London and Singapore, to the tax havens of the Caymans and to the oil-rich emirates in the Middle East – and eventually, all the way back to the meeting on the yacht Najib was floating on, off the coast of Monte Carlo, at exactly that time.

That was where it all began.

6. HOW TO START A NEWS SITE

October 2009, London

T HE truth was I didn't have a clue what to do. My chosen media
was TV, not the internet. Plus, I had absolutely no spare cash at
all. Journalism, however, is the art of persistence. So, after getting
back from Borneo that autumn, I began the job of working out how
to start a news site.

All I did know was there was a gap in the market. And while there
were plenty of angry Sarawakians venting about the injustice that
was going on, none of them were journalists and they hadn't yet
managed to make the story stick. My visit to Borneo had given me
a taste for more. It was clear that a monstrous injustice was being
carried out both to the local environment and to the people who
lived there – and that their plight required telling.

First up was the question of money. Every penny Andrew and I
had was spent keeping the family going. So I decided to seek help.
A benefactor in Switzerland, linked to the Bruno Manser Fund, was
interested in my idea. Generously, he agreed to give me £1,000 to
help design a website. I looked out an NGO-friendly web designer,
Christian Nolle, who got me up and running. And so it was that, in
October 2009, *Sarawak Report* came into being.

It had, I think it's fair to say, a slow start. Writing in the dining
room of my flat in Victoria, I began with a series of opinion pieces
about Sarawak's depleted environment. They attracted a few dozen
hits. But I knew what to do. A career in journalism had taught me
a few things about getting noticed. One is that if you can break a
story – if you can reveal information that somebody, somewhere, is
trying to keep hidden – then readers will come flocking.

So I got about four stories prepared on corruption in Sarawak, all
exposing how money from the rape of the rainforest was making its
way straight to the ruling family and then popping up in property

portfolios all around the world. My facts all straight, on February 11th 2010, I put the first story up. Nothing happened. I went to bed. Then, the morning afterwards, I got woken by a call from Christian. "Oh my God Clare, I woke up this morning and you've just got 18,000 hits."

I was up and running. Not making any money, of course; access to the website was free. But that wasn't my goal. The point was to make a splash and to make the Sarawak government's life as uncomfortable as possible. The website soon created its own snowball effect. The more I wrote – and as readers realised my facts stood up – the more emails I began to get from local people telling me they had information and would I like to check it out?

I soon became utterly engrossed. All thought of trying to make money through a freelance career in the UK went out the window – Andrew's salary would have to do for now. My average day would be looking after the kids during the day, getting them to bed, having supper at 9pm, before then starting work – writing until 2 or 3am at night, before snatching a few hours' sleep before the boys were back up at seven.

The problem was, however, that many of the communities whose stories I wanted to tell didn't have access to the web. There was an election coming soon and I wanted our reach to expand. So my thoughts turned to radio. A discussion with a Norwegian NGO told me that a similar enterprise, *Radio Free Burma*, was operating thanks to a UK broadcast outfit called World Radio Network (WRN), which I soon tracked down to just a mile from where I live in London on the south side of Vauxhall Bridge. So I had dashed over to see their manager Jeff, who turned out to be an ex-BBC radio producer. He could do a shortwave broadcast for $88 an hour, he said. It seemed financially within reach.

I learnt more. The whole former Soviet bloc was littered with under-used former Cold War broadcasting and relay equipment, and they were happy to take what business they could. It all felt close to my heart. Throughout most of my childhood in far-flung places, and then during boarding school holidays, my family and I would keep in touch with the global news via scratchy, crackly shortwave broadcasts from the BBC World Service. It represented a world of tradition long after the reality had evaporated, giving an outdated but very attractive sense of the best of British culture. It was not only the expats who loved to listen, so did people from other countries and of other mother tongues the world over. The crusty British broadcasters were honest, fair and decent in their coverage and as a fading power they seemed to approach subjects with more detached objectivity than other news outlets. You felt you were getting the truth when you tuned into the BBC, even if frustratingly you often could not hear it properly, owing to the whorls and fall-out of the shortwave medium.

So, having established that a radio station in Sarawak was practically and legally feasible (under international broadcast law I could shortwave whatever I liked from London), in September 2010 I was put in touch, thanks to the Bruno Manser Fund, with the philanthropist who agreed to support a few months of broadcasting in the run up to the state election with a grant of £33,000. It needed a local Malaysian to present it. And I had my eye on the right man.

I had met Peter John Jaban in early 2009, on another reporting trip to Sarawak (on that occasion, I had been caught filming the blockade and stopped by police.) A by-election had been taking place in Batang Ai, the site of the one of the oldest Iban settlements in Sarawak (the Iban, along with the Penan, were one of the dominant tribes in the region). I had made connections with members of the local opposition, and set about trying to film and interview as many local people as I could. A huge dam had been built nearby, in the heart of the Iban territories, destroying the communities and the environment that had thrived there for centuries. As I sat in a traditional longhouse nearby, one of the older fellows cried as he told me about a sad heap of ancient skulls that used to be buried beneath an older longhouse, now drowned under the deep waters of the dam – "those poor, poor people, so sad their end," he wept, and clearly meant it.

I asked them if there was anyone else who would speak out

about the corruption within the Sarawak government. "There is an opposition DJ here campaigning as well," my self-appointed guide, Tambat, had told me. "He had this very popular radio show, but then he criticised the chief minister and he got sacked. He is here this week talking to the voters."

We searched for him during the remainder of that afternoon. In town, it had started to become extremely busy and tense. Crowds increased around the town and the police presence thickened. Then the reason became clear. Chief Minister Abdul Taib Mahmud was about to fly in – Sarawak's powerful and notorious governing politician, about whom more in a minute. A new marquee had already been erected. Above, a small fleet of helicopters buzzed. We sat in our car, sweating in a traffic jam.

Suddenly, Tambat cried out: "There, that is Peter John!" An anxious looking character was running along the stationary cars putting leaflets in through the windows. As he stuck his head in ours, I called out, "Hey are you the opposition DJ I have been hearing all about, would you like to do an interview?"

"Too dangerous," said Peter, whose appearance (cigarette in hand) reminded me of student leaders back in my college days, "I need to run, BN [Barisan Nasional, the ruling Malaysian coalition] are coming!"

As Peter melted between the cars, a cavalcade suddenly came into view on the clear side of the road in the opposite direction: several black Mercedes, bearing the cream of the Sarawak establishment, then a grand white limo bearing Taib himself, swept past towards the marquee.

I had hung onto my leaflet from Peter, which contained his contact details, and later, hunting for my own DJ, I rang him up. No, he didn't remember me from Lubok Antu, he told me, but, yes, he was pretty interested in the idea of coming to work for a rebel radio station in London. I should come back and tell him all about it.

In 2010, when I returned to Sarawak, I did. It took a while to track Peter John down again. Eventually I found him, together with a bunch of friends, at an outside café under a flyover near the airport in Miri, one of Sarawak's bigger towns.

"So, it's like this," I explained, "I am going to set up this radio station in London to reach the rural folk who cannot get the internet and we are going to expose exactly what's going on here and how people need to use the power of their votes to change things. I can put you up and pay your tickets, but, apart from basic spending for food, I can't give you a salary and we aim to keep going for about six months."

Peter thought for a moment. "Ok," he said, "when do we start?'

"You do realise if they find out it's you then you might be in big trouble here with the authorities, because we haven't got one of their stupid licences and they won't give us one."

"Yes, I will use a stage name, but they will probably recognise my voice," he said. "How about start of next month?"

"Done."

I gave Peter a reasonable number of pounds to get himself as far as Brunei and a flight out and wondered if maybe that would be the last I saw of him. But, of course, it wasn't.

He arrived in London in mid-October 2010, shivering in the autumn chill (at the start of the coldest winter for decades). We went straight to Primark on Oxford Street to buy him a set of winter clothes that he lived in for the next few months. I put him up in a room I had rented from friends nearby. And Radio Free Sarawak began to broadcast, two hours a day, seven days a week – with Peter taking the name 'Papa Orang Utan'. We set up in the living room of my flat. Andrew would come home, not surprisingly, wondering what on earth had happened to his house.

Christian Nolle turned his hand from website design to radio. Our tiny team was then completed by a 19-year-old researcher, Amy Dodds, who would become an utterly indispensable fact-hunter over the years to come. Her first day in the job was to give her an idea of what was to come. I met her outside a large mansion flat overlooking Hyde Park owned by the same Taib Mahmud. I was there because I had received a tip-off that he was arriving for a secret visit. She arrived with a camera in hand. So, having a dozen other things to do, I told her to stay put and begin her first stakeout. Some hours later I rejoined her and set up a separate post behind some railings. Just then, a chauffeured car swept up to the mansion driven by a man we had earlier identified as one of Taib's henchmen. Spotting us, he grabbed five-foot Amy by the cord around her neck, twisting it to choke her while demanding she delete the shots.

We were, thankfully, rescued by two workmen who witnessed the entire thing. I was mortified to have placed my unpaid intern in such a terrible situation on the first day of her 'traineeship'. "Oh don't worry at all," said Amy, her eyes shining. "It's been the most exciting day of my life, please consider me on your team for as long as you will have me."

Team *Sarawak Report* was complete.

◆ ◆ ◆

We plugged in and started broadcasting. And, for the first two years, we aimed our sights directly at the man in the white Merc who had swept past us that steaming hot day in Sarawak, Abdul Taib Mahmud.

7. THE THIEF OF SARAWAK

TAIB, a lawyer by training, had entered politics in the sixties, intending at first only to devote five years to public life. In fact, after becoming Chief Minister of Sarawak in 1981, he was to become the longest serving politician in Malaysia – beating even Mahathir Mohamed for longevity. That lengthy period in office, at the helm of a burgeoning oil-rich, timber-rich state, was to prove a gold mine. Taib would take his cut from almost all major commercial contracts, using the proceeds to pay off tribal leaders, stifle opposition and enrich his family. He was to become fabulously wealthy.

He had started exporting his wealth in the early 1980s to Canada and the United States, following the paths of his children who were sent away as students. He used family members, like his younger brother Onn, to set up companies and disguise his funding as best he could. By the 2000s he had established, through his Canadian son-in-law and other close family, a vast international property empire, closely enmeshed with the fortunes of the local timber companies he controlled, including Samling, Ta Ann, Rimbunan Hijau, companies which have all diversified into oil palm plantation and have spread their destructive tentacles across the globe.

A good example was the huge Estrella property development near Phoenix, Arizona, which I would visit a few years later. In the late nineties savings and loan crisis, it ran into severe trouble, landing the federal government with a potentially enormous bill. Then the entire thing – fake lake, golf courses, prefab housing estates – had been snapped up for $2 billion by a company called Sunchase, the biggest sale by the federal government ever. Sunchase may have sounded to Americans like a homegrown US firm but the truth was it was owned by Sarawak timber barons linked to Taib. On my visit, I remember thinking about the irony of how a precious tropical rainforest had been eradicated and its proceeds spent on watering a desert and building up a clapperboard housing development. The development plainly represented just a fraction of the true value of the forest obliterated to create it. However, as far as Taib and his collaborators were concerned, at least that fraction was now in their personal possession and generating more cash in the developed economy.

A conservative estimate, arrived at by two separate analysts who examined Taib's network of timber kickbacks, monopolies and his control of state contracts in one of the wealthiest corners of the world, told me that after three decades of total economic dominance the diminutive politician had accumulated a personal fortune of 60 billion Malaysian ringgit, or 21 billion US dollars – all of it siphoned away from the people and the land to which it rightfully belonged.

The bill was paid by the poor tribespeople of Sarawak whose leaders betrayed them, and by the pristine rainforest which had stood for hundreds of years before Taib arrived to destroy it. Sarawak has over 42 separate forest tribal groups with their individual languages and cultures, all of whom were granted native customary rights to their territories within the wider constitution, as part of Sarawak's independence settlement overseen by the departing British. Over the ensuing 50 years all of these rights have been violated and abused, and an estimated 97 percent of Sarawak's virgin jungle has been cut around them.

Aided by brave Radio Free Sarawak sources on the ground, we tore into him. There was the illegal logging he had sanctioned, the corruption he fostered. Now he was preparing to cause more havoc, as he unveiled the misleadingly named 'Sarawak Corridor of Renewable Energy' which envisaged converting remaining rainforest into a money-making industrial zone. He had destroyed a rainforest and planted it with oil palm and planation wood and was running out of further opportunities. So industrialization it was.

From my dining table in London – as I juggled dinner times, pick up arrangements for my sons, and care for my parents – we began to bite. I have never worked so hard in my life. And come the 2011 state elections, it began to hurt. It was hilarious: everyone listening back in Borneo thought we were some huge media organisation. If only they had known that it was just the four of us, sitting around a dining room table, with me writing stories while making sure that the boys' fish fingers weren't getting burnt. Our *exposés* – in particular the revelations of his family's unexplained foreign assets – were held responsible for Taib's worst result in years. His share of the vote went from Saddam-esque 90 percent of seats down to just 50 percent.

It shook him. We learnt that he had sped to the governor's mansion late on election night to get himself sworn back in. I was told it was to secure his position in case of trouble when townspeople realised that only a raft of rotten rural seats had kept him in power. Gratifyingly, he blamed me for these travails when he stood up in the State Parliament shortly after. I was, he said, an "enemy of the state" who was acting on a "neo-colonialist agenda" as part of a conspiracy to hijack Sarawak's oil deposits. It was an insight into the mind of someone who had been pillaging his own country in an outrageous abuse of trust for the past three decades.

And yet he continued to cling on. And for two more years, into 2011 and 2012, we dug ever deeper. With Peter leading the radio bulletins, and me keeping the website active, we worked ferociously – to the increasing bemusement of my husband. Little if any money was coming in from my work: I didn't draw a salary from the money donated to us. But, most nights, armed with a glass of red wine, I would return to my desk in the living room of our flat, and try to find out more.

I began to look at Taib's business interests. A few years earlier, he had kept within his vast portfolio – all acquired through the abuse of his excessive political influence – a massive family stake in Malaysia's RHB Bank. It was one of the country's leading financial institutions and heavily linked to the government. For political purposes, Taib had been pressured to sell up. In 2007, the chief minister got the government-controlled EPF (Employees Provident Fund) to buy him out for a handsome profit. It left him with a huge chunk of money. Taib put it in one of his family outfits, the UBG

Group. Then who should come along to suggest some good ideas for where the funds should be invested? None other than a certain opportunist called Jho Low.

Jho's big thing, as he made sure everyone knew, was his apparent access to fabulously wealthy contacts in the Middle East. In a press article, Jho dropped the name of Yousef al-Otaiba, a flash young Abu Dhabi politician, who was later to emerge as an ambassador to the United States. Jho's business model appeared to involve making enormous payments to al-Otaiba in return for his opening doors to the Middle East. For him these were all investors or trophies, about whom he could boast to Malaysian oligarchs like Taib.

A deal was waiting to be done. Taib wanted foreign business investors to help him push ahead with his plans to build a staggering seven new dams in the rainforest. Jho opened up the possibility of contacts in the dollar-rich Middle East. At the same time, Jho persuaded Taib to put money into more government-backed development projects in West Malaysia, in which he had his own financial interests, thereby making tens of millions more dollars for himself.

At the end of their deal-making, Taib's company, UBG, had swallowed up several construction firms, had become attractive to the hoped-for investment from the Middle East and was now ready to take advantage of government-backed work in Malaysia. But the global financial crash was just weeks away and the investment bonanza never came. The project turned out to be a turkey.

Jho was in danger of getting the blame, especially after the old chief minister learnt of the profit the young man had made. But then – suddenly – the problems went away. In 2010, *Sarawak Report* learnt that UBG had been bought out, in its entirety, by the Malaysian government's flagship economic development company 1MDB (1 Malaysia Development Berhad). Using public money, 1MDB had been launched to fund strategic developments in energy, real estate, tourism and agribusiness. Out of nowhere, it had paid top dollar for Taib's teetering UBG group – thus relieving Taib and Jho of all their problems.

A well-connected source gave me a call. "Jho Low has used 1MDB to buy himself and Taib out of UBG, that's what happened," he said. But he had no proof. And nor did I.

8. THE BOXING DAY SCOOP

Christmas 2013, Geneva

YET the story had tickled my antennae. Taib and Jho's dealings pointed to a bigger picture which I didn't understand. And that made me restless.

For the four years after the launch of the blog and the radio station, I had concentrated on timber corruption in Borneo and the impact on its people and environment, an environment that had once been the most precious remaining natural wilderness on earth – richer in biodiversity even than the Amazon. I had unearthed stories concerning the staggering levels of corruption that was driving the devastation, exposing jaw-dropping levels of graft at the highest levels of state government in Sarawak and then Sabah. These concerned vast kickbacks from the timber and oil palm plantation industries (the overwhelming majority of the profits made went into the pockets of just a handful of politically connected people) and likewise the blatant abuse of power evident in the case of all government contracts. The structures of democratic accountability in these states and due process had been relentlessly eroded since independence for the benefit of a criminal local mafia run by politicians.

But I had also come to realise that the problems in Borneo were only part of a much bigger picture. All my exposés and all the evidence against the chief ministers of the two Borneo states, Taib in Sarawak and Musa Aman of Sabah, had been ignored, and all official investigations shelved because the Prime Minister of Malaysia, Najib Razak, needed those two powerful local potentates to deliver the votes that would keep him in office come election time. And while my stories had been followed up by the Malaysian Anti-Corruption Commission (MACC), these had rotted on the desk of the attorney general appointed by the prime minister.

Bravely, people across Malaysia were now coming together to protest against the rot at the top. The *Bersih* movement – a nationwide campaign for free and fair elections – had held several huge demonstrations in KL and had been met with tear gas and water cannon for their troubles. They were focusing their efforts on the 2013 general elections when Najib would face voters for the first time since taking office.

He responded with the dirtiest campaign in Malaysian history, with money thrown lavishly at voters in all directions during the campaign, even outside the polling booths themselves. Phony voters, immigrants with illegal identity cards, lost ballots, stuffed boxes, diverted postal ballots, double voters – the abuses recorded were colossal and all of them were on behalf of the powerful ruling coalition, which had also gerrymandered the election, an election where the size of the urban opposition seats outnumbered many of the tiny government-controlled rural constituencies ten to one.

He won but – despite all the corruption – only just. Najib's coalition (made up of his own party, the United Malays National Organisation, or UMNO, and other smaller parties) lost the popular vote for the first time in Malaysian history, achieving only 47 percent. It was a remarkable result, testament to the fact that so many ordinary Malaysians – Malay, Chinese and Indian – had simply had enough of Najib and everything he represented. It was a tragic irony that Najib had only won thanks to bought votes in Borneo. The people most oppressed by this vile system of money politics had been the ones desperate enough and uneducated enough to sell their precious votes for RM10 – the price of a bag of rice.

Now, at the end of 2013, it was clear that Najib's money politics was in the process of wrecking the entire country. The courts refused to address a single one of the flood of cases of alleged voter fraud brought to their attention. Further widespread protests over the blatant rigging were clamped down on with force. And then Najib pursued a spurious prosecution that was already underway against the moral victor of that election, opposition leader Anwar Ibrahim. Charges of alleged sodomy were brought against his political opponent (still a crime in conservative Malaysia). When that case was finally thrown out by the High Court for lack of evidence, Najib was implicated in an extraordinary decision by state prosecutors to appeal against that ruling of innocence (violating the principle against double jeopardy). The Appeal Court judgement was now looming in early 2014 and with the Malaysian courts subject to ever greater political pressure at the higher levels, the outcome was not promising.

Anwar had already suffered five years in jail after being convicted (on no evidential basis) of similar charges of sodomy in 1999. He was pardoned and found 'innocent' in 2004. The motivation of character assassination in this majority Muslim country was plain to see. The victorious but still vulnerable prime minister planned to destroy his main political opponent by any means possible. Meanwhile, in the background, more and more eyebrows were being raised over the outlandish behavior of Najib's Chinese fix-it man, Jho Low, and the staggering sums of money he suddenly seemed to have at his disposal.

◆ ◆ ◆

That Christmas, at the end of 2013, I was at a crossroads. It seemed that, no matter how many facts were uncovered and put out on the web, nothing would change. It was deeply depressing. I had done so much, but achieved so little. Along with Andrew, I headed to my brother's house in Geneva to try and get away from it all.

We had been enjoying a traditional Christmas time, wrapping presents and sharing out cooking chores at my brother's apartment, which looks across the lake towards the Evian mountain range. Malaysia and my work was beginning to slip into the background. But then, in one of those serendipitous moments that occur occasionally in life, an intriguing series of emails arrived from a Malaysian journalist friend based in Sydney. He had received a tip-off about Rosmah's latest excesses.

According to my friend, Rosmah had been urging education officials to take steps to enable every schoolchild in Malaysia to watch a particular film that was about to be released, as "a lesson in the sort of lifestyle to avoid". It was bizarre – the film was the sex-mad caper, *The Wolf of Wall Street*.

It was the first time I had heard about the movie. I was intrigued immediately. Why was Rosmah interested? The rest of the Christmas holiday disappeared. As I searched the web, the whole story unfolded. I read up about Riza. I discovered, with a tingle going up my spine, that Jho – Taib's business partner – was involved in this as well. I read how Riza had not just been funding expensive movies but had spent a staggering $33 million on a New York penthouse in central Manhattan.

Desperately, my mother tried to encourage a little more family time in what was a rare reunion for our dispersed family. I was utterly uninterested. All I knew, for certain, was that this story of Hollywood, the prime minister's step-son, and the ubiquitous Jho Low would go down a storm on my blog and would expand my horizons into the national Malaysian story which I felt needed to be told; a story of corruption at the very top of the political establishment of Malaysia, embellished by the tinselled trappings of a Hollywood setting. And if the full facts were still unclear, I could at least start to ask some tricky questions.

I began to write. "The wife of the PM, Rosmah Mansor, is apparently advocating that even Malaysian school child should be shown the newly released Leonardo DiCaprio film, 'The Wolf of Wall Street' in order to warn them against greed and immorality. One wonders how she proposes to get around the fact that the film has been X-rated owing to the violence and sex scenes, which extend to drug taking and mass orgies?"

Yes, I thought, this is going to get noticed.

I revealed that Riza's company Red Granite was behind the movie. I asked where his money had come from, noting he was a close associate of Jho, And I pointed out Jho's own rumoured connections to some of Najib's eyebrow-raising business deals. Was there a link?

In a photograph we had found of a partying Jho holding a bottle of champagne, I noted the remarkable similarities between him and the original 'wolf' himself, Jordan Belfort. I concluded: "If Malaysia was blessed with a free media this would be enough to provoke a barrage of questions as to exactly how the son of Rosmah Mansor has acquired these hundreds of millions of dollars to flush through major Hollywood movies? Because, if the money is Najib's, how did the PM get to be so rich?"

I pressed 'publish'. And as Malaysians came back from their Christmas break, the reaction was palpable – even from Switzerland. There was the sheer outrageousness of the wife of the PM interfering to suggest that public money in Malaysia be used to promote her son's film. Just as reprehensible in the minds of most Malaysians was the fact that the film in question bordered on pornographic. At home, Najib and Rosmah preached about religious values as much as they could. Now here was the wife of the prime minister suggesting children should watch a movie that seemed to glory in nudity, drug taking and hedonism.

Two weeks later, Riza and DiCaprio had their moment in the sun at the Golden Globes. It only served to place further scrutiny on the funding behind the film. And now I had questions of my own. "Skin in the game", Riza had said when asked about his investment in the film. Well what risk had he taken? And what risk had Jho taken too? How much had they put in? And where had the money come from?

And my story had brought forward more information: Riza's $33 million pad in New York was known about and was already causing a major stir in Malaysia. But, after posting my piece on the funding for The Wolf of Wall Street, one contact emailed me: "Did you know he also bought a £15 million house in Beverly Hills?"

I did not – nobody knew. My mind was made up – after years of chasing scammers, drug dealers, squeegee merchants, bent local politicians, Spanish con artists and the rest, I was going to make this my story, and I wasn't going to stop until I'd go to the bottom of it.

It was time to head west.

9. A HOUSE IN BEVERLY HILLS

January 2014, Los Angeles

THE truth is that, by this point, the question of money had come up a few times between my husband Andrew and me. As in, given all this work and travel that I was taking on, was I ever actually going to earn any? It wasn't an unreasonable question for Andrew to ask, especially seeing as, despite working all hours, we never seemed to have any. But Andrew knew the answer. As I told him, he knew what he was getting into when he married me, he had to have faith in me, this was just who I was.

I left for LA the moment we got back from the Christmas holidays. The blog I had written on Boxing Day had gone viral by then. It was obvious that, so long as I could keep the revelations going about Riza and Jho, the hits would follow. *Sarawak Report* was about to become big news.

Up till that point, Najib, Jho, Riza and Rosmah had all managed to hide under the radar by repressing the media at home, and by relying on ignorance abroad. Who, outside Southeast Asia, had even heard of Malaysia anyway? Did most people in the West even know where it was on a map? Based in London, and driven by my own peculiar, special interest in Malaysia, *Sarawak Report* would turn out to be their worst nightmare: unmuzzled *and* informed.

I began by exposing some of the misguided attempts back in Malaysia that were underway to exonerate Riza and Jho. In the *Malaysian Gazette*, a 'close friend' of Riza was quoted defending him by pointing out that he had "managed to break the monopoly of Jews in the world of film in Hollywood." Such a claim may have worked in Malaysia – where antisemitism was rife and, in many cases, officially approved of – but it didn't go down so well internationally, and my blogpost "Breaking the Monopoly of Jews in Hollywood" put more scrutiny on the pair. I was knocking on an open door since Riza and McFarland and Red Granite had already been making enemies in the Hollywood establishment. According to depositions in one legal case against the company, the pair had stepped well out of line as they had attempted to railroad existing interests in film projects they were buying over, thanks to their unexplained deep pockets. I also learnt that there had been one such spat over the development rights linked to *The Wolf of Wall Street* itself, which was eventually settled after ugly scenes.

In another case, involving the film series *Dumb & Dumber*, they were cutting mean on money too, according to the original producers Brad Krevoy and Steve Stabler. These two veterans of the movie business didn't need to read *Sarawak Report*, they were already enraged with the behaviour of these rookies, whom they were suing for breach of covenant for squeezing them out of the sequel and tens of millions of dollars in fees. Their court deposition ran:

> McFarland and [Aziz] lack the experience necessary to successfully produce motion pictures themselves. Although Red Granite apparently has family money from [Aziz], Red Granite will not succeed with money alone because McFarland and [Aziz]'s experience producing motion pictures during their short tenure in the industry consists of cavorting at nightclubs with Paris Hilton and making dinner reservations at posh nightclubs in New York and Los Angeles.

There was plenty more in the same vein. These were dangerous accusations against Riza, because again they highlighted, from the inside of the business, how unusual it was for such an inexperienced operator to have so much money put at his disposal by lenders, in what was already a notoriously risky industry. Furthermore, the producers' complaint drew attention to Riza's friend Jho whose excesses in LA's social scene were by now becoming notorious.

I got in touch with Brad Krevoy and Steve Stabler to let them know I was coming over to investigate Red Granite. And so it was that, a few days later, I found myself getting picked up by Steve as I arrived in LA airport. The anonymous source who had contacted me following my original blog had kindly supplied an address: 912 North Hillcrest Road. And in the heat of the LA winter sun, with new sandals tearing my feet to shreds, I hiked my way out to see Riza's empire for myself.

It was handily placed, only a short ride away was Red Granite's swish offices at 9925 Sunset Boulevard, which looks out onto a fabulous panoramic view of Hollywood. Riza had hidden ownership behind a third company (based in Delaware) – a well-known ruse for mega-rich foreigners looking to hide their wealth and their taxable income. The aim, presumably, was to stop people like me knocking on the door to ask how they had come by the money to afford it.

As I stood outside the plot of land, one thing was clear from the start: the owner had money to burn. A previous mansion that had occupied this chunk of prime Beverly Hills real estate had been demolished. A new house was now under construction. There was a guard's cabin by the gate and trucks of materials along the road. A team of South American workers were clipping at the hedge. They pretended not to notice this strange middle-aged *gringo* lady on foot watching them at work in the blazing sun.

A gardener in a nearby property came into view. "What's going on there?" I asked congenially. He shrugged: it had been bought for a fortune not so long ago by some foreign guy and then completely rebuilt, he replied. Then, the gardener added, he had flipped it on, even more expensively, to another foreigner without having even lived in it. Now it was being pulled down all over again to be rebuilt a second time. He disapproved and so apparently did the neighbourhood. I hobbled off and pondered how best to nail the story. Sitting on the kerbside, I called the source who had contacted me a few days earlier. He knew the name of the building firm being employed to construct the new house. He now suggested I ring up Riza's personal wealth manager, one Debra Whelan Johnson at her firm, NKFSB.

"Ring up Debra at her office and say you work for Riza Aziz's builders. Say you have to get materials delivered for his works and you have conflicting addresses – can she confirm the correct address for Riza Aziz on Hillcrest Road?" my anonymous friend suggested.

"I can't do that," I retorted. "Why not?" he said. "I sound too British," I gulped. "This is Hollywood," he snapped, "the place is full of Brits working for delivery companies. She won't turn a hair, trust me."

The source was right. A bored assistant at NKFSB kindly confirmed for me the exact correct address of their acknowledged client Riza Aziz to be 912 North Hillcrest Road in Hollywood.

Time to get a cameraman. Together, we compiled the evidence. First I managed to confirm that, while waiting for the house to be finished, Riza was living in a $45,000 a month apartment (the most expensive in LA, according to press cuttings) at nearby 8500 Burton Way. Then, back at the building side at North Hillcrest Road, we decided to try our luck. The gate was open with no guard present. And with a ladder helpfully lying around outside. I climbed up a tree (in my summery frock), to find a perfect view right into the property. It had been virtually razed to the ground and was covered in tarpaulin.

"Let's take a look inside," I suggested to the cameraman.

He blanched: "What if we get caught?"

"I thought you were a news cameraman in your day job," I replied, now feeling that I had got well into my stride within what had been new and daunting territory just the day before, "Come on!"

We spent ten minutes darting into the covered cavern of Riza's dream Hollywood mansion. The workmen seemed to be having lunch somewhere outside at the bottom of the garden. I snapped away at the vast open plan areas and luxury bathrooms along with a huge pool that was being completely re-dug. High up the hill, this property again had a 'prestige view' over Hollywood. Riza had plainly made it big time. But how…?

The cameraman had been filming me snapping shots of the interior. Suddenly an engine started. "We're trespassing," he whispered, panicked. I was nonchalant by then: "What can they do? Take your expensive camera?"

"Yes exactly," he hissed back. I sighed. It was fun, but we had photographed everything we needed and I had no excuse for further risk.

We bolted.

◆ ◆ ◆

By the time I got back to London, on 24th January, Riza's lawyers, Loeb and Loeb, had caught up with me. Two letters awaited me. They were to be my first experience of something I would become very familiar with over the following years: the threatening lawyers' missive, designed to frighten off prying journalists.

The first, written by lawyer Sunny Brenner (who just so happened to be married to Riza's wealth manager Debra Whelen), was a proper rant. My Boxing Day blogpost had made "numerous false, misleading, defamatory and malicious statements". It was plain that I had a "naked political agenda". The second focused on my trip to LA which had now been widely picked up in media elsewhere. Over nine pages, Sunny attacked me for my "outrageous and unlawful" activities. Naturally, I was to remove the article from my website forthwith and issue a grovelling apology for all the above transgressions or I could expect to be a pauper in a very short time indeed. Naturally I intended to do nothing of the sort. I was not very worried; did they really want to explain to a UK court how this politically connected individual from Malaysia, of no apparent means, was spending so much money around Hollywood and the US? I suspected not.

More revealingly, I was soon to discover why the letters had been sent. A few weeks later, I met a close confidant of the Najib family who was prepared to spill some information. Sharing a bag of McDonald's chips in a corner of an international airport lounge, where we had both arranged to briefly coincide (I experienced a surprising number of similar airport assignations over the course of my Malaysian investigations), this person told me that, unknown to me at the time, Rosmah had in fact flown the prime ministerial jumbo jet over to LA that very New Year's period to visit her son and enjoy the preparations for the launch of his movie. From a separate source, I learnt she had taken up residence in a suite at the Beverly Hills Bel Air Hotel, where she had proceeded to run up a bill of over a quarter of a million dollars. Part of the bill might well have been accounted for by a reported 220 bottles of champagne ordered for New Year with Rosmah's name engraved on the label, according to what I was told.

I was also to discover later that she had met up with Jho who, at her behest, had brought top jeweller Lorraine Schwartz to see her. At a private sitting, Rosmah picked out no fewer than twenty seven bracelets and necklaces, at a total cost of $1.3 million. Discreetly, Jho picked up both the tab for this, and the Bel Air hotel too.

Back in Malaysia, Rosmah's husband had been courting the strict PAS Muslim party, which was then aligned to the opposition, by playing holier than thou and fomenting increasing social and legal intolerance of non-Muslims. So presumably Rosmah enjoyed the break from the pretended disapproval of all things considered by purists *haram* (forbidden).

The New Year atmosphere had been punctured by my article, explained my informant at the airport. It had left Rosmah raging. She wanted me sorted out, destroyed. Jho counselled that they should just keep quiet. But, Rosmah would not have it, so Riza did what his mother wanted and called in Loeb & Loeb. Riza is a mild and nice enough chap, according to my sources. The whole Hollywood dream was largely his mother's obsession and grand idea.

With the Hollywood press now going to town on the controversy around Red Granite and its funding, many more were now publicly questioning the sudden extraordinary spending and apparent wealth of Jho and Riza: men not yet 30 years old, who were being fêted in Hollywood and thanked by Leonardo DiCaprio by name for "taking the risk" in making the hundred million dollar movie *The Wolf of Wall Street*. And it was the same question: how on earth had they got all this cash?

I could rule out Joey McFarland immediately. He had been absolutely "*nada*" in Hollywood, all agreed, until Jho and Riza had turned up with their money bags and funded his transformation into a major producer. No – the money trail pointed to the Malaysians. Jho had been bragging about associations with the likes of DiCaprio and Jamie Foxx as far back as 2010, just as Red Granite was getting started, telling journalists that he was keen to promote Malaysia as a film location. The dots were joining up. Could it be that it was Rosmah who was really behind this Hollywood venture of her banking apprentice son and that Jho was essentially her walking cheque book? And if the money came from Jho, where had he got it from?

Back in Malaysia, Rosmah's husband, Najib, was settling comfortably back into power. And despite having publicly embraced the idea of reform, it was now clear, four years after coming to power, that Najib was turning out far worse than any of his predecessors in terms of greed and corrupt practice.

It was clear, too, that this was a double act. Schoolfriends say Rosmah had announced as a young girl that she would wed a prime minister. So determined was she that she divorced her first husband in order to bag Najib. That done, she then thrust herself deeper into the running of his government. "Anyone who wants a contract knows to see her first," I was told by one well-placed source . I was also told that she would then demand a cut in the form of suitcases of money to press the causes of her business suitors. "She has a wall of safes, different ones for different currencies," more than one person had told me.

Together the couple made a fearsome political double act, filling the key positions in the administration and government-linked companies with their own henchmen. And they had the power to do pretty much as they pleased. After all, Najib was in direct control of most of the nation's public finances, including pension funds, sovereign wealth funds and the national oil company Petronas, a key component of the country's wealth. None of these entities were truly independent of political interference. It was the prime minister who decided all the key appointments. Furthermore, government funds also hold controlling shares in around half of the country's listed companies, which gave Najib immense decision-making power in the private sector as well.

Najib and Rosmah's hold on power was total. And, along with having a lock grip on all these government-backed firms and private companies, they also had an iron hold on an innocuous sounding KL-based entity called 1MDB.

PART TWO

THE SCAM

10. 1MDB

AROUND the same time as my ladder-climbing expedition in LA in early 2014, Jho Low was on a very different kind of mission: how to bag a supermodel.

The star in question was Miranda Kerr, an Australian by birth, who had now conquered the American fashion scene. Having just divorced actor Orlando Bloom, Kerr was seeking a fresh start by launching a new skin care line, KORA Organics. She met Jho in January 2014 and, hearing he was cash-rich, struck up a conversation to see if he might want to invest. Apparently, Jho was smitten and, in August that year, he decided to give her a treat.

He flew her to the Bahamas and invited her on board his new toy: the $250 million, 300-foot super-yacht *Equanimity*. Capable of carrying as many as 26 guests, looked after by a crew of 33, it included a helicopter landing pad, an on-board gymnasium, a cinema, a massage room, a sauna and steam room, and a plunge pool. Jho had just taken delivery of it in June. He wanted to show it off.

But how to impress a supermodel? Jho went big, presenting her with a specially commissioned set of diamonds: an 18K white gold diamond necklace, earrings, bracelet and ring, designed by top jeweller Lorraine Schwartz and costing a cool $1.9 million. We would later learn of the lengths Jho went in order to get it all just right; everything had been meticulously planned through a high-end concierge service. The jewellery was engraved in Kerr's own initials. These weren't the only gifts he lavished on her: Jho's other tokens of affection included an 11-carat heart-shaped diamond worth $1.8 million (given to Kerr on Valentine's Day), an 8.8-carat pink diamond costing $3.8 million and two 5-carat "internally-flawless, pear-shaped diamond earrings" bought in October for just over $1 million.

Poor Leo DiCaprio, who was only given Marlon Brando's $600,000 Oscar and a $3.2 million Picasso entitled *Nature Morte au Crane de Taureau*, must have felt relatively short-changed.

There are many stories like this of Jho's excesses from that crazy period between 2009 and 2014. As early as October 2009, gossip columnists were already reporting on how he was dropping tens of thousands of dollars a night at hot spots around America, spending $160,000 in one night at the Avenue, New York, during Fashion Week; then buying Lindsay Lohan 23 bottles of Cristal champagne at her 23rd birthday bash; then marking his 28th birthday with a four day bash at Caesars Palace in Las Vegas with Paris Hilton, Megan Fox, Jamie Foxx and Usher, flown in to add glamour by a hotel pool surrounded by caged lions and tigers, and girls in bikinis.

There was the night at the exclusive Les Caves du Roy in St Tropez in July 2010, mentioned earlier in this book, when, after sailing into town on board the 303-foot yacht *Tatoosh*, Jho and his entourage spend $2 million in one night on champagne. There was Jho's attempt to woo the Taiwanese pop star Elva Hsiao: Jho took her to the Atlantis hotel in Dubai for a private dinner on the beach. As they finished eating, a helicopter suddenly appeared and two men parachuted out wearing tuxedos. After landing, they then walked up to the couple and presented Hsiao with a Chopard necklace. Fireworks followed for a date night that reputedly cost $1 million.

Then there was the extraordinary excess of the party Jho threw in Vegas on the 3rd and 4th of November 2012 to mark his 30th birthday, described by the very few journalists who were able to attend as the most extravagant private celebration ever held in the capital of excess. First, Jho erected a huge marquee on a lot next to the Vegas strip. This "party playpen" was divided into two sections: an amusement park replete with a Ferris wheel, a fairground carousel and a circus trampoline, and a nightclub-style dance floor where the main stage acts performed. An army of scantily clad women handed out free drinks all night to the guests, Cirque du Soleil-style dancers performed, while Jho even hired a group of dwarves to act as Oompa-Loompas to add to the fun. The highlight was the stage show – hosted by Jamie Foxx, the show was opened by South Korean star Psy singing his hit *Gangnam Style*, continued with Swizz Beatz, Busta Rhymes and QTip, before Brittney Spears rounded it off in time for a massive fifteen minute firework display. Only VIP guests (including the ever present DiCaprio) were invited and allowed in through the airport-style security. Jho also ordered a lock down on publicity, demanding that attendees sign a non-disclosure agreement. To cap it all, it was reported that, at the end of the night, Jho was presented with a $2.5 million Bugatti Veyron as a birthday gift. Robin Leach of the *Las Vegas Sun*, who managed to gain entry, declared: "I have been to many jaw-dropping 'Lifestyles of the Rich & Famous' parties around the world over the years, but this one topped them all." The estimated cost was "double-digit" millions.

Not satisfied, the following month Jho chartered a Jumbo Jet to take him, DiCaprio, Jamie Foxx and a group of models first to Sydney and then to Vegas to see in the New Year – twice. (Foxx, one of Jho's most adhesive cronies, declared afterwards: "I got a friend and he flew me, Leonardo DiCaprio, Jonah [Hill, the actor], and we flew to Australia, right. And we did the Australia and then we jumped back on a plane and then did the Vegas. That's crazy! That was nuts!")

Jho was spending millions in casinos in Las Vegas. And he was looking after his political friends too. In particular, he was careful to sate Rosmah's lust for material excess. The purchase of the diamonds in LA mentioned in the previous chapter was small change. It would later emerge that, in July 2013, he invited the Malaysian First Lady on board the *Topaz*, a super-yacht owned by the UAE's Sheikh Mansor (whom we will also meet later in this story). Schwartz – his favourite jeweller – had been flown in from New York. She was there to show Rosmah a beautiful pink heart 22-carat diamond. Two months later the diamond was placed in a necklace of interlinked smaller diamonds. It was then presented to Rosmah in September. The cost? $27.3 million – one of the most expensive pieces of jewellery anywhere on the planet.

I was to report on much of this over the coming months. And, thanks to the work of some superb opposition politicians in Malaysia – and my blog on Boxing Day 2013 – questions were already surfacing. Jho had come up with a series of odd explanations, including suggestions that his new-found mega-wealth was all cash built on the prudent success of his father and grandfather. It was all rather hazy, however. Only on one thing was he categorical: the rumours that he was involved with Malaysia's sovereign wealth fund known as 1MDB were absolutely wrong. Yes, he acknowledged, he had played a role in setting the fund up at its early stage. But suggestions he was still involved in any way after that were entirely false, he insisted.

It was, of course, a complete lie, but a revealing one at that. Because, by the beginning of 2014, he wasn't alone in trying to wash his hands of this mysterious body.

◆ ◆ ◆

I had first come across 1MDB in 2010 when I was investigating the finances of Sarawak's Taib Mahmud; it was 1MDB which had bought Jho out of trouble over his investments in the state – paying Taib for one of his own troubled businesses, thus releasing both him and Jho from imminent difficulty. It had raised a red flag, but I hadn't – yet – enquired too deeply. Now, however, three years on, the questions were stacking up.

1 Malaysia Development Berhad, to give it its full name, had been set up in 2009, with the stated aim of driving long-term economic development for Malaysia. Just like many similar publicly owned wealth funds around the world, the idea was simple. The state would throw cash into the fund – either through borrowing or through publicly owned assets. These would be held in trust and invested in anything from stocks and shares to capital projects, with profits returning to be used for the public good. Perhaps the best known such fund is Norway's, which has sunk an estimated $1 trillion of oil reserves into its own sovereign wealth fund. The aim is to fund long-term projects for generations to come.

1MDB's mission, upon its creation in 2009, was to invest funds in everything from energy, real estate and tourism to agribusiness. It was flagged up as a genuine attempt by the Malaysian government to plan for the long haul. And it was, from the outset, controlled entirely by the minister of finance – one Najib Razak.

Upon becoming prime minister, Najib's first act after taking control was to sanction a borrowing binge. First, a billion dollars, using local banks. Then, in 2010, another billion on top. Nothing untoward there: it was to be expected that such a venture would borrow to invest. Then, in 2012, a further $3.5 billion was borrowed and thrown into the fund, and the following year, yet another $3 billion on top.

By this point, eyebrows were being raised and opponents were beginning to ask what exactly 1MDB was doing. The questions were led, doggedly, by a local opposition politician called Tony Pua. Tony had a background in finance and, unlike most of his colleagues, he knew how to read a balance sheet. Poring over those accounts that were available, he laid out the picture. 1MDB's initial borrowing had gone straight into a joint venture with a mysterious firm called PetroSaudi. Yet this joint venture had yet to reap any benefits whatsoever. All the while interest was stacking up on the borrowing that had been made.

Indeed, the only thing 1MDB actually had definitely bought with all those billions of borrowed cash were two electricity generating plants in Malaysia called Tanjung Energy and Genting Energy, costing $3.5 billion. These purchases seemed puzzling, to say the least. Both were owned by businessmen close to the ruling elite. And while Najib and his allies claimed that the purchases would provide value for money, it was quickly apparent, and pointed out by Tony, that the purchases were a dud. The Tanjung Energy plant had been nearing the end of its contract with the government to supply electricity to customers, and Najib could have obtained a far better deal if he'd tried. Yet 1MDB paid top dollar to buy it – unnecessarily so.

And then there was the weird cost of the borrowing itself. Governments usually only pay a low interest rate on bonds, because they can pretty much guarantee they are going to pay the money back. Yet the charges for much of the borrowing – arranged by Goldman Sachs – were staggering.

Goldman arranged the two big billion dollar bonds in 2012 and 2013 (where cash is lent to a government by investors, who then receive a guaranteed rate of interest in return). It emerged that they had earned staggering sums for doing so. For example, the first $3.5 billion bond purchase in 2012 was divided into two $1.7 billion chunks. On the first, Goldman would make eleven percent of its total value, amounting to $190 million. On the second (following questions as to why Goldman had earned quite so much first time round), it accepted a lower fee, but still took home a huge $114 million. Once the cash was counted on both the 2012 and 2013 bond deals, it would be paid $590 million in fees, an unbelievable pay day.

The questions piled on. Why had 1MDB agreed to such crazy fees? What had it actually got for all this enormous debt? Why had it snaffled up the two power stations which weren't even generating nearly enough income to meet looming debt repayments? And what on earth was PetroSaudi?

In short, Malaysia's big sovereign wealth fund, which was set up to provide steady investment to the country's citizens, had borrowed billions and billions of dollars (and paid huge fees for the privilege), had taken part in a joint venture with an unknown company, had bought two duff power stations, and was now having to borrow more in order to service the debt interest on the original borrowing it had made.

No wonder questions were being asked. As a briefing noted from wealth management firm Merrill Lynch concluded: "1MDB's aggressive expansion and acquisitions have been financed largely by debt... 1MDB remains somewhat of an enigma and will be closely watched, given its fast growing leverage and aggressive expansion."

◆ ◆ ◆

I had returned from LA. It was now mid-April 2014. I had spent the year since Najib's election plugging away on my stories of choice: Taib's gross corruption in Sarawak, and Najib's equally dubious practices in KL. Late one night in London, with supper cleared, homework checked and the boys bedded down for school next day, I had holed up in my cosy kitchen for an extra hour or so, as was my wont, ferreting on the internet. I was curious about 1MDB, given its link to the UBG buyout. I didn't understand what was going on, however. Surfing the web, I suddenly stumbled on something which, to my mind, made a decent story. It was to prove to be the moment I hit the jackpot. I found a provable connection between 1MDB and the big spending Jho Low.

Scanning articles relating to 1MDB, I found a reference to "Irish court papers". The case involved a recent battle over the purchase of the Maybourne Hotel Group, owner of some of London's poshest hotels such as Claridges and the Connaught. A group of Irish investors had tried to buy the group, but had been stung in the crash of 2008. The ruling concerned an attempt of a rival group who were now trying to exploit the situation by taking control themselves.

It was called Wynton group. And the documents showed that the group was run by none other than Jho. I frowned as a question formed in my mind. How on earth could Jho afford to get involved? The answer was bizarre. Letters to the court revealed that Wynton group's assets were backed up, in writing, by 1MDB. Indeed, as the bidding war continued, Jho had submitted a further letter in January 2011, stating that the financing of the entire offer had "in principle" been fully underwritten by it.

I poured myself another glass of wine. So Jho was going around KL claiming he had nothing to do with 1MDB. Yet, here he was, in private, up to his oxters – using 1MDB cash to back up a spending splurge by his private equity fund on some of the world's most expensive real estate. How to explain that?

Reviewing the situation at my kitchen counter around 2am that April night, I remember thinking, "Wow, how do they get out of this?" I began to type.

"Why is Malaysia's sovereign wealth fund, which is supposed to be investing in development in Malaysia, evidently funding risky private equity ventures by Jho Low's companies?" questioned *Sarawak Report* the following day:

> Does it all mean that Jho Low is in fact a lead investor for 1MDB and if so what is his profit margin?
>
> Or is Jho Low in fact just a front for other investors who can't be named? Finally, does not Jho Low's involvement with 1MDB and his known close friendship with the family of its chairman, Najib Razak, provide the most convincing explanation to date for his, so far undisclosed, sources of investment income and his extraordinary sudden wealth?

There, I thought, a few rocks lobbed. Now it was time to see if they smashed anything up. I pressed send, and went to bed.

11. THE SOURCE

Spring 2014, London

AS with my story about Jho and Riza's shot at Hollywood fame a few months before, the story went viral. And most importantly, the very fact I was now breaking news about Jho and 1MDB meant that *Sarawak Report* became the go-to news outlet for the many insiders in Malaysia who wanted to find a way to get information out into the public domain. I was proving a point to people: I would publish and be damned and I didn't give a toss for lawyers' letters trying to close me down. My sources therefore knew that, when they leaked something to me, they'd get full value in return.

In May, I unearthed another story about Jho's mega-expenditure. He had donated no less than $50 million to a Houston-based cancer research initiative. Why was Jho dispensing such vast charity in this prosperous place, when there was so much need and suffering back home, I asked? Then, not long after, I uncovered the fact that, in November 2013, Jho, partnered with the Abu Dhabi wealth fund, Aabar, had bought out a concern called Coastal Energy from a previously jailed Houston oilman, named Oscar Wyatt, for $2.3 billion. The sums were absurd. And my stories were getting noticed.

There were now three questions which I was raising constantly on the site. Was 1MDB the source of Jho's crazy spending frenzy? Was he acting on Najib's orders? And could anyone prove it? That June, the story began to crack open.

Anwar Ibrahim, Najib's defeated opponent in the general election, had come to London. Seeking support over the prosecution he was facing in Malaysia, he spoke at a number of events involving expat Malaysians in London. I attended one at Chatham House. Afterwards I joined some of his entourage in a quiet Bayswater restaurant.

Anwar had gone on to prayers and some further meetings.

Meanwhile, his aides and I swapped stories about the various political scandals involving Najib back home. It was rather flattering: they wanted to know what I was writing next. I wanted to know whether they had any further information on 1MDB. And to my left, one of Anwar's colleagues sheepishly began to tell me what, initially, sounded like a far-fetched yarn: he had been approached by someone who claimed to know everything – and could prove it.

"It is far too bizarre and it is probably just a trap. The source wants money," the man said.

In my experience, many of the best stories come from information that can be easily dismissed as 'too strange' or 'probably from a fantasist' or just 'too hard' to get to the bottom of. So, I pressed for more detail. The man shrugged and pulled out his phone.

"They sent us this strange document and I photo'd it," he said. "If you give me your mobile number I will send it."

We continued to eat our noodles. But, as we did, I began scrolling down my iPhone at the picture he had sent me. It was a snapshot of a single sheet of A4 paper. It had been sent anonymously as a 'taster' to various people in Malaysia, who might be considered sufficiently interested in information that might damage the present prime minister. It read as follows:

Thousands of documents related to the deal 1mdb-ps (emails, faxes and bbm transcripts) All documents showing that the main goal of the deal was distribution of commissions. Names of all companies used, all emails, addresses used, etc.

The writer then listed excerpts of what appeared to be emails:

First discussion following the meeting in London between JL and PS for structuring the deal:
"Jho/Seet/Tiffany,
Many thanks for your time the other day. As discussed, there seems to be a number of things we can do together. However, I think we should try to focus on the more actionable ones for now

and we can then spend more time exploring some of the other areas where me might be able to cooperate.

The email was cut short at that point and the document moved on to a second snippet, where a telling French spelling in the heading gave me a first clue about the compiler of the document:

Evaluation of PS assets, instructions given to the evaluator and paiement
Report evaluating the Petroleum Exporation and Production Assets of PetroSaudi International Limited submitted 29 September 2009,

was all it said. On to an even more intriguing snippet:

BBM transcript beetwen JL and PS
_____: *Please send me your account details*
_____: *So I can sent you final instructions*
JL: Okay
_____: *Thanks*
JL: Asked bank n friend for it
JL: Will have it sent today once I get it
JL: Good progress?

Next:

Paiment done by 1MDB-PS for hundred of millions in Switzerland used for commissions:

Under this heading there appeared to be a screenshot of an electronic statement:

Payments to HRH_____
13-Sept-10 USD -25,000,000.00
04-May-10 USD -25,000,000.00

02-Mar-10 USD -3,000,000.00
18-Jan-10 USD -14,000,000.00
Please transfer CHF _____ with value date
_____ Zurich, Switzerland _____
Favour of _____
IBAN: CH _____

Following on from these heavily redacted fragments of documents was a list of other documents, including:

copies of JV agreement and Murabaha Financing Agreement dated 14th June 2010 between 1MDB PetroSaudi Limited and 1Malaysia Development Berhad

allowing for half a billion dollars to be drawn upon:

Amount: $500,000.00

The mystery compiler next assured his reader that he would be able to provide all the email addresses for the above deal, which he said was named 'Project Uganda'. A screenshot heading of an email from the sender 'Project Uganda' was included, sent to the following addresses:

shahrol.halmi@1mdb.com.my,
nik.kamil@1mdb.com.my,
casey.tang@1mdb.com.my,
radhi.mohamad@1mdb.com.my

The subject of the email was "Re:Signed Resolutions 1MDB PS/ JV Co – US250m." Finally, the base of the page indicated that the sender had details of the Sarawak "UBG deal" and "Important names involved". Linked to the important names was a last snippet of email:

"VERY PNC NOTE, delete post reading:

From MDM:

This is a very 'focused & effective' trip. Objective is not MOU or general business ties.

Specific that PM is seeing the 3 highest levels in Saudis (one to one) being the King, Crown Prince and Prince Naif while First Lady sees the Queen and Crown Princess to build "effective ties"

And to the side of this mysterious note was a little square of information in the bottom right hand corner of the A4 page and barely legible, which appeared to be a screen shot of a segment of a document ready to be signed. It read:

for and on behalf of
[PETROSAUDI INTERNATIONAL LTD]
in the presence of
[HRH PRINCE TURKI]
Signed by
SHAHROL HALMI
for and on behalf of
1MALAYSIA DEVELOPMENT BERHAD
in the presence of:
DATO' SRI ABDUL RAZAK
PRIME MINISTER OF MALAYSIA

And that was the document.

By now my dining companions had finished their noodles. I had still barely begun to eat. I tried to summarise mentally what I thought I had read. The document appeared to suggest that large bribes had been paid by 1MDB. And, what's more, whoever had sent the document was saying that he had Jho bang to rights as the main player. The documents were a mess, but that, for me, only pointed to their authenticity.

My dining companion was, however, less convinced: "Yes, but it could all just be rubbish. Those bits of documents are all a mess. They could be made up. And he [the source] is saying he won't deal with us any further unless we can promise to pay him $12 million. It's ludicrous."

I nodded. I have a tendency not to give in immediately when presented with obstacles on the path to a good story. Although, admittedly, a request for $12 million was a pretty big obstacle.

"If you are not prepared to have anything more to do with him, would you mind if I perhaps got in touch and tried to see if I could find out a little more?" I wheedled.

"Sure," replied my friend and he texted me the number of the contact and promised to message him or her that I would be in touch.

"Will you ring him first and let him know who I am and that I will get in contact?" I asked.

"Sure, I will tell him you are negotiating on our behalf," my lunch partner chortled, "What are you hoping to knock him down to?"

"Zero", I replied.

The following day, I chased up Anwar's aide. He had contacted the source on my behalf, in Thailand, where he was living. But his tone was no longer quite as jovial as the day before.

"I passed on the message, but I suggest you don't get caught up in this," he told me. His amused tone had disappeared. "He is in Thailand and when I spoke to him there was a Russian radio playing in the background. He has a strong accent from somewhere and my guess is that he is actually Russian mafia. My intelligence contacts in Bangkok tell me they operate all number of vicious, high grade con tricks out of Thailand and they are very dangerous. This is a classic ruse and I warn you to step away."

You can't get eaten down the phone, however, so I asked for the source's number and said I'd take it from there. I dialled. A man answered. He definitely wasn't Russian; his voice sounded French. Yes, he could prove everything. Yes, he had evidence, and yes, he would be happy to meet.

I called my husband at home. Andrew had a default position with me by this point: yes, he could remonstrate about me disappearing, but what was the point when it was obvious I'd made up my mind?

The next day, I was on a plane to Thailand.

12. TEN NOUGHTS

June 2014, Bangkok

I did feel a bit guilty by this point. I had already ruined one family Christmas holiday chasing this story. Now, in the middle of June, my younger son was sitting his AS Level exams and my older one was tackling Higher Maths. A time for a mum to be around.

Furthermore, there was a rather fundamental problem whenever I went away. My husband and the two boys were rather unreconstructed when it came to the kitchen. Andrew simply didn't know how to cook and had even, on one famous occasion, tried to microwave an egg – with explosive results. Following this episode, he had decided that, whenever I went on a trip, he would go to M&S and buy several ready meals, instructing the boys to help themselves and remember to heat them in the microwave. But the boys were now protesting at their parents 'neglect', complaining that days on end of ready meals made them feel depressed, which was all very understandable. Whenever I could, I tried to pre-prepare some popular re-heatables to leave in the fridge, like shepherd's pie and bolognaise so their diet was at least passable. The trouble was that the tempo of my work had increased. I reasoned that it was best just to pack everything possible into as short a trip as I could and to get back as soon as possible.

Perhaps a little too easily, I put my guilt to one side, headed to Heathrow, and got on board the flight to Bangkok.

My conversation with the source had been brief. Yes, he was aware of who I was. Yes, he would be willing to fly in to Bangkok to meet me. I should text on arrival. We'd meet on the 15th.

Truth be told, I didn't know whether to trust him or not. As Anwar's contact had said in London, I could be walking straight into a trap.

I got into Bangkok, checked into an airport hotel, and –

apprehensively – called him again.

"I would prefer to meet somewhere public and well-guarded," I said. "Is there a central hotel you can suggest?"

"I fully understand. I was going to suggest the Athene Palace [a 5* international hotel] at 11am," was the reply.

Perfect.

I felt reassured that he accepted my concerns about the idea of going into a dark corner of Bangkok to meet a stranger. The next day I took at cab from the airport and found a seat in what I hoped was a reasonably exposed but quiet position in the large and rambling foyer of the hotel. I opened up my laptop and killed some time as inconspicuously as I was able. I had by now conjured a mental picture of my contact, mainly to reassure myself. My image was of a pasty, bookish, office worker, who had stumbled on this information and, since he resented his bosses at PetroSaudi, had determined to share it. I decided he would be small, shy and mild.

"Are you Clare?" echoed a deep voice from behind and above. I physically jumped.

Far from being the man I had expected, I was greeted by an extremely tall, muscular, beach-bronzed individual looking down on me, who could clearly have eliminated me with one blow. He looked uncomfortable, almost as uncomfortable as me.

"Yes," I replied. "And you?"

He refused to give me his name. Looking around the hotel foyer, he explained his presence. He represented a group who had information available that would, if made public, bring down the entire Malaysian government.

I tried to maintain an air of scepticism, pointing out to him that people back in the UK who had put me in touch with him didn't think anything would come of it.

"I will be honest," I said. "They don't really believe that you have the information you say you have and they are fearful you are a trap. I am here because I have done a lot of background on this story and was persuaded by the material you produced that you may very well have the evidence you say you do, but they themselves are not that interested right now."

He nodded but didn't seem perturbed in any way. "I have hired a meeting room upstairs. Are you comfortable with that as we will need some privacy?"

Slightly nervously, I followed him up to the first floor and the business unit, guarded by its own reception. He sounded Swiss-French but looked more southern, particularly given his tan. He was in his 40s. I guessed he might possibly be Arab – was he one of the Saudis involved in all this? He wasn't saying.

Placing his laptop on the desk he sat down and looked hard at me. "I want you to know straight up," he said. "This for me is about the money. Nothing more and nothing less. I am prepared to come down to $2 million, that is a figure I am owed, but no further. This for me is a very dangerous enterprise and I need the money to protect myself and I have other issues. There are also people I need to pay. There is no room to negotiate and frankly this material is gold for Anwar or anyone in the opposition who wants to expose that greedy bastard Najib."

$2 million was certainly a very long way down from the $12 million I had been earlier cited, so it was progress in the right direction. But it was also a long way from zero. I tried not to swallow. I knew that I had a very tough job on my hands trying to broker any sort of understanding between a man who said he cared only about the money and opposition politicians who had no money and were terrified above all of being caught in any kind of compromising activity.

"I agree, they need this kind of evidence if you have it. But, I don't think they have this sort of money to be honest. All I can do is try to assess what you have on the basis of my research into 1MDB and then discuss the matter with them," I parried.

"Of course they can find the money. We are talking about the chance to take power in Malaysia. There is a huge sum of money at stake and they can find enough to see me right in return for what I can do for them."

"Weeeell, I think they want to do things differently," I replied.

"Their platform is about reform. But, let me try to understand what you have. I promise now that I will not publish any of what you show me without your permission and I will not betray you as a source. I will act towards you with integrity on these matters, whether or not any of this comes to anything. I ask for your trust, based on the fact that you can see from my work that I have been given many confidences and do not betray my sources." I looked him in the eye, because I meant it.

By now the pair of us were easing up. I felt he could see that my intentions were honest and I had also started to sense that his cold, financial stance was a mask for a more emotional and widely motivated person. He knew about the situation in Malaysia and he had a moral view on it. I could feel there were plenty of things we could probably agree on. He opened his computer to give me a taste of what he had. "Don't take notes," he barked, but soon I was taking them and he pretended not to notice.

I jotted down anything I could for future reference, to jog my memory or to prove a connection – bank numbers, dates, company names. He spun through a bewildering number of documents, opening and closing them at enormous speed. These could only be genuine emails, as there was simply too much data jumbled up in the file he had opened for it to be some kind of fraud – I was by then 95 percent convinced it wasn't a hoax, but we would still need to prove it.

In total, there were a staggering 330,000 emails. I asked him about the time period covered.

"Two years, from 2009 to 2011, the period of the 1MDB deal. They were like amateurs at the time, with all that incriminating material just there on email. Afterwards, they realised how compromising all this was and so they physically removed the servers both from London and Geneva and shipped them over to Jeddah, where they could be held out of sight."

I was only partially listening. My eye had been caught by a particularly large figure noted down as a bank transfer. To begin with, I had read it as $700,000. But then I noticed an extra line of noughts, three of them. We had skimmed past it but I wanted to double check.

"That wasn't a payment for $700 million dollars I just saw, was it?"

That tingly feeling had started raising all my follicles again.

He scrolled back, trying to find the figure in question. "Not sure I can find it again for now," he said, "but yes, that was the first payment to Good Star – the first big bribe to Jho Low".

I felt almost winded. A $700 million bribe to Jho Low? "Please, please can we try to retrieve that document, because I need to be solid about what you have if I am going to be able to try and convince people to open negotiations," I begged.

He looked again, as exhausting and nerve-wracking minutes passed. "Here. Here is another version of the same transfer."

Sure enough, the figure had a resounding eight zeros followed by a dot and another two zeros. Ten noughts. I scribbled down dates, bank numbers, but there was no stated recipient beyond Coutts Zurich. Surely the Queen of England's own bloody bank wasn't taking whopping sums like that on behalf of a notorious shyster like Jho Low?

If only I could pore over all this data straight away. It was tantalising: this was what every journalist dreamed of – unvarnished private documentation, here in black and white. I felt sure, just looking at it, that it would show the full secret of the 1MDB scandal. And yet it remained just out of my grasp.

"How do we know the account belonged to Jho Low?"

"It belonged to the company Good Star Limited, based in the Caymans [on this he turned out to be slightly incorrect; the company was incorporated in the Seychelles]. Jho Low owns Good Star."

My contact, who had still not given me his name, suddenly drew himself up. "You know, I have worked in the oil business. Commissions are normal, maybe five percent, maybe even fifteen percent, but this is disgusting. It is outrageous. Out of a billion dollars they took 70 percent and that was just the start. And where did the other 30 percent go? That went into the legitimate business, the side I was later involved in, but how could they justify such a huge theft of money?"

I tried to get a handle on what I was looking at. "This was money raised in the name of lifting up poor Malaysians. Are you now telling me that $700 million of borrowed cash, on which the country was paying very high interest, was diverted to Jho Low?"

"Precisely," he replied. He then shut his laptop. "That's enough," he said. "You can see this is for real and that I have it all. Go and tell your friends they have the weapon they need to help the right people in Malaysia take back the election they should have won. I need to move now to catch my internal flight, otherwise I will be another night away from my wife and she is pregnant with our first child – it will be a boy."

His handsome face lit up with irresistible pride and within moments we were chatting about sons and parenthood. We had the beginnings of an understanding by the time we had shaken hands and parted at the lift.

It felt surreal. The figures seemed absurd. You didn't just steal $700 million like that, and get away with it. Who in their right mind would ever think that was possible? And surely, given the vast sums involved, someone would already have exposed this? Why wasn't every financial journalist on the planet currently poring all over this? Why hadn't the judicial or political authorities in Malaysia opened up a full investigation? Why did it, apparently, all depend on a freelance journalist like me finding $2 million to pay to this anonymous man in order to get the story out? I walked back into the hot Thai sun, still jetlagged, and wondered what to do next.

And yet, here was the most surreal bit of the whole story: it all felt genuine. His information was all too detailed and too thorough to be a hoax. I was a trained sceptic, I knew how to spot a fraudster. This man wasn't one. I called my source back in London.

"How can you be sure about it?" he said.

"I am not completely sure, but so far everything fits. There are no discordant notes," I said. "Have you no rich party faithful who might just step in and pay this guy, given how high the stakes now are?"

"No", he replied. "They think Mahathir is behind all this. They think it's a trick."

"How so?"

He sighed: "Let me introduce you to the person who told me about this story."

13. XAVIER

Summer 2014, Bangkok (again)

THIS was becoming very serious. I got back from Thailand and, within a few weeks, Anwar's contact arranged for me to go back to Heathrow for the meeting with his own source: the man who had first sent him the taster material about 1MDB. Almost literally, I could feel myself going higher and higher up the ladder of Malaysian politics. Three figures dominated it: Anwar, the jailed opposition leader, Najib, the prime minister, and – above them both, still – Mahathir. Now nearing his 90s, he might have been expected to be in a retirement home. But fit, healthy, and politically active, everyone knew that this Asian tiger was still a force to be reckoned with, and feared.

The man – who I am calling Din – had contacts with both Anwar and Mahathir when the two men were rivals, and had trodden a fine line between the two. He had been passed the information about 1MDB and had then given it to Anwar (from where it made its way to me). He was treated with suspicion by Anwar's team. But they now had a common goal: to flush out Najib and get to the bottom of the staggering corruption now being uncovered.

He arrived in a chauffeur-driven limousine and we began to talk. He had been passed the information from a contact in business who was friendly with my new Bangkok source. No, he was not willing to spend $2 million to buy it from him. But, yes, he was deeply concerned about Malaysia, wanted to see a reconciliation between Mahathir and Anwar, and wanted to do what he could do put the country back on an even keel. Din knew little of the content of the documentation which he had steered in my direction or what further information there might be. It was I who would eventually start to tell him what I had learnt – all of which he passed back to Mahathir, I soon began to realise.

The meeting broke up inconclusively. It became clear to me soon after that it would be up to me to try and find someone prepared to stump up the necessary payment to release the information into the public domain. So began a frenetic and frustrating six months as I scoured the earth for takers on the story, spent delicate hours probing to see if I could switch the strategy of the source (get him to give me the material, in other words).

I don't think I have travelled so much in my life as I did those following months in 2014. There was the radio project (now based in Brunei) to keep tabs on, conference invitations resulting from all that profile and various NGO events in Jakarta and Japan. I tried to weave it all into connected trips, taking every opportunity to see if I could entice someone into helping me lay my hands on what I was certain was a huge international story. I was now increasingly convinced that this could become the case study that would shine a glaring light on just how the global financial players, our banks and other institutions, were assisting kleptocratic leaders like Najib Razak and, of course, Taib Mahmud, to destroy their countries through unimpeded corrupt practice.

Put simply, if a mega-thief can't move his money out into the world economy, store it in a respectable bank and enjoy it as if it were clean cash, what's the point in stealing it in the first place? All the evidence in this case showed that, thanks to the offshore system and compliant local banks, laundering cash was still perfectly possible for a half-competent kleptocrat. This was a truth which lay behind the misery of so many victims of corruption and I wanted to prove it. Yes, I had been excited about taking on a story that would create a storm in my backyard of Malaysia. But now I felt that this might be a story that could take on global significance – and that is what any journalist lives to get their teeth into and uncover.

In mid-July 2014 I even shuttled back over to LA in the hope there might be takers there. There weren't and every time I sounded out a new potential party it extended the risk for the source and the story itself. The tension of those months was maddening as I could feel my source was losing faith that I could deliver on a deal or that his mission was something he could ever carry through.

In August, my mother died suddenly. As we mourned, I spent time with my father. He and I had often quarrelled about the fate of Borneo. Even as an 8-year-old I had demanded he do more to prevent the cutting down of the jungle. He, however, had insisted that there was nothing we westerners could do. Now, however, he encouraged me. He was interested and engaged. He wanted me to keep going. Two weeks after my mother died he and I therefore agreed that I should get back onto the story once again.

I called up my source in Bangkok and told him I was coming. He agreed to meet me. We met at the same hotel as before. And, this time, he began to open up.

◆ ◆ ◆

His name was Xavier Justo. He was a citizen of Switzerland. He was a former senior employee of PetroSaudi, the mysterious firm which had entered a joint venture with 1MDB a few years earlier. He had left the company in 2011, three years before. Not long after we sat down, he began to talk about his time in the firm.

Xavier's way in to PetroSaudi had been his longstanding friend Tarek Obaid, one of the men who welcomed Najib and Rosmah onto the boat off the coast of Monaco in 2009.

"He was like a younger brother to me," Xavier said. "Let me explain the background to this."

In the early 2000s, Xavier and Tarek joined up with another friend and a British/Swiss businessman called Patrick Mahony to try and make some money.

"We were like four Musketeers," said Xavier, "Tarek, myself, another friend and Patrick Mahony. We all hung out. Tarek had pretty much nothing, since his father had frittered away his fortune. There is one cleverer older brother, who has got jobs in the Saudi administration, there is a younger one, who just hangs out in Geneva and there was Tarek looking for opportunities. They had been to school in Geneva and Tarek's big contact was Prince Turki – he is the seventh son of the current King of Saudi. The idea was to make some big business using this contact. I was having a success in business in my own right with my company and together with our other friend I loaned Tarek SF100,000 to set up the company PetroSaudi."

Xavier laughed: "What a fantastic band name! That is all it was, a shell with a fantastic name that sounded like a billion dollars. We reckoned with that name, with a Saudi Prince on board we could make some deals. That was the idea."

I was scribbling notes.

"The clever one was Patrick Mahony. He is the cleverest businessman I have ever encountered," said Xavier.

"Never underestimate him. He is very dangerous. He was working for the private equity group Ashmore at that time. In fact, for months he was running the PetroSaudi venture and working for Ashmore at the same time. We were all like brothers."

Xavier sighed. The idea had worked but, around 2009, Xavier had dropped out. The crash had wreaked havoc with his company and he headed off to Thailand with his new girlfriend, whom he had met through work. They had travelled for many months and fallen in love with the country and each other. The pair had decided to settle down and find a new life working in the tourist sector on their savings.

Xavier continued the story. "Then Tarek calls from Geneva. He tells me to get off the beach and get back to Europe since they had hit the jackpot – a huge deal – and now they needed to put the company into action. He needed me to run the show. At first I rejected him, not interested and happy where I was, but he said he would offer me £400,000 a year and all expenses paid. There would be a central London flat for me and Laura near the new London base in Mayfair that was now housing the company. I should be the director, there would be international travel, there was money and they needed to expand fast – there was already a project in Venezuela and I needed to get over immediately. They needed someone who knew business, whom they could trust. OK, so I agreed and we moved over to London. Big mistake."

What had happened, I presumed, trying to draw a timeline, was that Tarek and Turki had just got together with Najib and Jho Low.

"When I got there they were cagey. Of course, there was something that had been going on. Suddenly there was all this money, it was madness. I knew there was shady stuff, but on my first day, when I was introduced to the new president of the company I pretended I was happy. Rick Haythornthwaite – you know him?"

I shook my head.

"He is a really big name in business. Big positions. Look him up. Rick called me in to talk and the first thing he asked was, 'this Malaysia deal, is everything OK with that?' I said, 'Sure, I know them all, it's all above board.' Of course, I was sure it wasn't, but that was that, we did not discuss it further."

He carried on: "It was a really exciting job for that year, don't get me wrong. It was not good for me and Laura, because I was travelling so much, but for me it was very intense. I was heading up the new Venezuela operation, we were raising more investors and we had this huge contract, a drilling ship that was making $500k a day. How we got the contract was suspicious. They took the Saudi prince over to impress people and there were bribes for certain. But by the time I got there it was just operational stuff and money to raise. I didn't feel comfortable with the lifestyle they had slipped into by then, however. It was embarrassing and tacky. Wild parties, whores, stuff going down – not my scene. I had a nice girl at home.

"For the main, though, it was the dream job. I would go round with this Haythornthwaite, who would play the classic English gentleman as our figurehead and the investors all lapped it up and then I would clinch the deals. But, there were problems."

What problems, I asked?

"It was like there were two sides to the office and I was no longer within an inner circle of friends, or wholly trusted. And Tarek, he had not just made a great deal, it was more than that – there was a huge amount of money. I was dealing with all the formal company accounts, these were with JP Morgan and I managed all of that. But there was other money and there were other deals where I played no part – they kept me out. And they had become arrogant towards me. Tarek had gone from a penniless young guy, who borrowed from me, into this spendthrift millionaire, but he started to short-change me and treat me with disrespect. He had promised me £400,000 before I left Thailand, but when I arrived it had changed to £300,000. I am not so greedy and I didn't challenge that, but then I found that the rent on my property, my business class flights, these weren't being paid. I had to sort my own expenses from my pocket and it was becoming frustrating – the company owed me a lot of money by the end of that year. Also, Tarek had become a mess. He was hard to speak to, he flew into rages, he was on painkillers and drinking wildly – he would insult me to my face and demean me. It got too much."

He had got too rich too quick, I asked?

"Yes, it had all gone to his head. He had become wild and arrogant and he was taking substances. He was not the friend I had known. One night he just sent me all these texts – it was too much. I was finished with them. The next day I told them I was leaving. I refused to change my mind. I cut a deal with them, it included paying me the money they owed me. But, when I got back they cheated me and cut it again. I was so sad at the time, so cut up I just walked away, but soon I felt very angry. I want revenge and the two million they owe me."

Xavier could not have been more frank and informative. And now I understood his motive. He and Laura had returned to Thailand where they had married and bought a beachside property, which over the past year they had been developing into their dream guesthouse business. There were seven apartment suites, a pool over the sea, tennis courts. It was massive and they were ready to open, but the money was running dry and now their baby was on the way. Somewhere along the way Xavier had come by the means to exact his revenge and rescue his situation – he had got a copy of the data from the server which, he said, PetroSaudi had later decided to export to Saudi.

My pad replete with my scribbled notes, we repaired to the business centre for a few remaining minutes to take another look at what Xavier was trying to offer the Malaysian opposition.

"I love this part of the world," he told me, again opening up his files. "The Thais are lovely people and so kind. We are very happy here, but so many people are poor in Asia. It makes me so angry to think of all that money that was borrowed to supposedly help the poorest Malaysians being spent on booze, drugs and whores – ridiculous waste and excess like that. It is morally disgusting."

I heartily agreed. Xavier had a financial motive, but also a moral compass. As we flicked through documents again, I looked out for key words. There were emails from Jho to people at 1MDB, in particular the chief executive, Shahrol Halmi, years after he had claimed he had nothing further to do with the fund. And there were messages from him to Patrick Mahony, referring to orders from the 'Big Boss' (which had to be Najib) and to 'Madame' (Rosmah). Financial transactions with 1MDB were being back-copied to him by Mahony and Tarek. It was obvious there was mounds of evidence here to prove that Jho and Najib were lying about 1MDB and maybe more. But was there also real-proof that that $700 million had been diverted from the PetroSaudi deal to Jho's company's bank account?

"I have been looking through these for months. Yes, I think you have all the proof you need," said Xavier. But he wasn't giving it till I paid him the money I still did not have.

We parted company once more. Xavier and I had developed a variety of means of messaging by now and as we communicated over the next few days he agreed to let me write up a story to indicate that I had started to learn more about 1MDB and its relationship with Jho. I wanted to get the message out that Jho was up to his neck. After all, the fund was still gearing up for a planned floatation on the stock exchange in the latter half of 2014, and claiming that the role of Jho in 1MDB was "zero".

But without the actual documentation, it was difficult to nail the story down. And no one I spoke to was sufficiently interested or deep-pocketed to engage with Xavier and offer him cash. After twenty years of ferreting out stories, I knew that, above all, persistence pays (I would later therefore accept as a badge of honour an angry

comment from PetroSaudi's Mahony calling me a 'persistent pest'.)
Yet, despite my most persistent efforts, I was starting to lose hope
that this huge and revealing stash of information would ever be
brought into the open.

In the middle of the month I was invited to Australia with Peter
John, to accept, on behalf of Radio Free Sarawak, the University of
Queensland's Media for Social Change Award. Afterwards I flew to
join Bruno Manser Fund campaigners in Japan to launch their book
on Sarawak's timber corruption in the country where it mattered
most, the chief customers for the wood itself. In between I fitted in a
short journey to Bangkok to see an increasingly exasperated Xavier
once more.

We nearly missed each other after a series of delays and catching
up at our now familiar venue in the business centre of the Hotel
Athene we flicked again through the material I had previously
seen. No time for details, just the overview as ever – we had only
20 minutes.

One name suddenly caught my eye. "That contract you just flicked
past... can we go back to that?"

"We don't have much time," said Xavier. "You know the whole
story now. Either get me that buyer or we leave it. These people are
beyond dangerous. I need the money to escape them when I need
to. They may come after me. And I need it for my kid who is coming
soon. I feel I am making a big sacrifice bringing this to the open and
I should receive some protection."

My mind was still on the document. I scrolled back to it. Yes: there
was a familiar name. "I do understand and I am really doing my best
on this. But, that contract there...." I pointed to a familiar name.
"Did these PetroSaudi people hire Blair?!"

Xavier looked at me nonchalantly. "Sure, he was great window-
dressing for them. And also to get some deals. They needed to
expand their business and it is all about mutual access."

There, on the screen, "Tony Blair Associates" was written in black
and white. I gulped.

"I know that is not very central to our story and maybe not very interesting to you, but back home in the UK that contract is bloody dynamite. The entire UK media have been trying to find out what the hell he's up to and how he's making so much money. Can I look at what they were paying him?" I asked.

"Sure, here you can have a couple of the copies – there are lots of red lines, but this looks like the finished contract."

Xavier swished a couple of documents onto a pen drive and then onto my own laptop. If I had received nothing more these would have justified the trip.

For Xavier, the Blair connection was a sideshow to the much bigger story of corruption. For me, however, it was a thread that might help me unravel the whole thing. Blair's earnings were, at the time, the subject of huge interest within the UK. I could now use this data to push the PetroSaudi/1MDB story into the UK media – which, like everyone else up till then, had ignored it entirely.

Blair's deal was quite something. After an initial approach to his company, his close aide Mark Labovitch had initially solicited for a retainer of $100,000 a month. In the end he settled for a $65,000 a month retainer from PetroSaudi for his 'advisory' and 'negotiating' services, plus a staggering two percent of the value of any contract negotiated, uncapped. The deal, organised by Mahony, was simple: Blair's job would be to use his own contacts in China to point potential investors towards PetroSaudi. For its part, PetroSaudi would, thanks to its grand Saudi connections, offer these Chinese investors the chance to access oil and gas reserves in Saudi Arabia and gain access to government contracts. Writing to Blair's office in 2009, Mahony blithely declared: "We are very happy to… work with the relevant Chinese companies to bring them to the Kingdom and give them full access to our shareholders' ability to win large government contracts." He was bluffing outrageously; PetroSaudi was, according to Xavier, still a shell at this point and had no expertise in exploration and extraction. But Tony Blair Associates did not appear to be digging too deeply. Indeed, they appeared to be wholly comfortable with a relationship with a company whose business model was purely and simply about political influence.

It was, though, an awkward story for me to sell; Tony had been a Labour prime minister and my brother-in-law his successor. Suspicions and accusations would be rife, especially amongst the circles of hangers-on, that this was a plot, when in fact it was merely the product of Tony doing business with a company I was investigating over their unsavoury practices in Malaysia.

I decided to stay in the background and instead passed the story onto contacts at the *Sunday Times*, contenting myself with merely picking up on their article for my blog. That suited my agenda with Xavier as well, since neither of us wanted to draw attention to the real source of this material at that stage.

There was another significant point to this exercise, which was that it tested Xavier's data and proved its accuracy. The *Sunday Times* ran the documents past separate sources and corroborated that they were genuine and correct. Moreover, whilst Blair's office protested over the story, it did not challenge the authenticity of the documents. If such a hugely sensitive, secret, unexpected and important piece of data retrieved at random from Xavier's database had been proven to be correct, then I could rest assured that we were dealing with a genuine source and a genuine product – the rest of the data needed to be corroborated, of course, in the normal way, but this was no grand hoax.

It just remained to either persuade Xavier to give it up or to persuade somebody else that now we could be sure that his information was genuine, it was worth the price in terms of exposing corruption at the very top back in Malaysia.

Thankfully, I was about to meet a man with a very big cheque book.

14. A DEAL

January 2015, Singapore

FOR most journalists in Malaysia, freedom to challenge the government had long been strictly conditional. In theory, there is a free press. But, as all titles know, overt criticism of the ruling authorities was certain to be met with their licences being pulled. Despite this, there were still some titles and websites which, bravely, sought to dig out the facts. Among them was a Singapore-based financial newspaper called the *Edge*.

By the beginning of 2015, it had already produced plenty of exclusive stories which raised major questions about 1MDB. It had examined the crazy payments given to Goldman Sachs for the two bonds it organised in 2012 and 2013. Why had 1MDB paid over the odds? Perhaps, people were asking, it was on the understanding that no questions would be asked about the use of the money. The *Edge* also focused on two businessmen known to be close to the ruling BN party: Ananda Krishnan, owner of Tanjung, and the Lim family behind the Genting business empire, from whom 1MDB had bought two power stations at an inflated cost. The paper reported that, subsequently, Ananda had handed over 400 million Malaysian dollars to a 'charity foundation' linked to 1MDB, while Genting had thrown in a further 190 million dollars. And the *Edge* was also reporting on the losses at the fund, and on Jho Low's connection to it all.

Now, at the start of 2015, with a plan to float 1MDB on the Malaysian stock exchange – pencilled in for April 2015 – seemingly a deal in the water, the *Edge* was reporting on its terrible condition. As my sources were also telling me, nobody in their right mind would buy shares in a turkey like this. To add to the sense of crisis, Mahathir threw in his own bombshell, demanding that UMNO sack Najib. Meanwhile, rumours circulated of a secret dossier being held by a whistle-blower which, it was said, threatened to blow the whole thing apart.

It was intensely frustrating. I had seen that dossier. It was being held by my source. But I had just about run out of ideas on how to give Xavier the funding he wanted. Without some cash, it seemed that the story was doomed to stay hidden forever. Then, however, I caught a break.

I was back in the cold of London. Out of the blue, I got a call from Tony Pua, the Malaysian opposition MP who had done so much to pursue Najib over the 1MBD affair. That day, Tong Kooi Ong, the publisher of the *Edge* had taken out legal proceedings against Jho after an anonymous blogger that Tong was sure Jho was behind had called him a traitor. Tong's blood was up – and he wanted to attack. "I have been asked to pass you Tong's number," said Tony. "My guess is that he is aware of the material you have been pursuing and he may be interested in acquiring it."

Tong was wealthy. He had made his money in finance, lots of it. He had then decided to use his windfall to set up the *Edge* – which, unlike many other self-censoring Malaysian titles, was more or less independent. Yet he presented a contradiction too. It was clear he enjoyed using his title to ruffle feathers. At the same time, like any rich Malaysian, he was a party insider who had shown he was not at all averse to playing Najib's game (he had earlier played an important role in the setting up of Sarawak Securities, a Taib family company, which had made yet another fortune for them by monopolising access to the stock exchange in the state). I thought of him as a Southeast Asian equivalent of Rupert Murdoch: a media baron, who was prepared to pay for stories when they were big enough, like this one was, but ruthless enough to bury it too, if is suited his purposes.

I dialled the number Tony had given me and Tong answered immediately. He got straight to the point. Was this really the inside information on 1MDB and did it prove the ongoing association of Jho with the fund, he wanted to know? Good, he replied, then let's talk. I ran off and texted Xavier. "I think I have your deal," I told him.

The following week, I was back in Southeast Asia, this time in

Singapore, to introduce Xavier and Tong to each other.

♦ ♦ ♦

The tension was hard to bear, and the scale of what we were discussing was brought home to me when I checked into my hotel in Singapore and ordered room service. Shyly, the waiter bringing the food held out his hand. "You are the editor of *Sarawak Report* aren't you?" I nodded, surprised to be spotted in Singapore. He continued: "I am from Sarawak myself and I just wanted to thank you for doing what you do. We are all very appreciative." It was these encouragements that kept me going and the knowledge that real lives were affected by the stories I was writing. If I could pin down 1MDB, it wouldn't just affect people in Sarawak, the impact would be felt globally.

Furthermore, the next day,10th February, was the day Anwar Ibrahim was due in the Federal Court to hear the final ruling on the charges of sodomy he had faced over the previous six years. Many had advised him to leave the country rather than face a politically driven judgement that threatened yet another lengthy sentence. But for him to have run away would have counted him out of politics – a victory for Najib he was not prepared to concede.

To this backdrop, I made my way to Tong's lawyer's office, high up in one of Singapore's endless tower blocks, which even the taxi driver could not identify without multiple enquiries. Flustered and somewhat late, I was pushing the buzzer, when I was joined by a diminutive, rather dishevelled, middle-aged individual, who looked as if he had slept overnight in his crumpled bright orange shirt and baggy jeans and had forgotten to comb his hair.

"You must be Clare," he burst out agreeably, progressing into a slightly manic high-pitched laugh. "I am Tong. At least this is not boring," he said. After a pause, he added: "I can stand anything as long as it's not boring." He hooted with more of his eccentric, intelligent laughter. I liked Tong immediately.

We were joined soon after by Ho Kay Tat, the editor of the *Edge* and the man responsible for so many informed and insightful articles on

1MDB over the previous months. The three of us, several lawyers and advisers then sat down in the law office's boardroom, around a vast oval table, with windows looking out onto the concrete jungle of Singapore.

I was invited to explain my case. I took a deep breath and kicked off. The content of the data I had seen, I told them, related to politically connected thefts from 1MDB and would prove the criminal circumstances that had landed the fund with $12 billion in debts it could not service. The source wanted $2 million to hand it over. I made clear that I wanted no involvement in the financial aspect of the deal and sought no payment either. However, I suggested that if I could introduce the newspaper to the source then I would ask merely for a promise that I too would receive a copy of the data. I pledged to cooperate with them in publishing it so that I would not jump their scoops. On the other hand I would want to be in there on the first day of the story.

I concluded, "If you do settle on his price then I reckon this will turn out to be the record amount ever paid for a single story ever, anywhere. Given the magnitude of the story, its international and political ramifications, I actually happen to think it's worth it."

I finished. "Sensitive material" one of the lawyers muttered. There were many smiles around the table, but little more. This was not the UK, where lawyers and newsmen might have leapt at the challenge of negotiating such a high-profile situation; it was Singapore, where official secrets are treated as sacred, companies and banks are the source of all income and the media controls were possibly even harsher than in Malaysia.

Kay Tat broke the silence. "How can you be sure this is genuine material?" he demanded, as any editor would. I told him that after months of scrutiny and discussions with the source, I was 99.9 percent convinced. Further all-round silence.

"Time for some lunch?" suggested Tong. "Maybe I can discuss matters further with my lawyers and we can meet again in the afternoon?"

I took my cue. It was agreed Tong would call me later. Meanwhile,

Xavier had texted me to say he had arrived from Bangkok and was making his way into town from the airport, so we agreed to meet for our own lunch at the Fullerton Marina Hotel, which sits along the waterfront from the main Fullerton Hotel, itself a conversion from the stately Old Post Office building and one of the landmarks of traditional Singapore.

Xavier was late, so I ordered for myself at the glass-walled café that overlooks the picturesque marina, fringed with boardwalks that lead along the waterfront. Munching on my salad, I glumly concluded this was not going to be easy. Plus, I was in danger of being squeezed out of the story. Ho Kay Tat, Tong's editor, would presumably not want me interfering in a potential scoop. We were both journalists chasing the same scoop after all – I was the one who had landed it, but it was he who had the wherewithal and clout to clinch the deal.

Xavier arrived and after months of being in touch it felt like a meeting of old friends. I filled him in as best I could. Tong definitely had the money, I said, and he was clearly keen on landing a major story. But I felt we were a long way off a satisfactory transaction. Xavier had broached the question as to whether I wanted a cut and I had told him I did not want to be compromised in such a way. I wanted that clear on all sides.

Tong then called; he was coming in through the door at that moment with Kay Tat and they wanted to talk to me alone. I told Xavier to stay put and I shifted quickly to another part of the foyer. "Is he here?" Tong hissed, looking around conspiratorially.

"Not far away at all and we have spoken," I said.

"Look. I have discussed with the lawyers and they say it is better they don't get involved. Let's keep it informal," he said.

"What about the risks?" I asked. "What if the data sucks?"

"I trust you and these are troubled times." It was an oblique reference to the fact that, minutes earlier, over the border in Malaysia, Anwar had been found guilty by federal judges and was being taken away in a police van to jail to serve another five-year term on a trumped up sodomy charge.

There followed a bizarre afternoon and evening to rival anything

I had experienced in the 1MDB affair. First, Tong wanted to know whether Xavier would budge from $2 million.

"Well, to be honest," I said, "he seems pretty fixed on that particular sum."

I pointed out that $2 million wasn't a long way off the legal fees of a libel case. Maybe even a little less.

There was a pause. And then: "OK, let's not quibble. Where is he?"

Introductions followed. Tong's computer experts checked the data, which Xavier had brought on a hard drive, and confirmed it was genuine (though because the files were security-protected they were struggling to make decipherable copies). Xavier didn't have a bank account set up which could accept a sudden $2 million payment. I ended up ringing a broker friend of my brother, whom I knew in Singapore, to see if he could help manage the transaction, but to no avail. Xavier then announced he wanted to leave as soon as possible to get back to his family, and that Tong and Kay Tat could take the hard drive on trust. Kay Tat put the drive in his suit pocket. By way of a guarantee, Tong then suddenly declared that, if Xavier wanted a sign of their good faith, he could take one of his Monet paintings which he had hanging in the office.

Xavier frowned: "How could I just walk off clutching a Monet in the street and through the airport?" It seemed a fair, if unreal, question to ask.

Forget Monets, I thought. I had other concerns. As we prepared to split, I piped up: "Can I ask about me? Do I get a copy of the data and to do the story also?"

"To be honest that works for us," said Tong to my intense relief. Probably he and Kay Tat had agreed it would give them some cover if I was writing it up too, given how sensitive the material was. Tong then took me aside to make clear that while he wanted to expose this scandal, neither of us should seek to take it to Najib's door.

"We need to hold back on the full story, on some of the information. It must not touch the top. Do you agree and can you pledge to work with me on that?"

Tong had returned to being a banker rather than a media man. "We must not touch Najib," he said. "This is about a financial scandal, but we must avoid the politics."

I smiled sweetly and innocently, a lifetime of white lies behind me in the greater cause of journalism. "I understand your concerns and we must certainly tread cautiously and move together on what we publish," I replied carefully.

I sort of meant it.

Xavier then passed me a little pen drive. Kay Tat's eyes followed it and I tensed. "What is it?" I queried.

"Well, you mentioned how it would help if I selected perhaps the top 100 most important documents and items on the database for you to look at, to help you cut through all the material, so here they are as far as I can make out," he said. "I have been going through this stuff for months. These are the key documents that show you how they stole the money on the original deal; the later loan arrangement under which more money was taken out and then how some of the money went into buying out UBG as well."

I glanced up at Kay Tat and noticed his attention had wandered elsewhere. After all, he had that full hard drive in his breast pocket. I thanked Xavier quietly and copied the material onto my computer, then slipped the pen drive back to him: my competitive nature told me that I had just got the edge on the *Edge*.

A cordial enough dinner followed, the tension having lifted with the transaction apparently now in order. But I remained uncomfortable that our very recently met new friends were the ones who looked poised to leave our gathering holding on to the full, unabridged data file. That hard disk was in Kay Tat's pocket. What if they simply walked? I took Xavier to one side as we squeezed out between the tables.

"You're leaving tomorrow, but I don't have a copy yet," I hissed. "Would it not be better if I guard that data overnight until we are sure we have copied it all round?" He took the point immediately and turned back, towering over Kay Tat.

"It is better that Clare takes care of this for me overnight – you can complete the copying tomorrow, do you have any problem with that?"

"Oh yes, of course," exclaimed Kay Tat, smiling through his teeth. "Please do take care of this Clare and we shall meet here again tomorrow perhaps?"

We arranged to do so, bid Xavier goodbye and I caught a cab back to my hotel, with the data burning in my handbag, triumphant.

◆ ◆ ◆

The following morning, Kay Tat was waiting at the Fullerton alone. "How are we going to pay this guy?" he asked. The issue was plainly worrying him. "We would feel much happier to pay you."

"No way," I responded, absolutely appalled. How could I explain a sudden influx of $2 million dollars into my modest bank account and then the need to transfer it immediately to Xavier?

"Well, it's also a disappointment the data only covers PetroSaudi," said Kay Tat. He reckoned that the real dirty business was the later dealings he had examined, especially around the two mega $3 billion bonds arranged by Goldman.

We repaired to yet another commercial tower-cum-office complex where the computer experts were at work and waited downstairs for Tong, who eventually arrived in a black chauffeured limo. We drank coffee on the ground floor and talked.

"I would much prefer to pay you," Tong said, continuing where Kay Tata had just left off. "I could buy your company, which would be a sensible media acquisition, since you have become known in Malaysia. Then you can solve this issue with Xavier and it won't be anything to do with me."

Xavier had by now boarded his plane, we had what appeared to be the data and this was an issue I wanted nothing to do with. It was only as the whole 1MDB crisis became a witch-hunt in Malaysia that I started to realise how sensitive the issue of payment would be. Tong did not want to be caught up in it any more than I. It would bring the wrath of UMNO on his head.

Meanwhile, it seemed that Xavier's gentleman's agreement was already under threat and I was worried. We headed up to the offices.

After an hour or so, the technicians declared they had cracked the encryption and presented us with our copies, as agreed. After the best part of a year I was quietly jubilant that my maxim, persistence pays, had proven true once more. Finally, after months traveling from Europe to Asia and back, of hunting down contacts and pestering everyone I could think of, I was able to pour through Xavier's files and examine the documents and emails that I had been yearning to scrutinise.

◆ ◆ ◆

I had a final meeting at the airport before heading home.

Tony Pua had hopped over at my persuasion from KL and we met in the transit lounge to take a first look at what information the data might hold. Tony was by now firing out precision guided press statements, tormenting the fund's managers. Every inconsistency and lie was pounced upon, all their arguments unpicked and the facts laid bare.

"I have hardly had a chance to look at this stuff," I explained as we consumed a bowl of wonton soup in the food court and I told him about the technical frustrations. "But I think it will tell us everything in the end."

I had already scanned through the top 100 documents that Xavier had passed to me. One was the original contract for the joint venture partnership between 1MDB and PetroSaudi. Had that always been kept a secret?

Tony nodded. "No one has had access to the document, even though it's a public company."

I suggested Tony take a look. The documents were embedded in emails going back and forth between PetroSaudi's Patrick Mahony and a series of lawyers in New York, London and KL, two of whom were linked to Jho Low. And the emails showed this group of corporate lawyers working at breakneck speed to draw up a contract that would, in essence, give PetroSaudi just about everything it wanted. It – not Malaysia – would get a controlling stake in the new joint venture (called 1MDB PetroSaudi). And Malaysia – not it –

would then throw a billion dollars into the company. To cap it all, PetroSaudi would have the right to an immediate repayment of an alleged $700 million 'advance' made just before 1MDB bought into the venture, to be 'paid back' out of that very billion dollars.

Tony turned to me and laughed. All this, he added, had been sorted out by Jho's lawyer in New York, who sent it to Mahony at PetroSaudi, little more than a week before the entire billion dollar deal was signed.

"Why would any management team in its right mind buy into a deal like that?" I asked Tony. I searched for a metaphor: "It's like buying a house when there is a massive loan out on the property."

"Well, in such a case there might be some value at least in the property" replied Tony. He was right, so what value was there in this new company 1MDB PetroSaudi? This was the company the bosses back in Malaysia were preparing to stuff hundreds of millions of pounds into.

"It's totally insane," I kept marvelling. Not only was it just a crazy risk to take, it had all been sorted out in about a week. The first joint venture draft was sent over on 21st September and the deal was finalised on the 29th.

Tony laughed again. "Because this is Malaysia," Tony said. "If the boss man says OK, then OK."

"So, can we be sure Najib was boss?" I replied, scrolling through to the second draft that Xavier had pulled out for me. In the documents we were hurriedly scrolling through, he continuously claimed he was merely a distant chairman of 1MDB's advisory board.

Najib had also secured the equivalent of alibis, with reputable names such as Goldman Sachs prepared to vouch for him (as they would continue to do: it was Goldman which had assured its buyers when it issued bonds in 2012 and 2013 that 1MDB had robust management free from political influence.) But the idea that Najib hadn't been involved was not plausible. "So, CEO Shahrol Halmi, he does this without checking with the finance minister, who is the guarantor for all the money? Rest assured Shahrol is acting on instructions from The Boss. This is why he makes no checks and asks no questions. This is Malaysia," Tony repeated.

It was true and of course it had been obvious from the start, which was why I had known this was such a major story. There was no other possible explanation for this extraordinary PetroSaudi deal than the fact that the prime minister-cum-finance minister had assented to Jho removing the money. The question was whether, with this data in my possession, we now had solid proof of Jho's pivotal role at last – and the prime minister behind him.

My flight was about to go. Tony and I continued to pore through the data. Next we came across a second draft of the joint venture agreement, which gave a further insight into the chain of events. It was simply plain and obvious that the central purpose of the entire joint venture was to siphon out the $700 million into Jho's account. Of course, the drafters needed to hide this fact – so the new agreement now extended to 26 pages of legal long grass, all the better to hide what was going on.

My flight was being called. "I need to do this story together with a major press publication," I said to Tony. "I don't know what the *Edge* will really dare to use, and if I do this just via my blog then the crooks will think they can ignore me, discredit me and smother the story."

"For now, I suggest you stick to this one document," he advised. "In itself it is a dynamite story… and anyway, I think we should peel this story slowly bit by bit. Like an onion." He was starting to sound like Tong. I looked at him stony-faced.

"If this is a socking great scandal then it should all come out," I said. "As soon as possible."

Tony sighed. "It's the problem in Malaysia. We are not a democracy, we are a sham democracy. Najib has inherited dictatorial powers and no one wants to stand up to him. He will be hard to budge even when this comes out. We have to move carefully and try to win the next election based on the public disapproval of what has been done."

I scoffed. "You cannot treat this like a game of chess," I complained. "Come on. It's a once in a lifetime story to have a prime minister caught red-handed stealing a billion dollars. It's completely huge. It makes Watergate look like a tea party. Let me be absolutely clear, now I have this story I am not going to sit around peeling onions bit by bit, I will take aim and fire."

"Typical Westerner," Tony sighed theatrically.

"Typical Malaysian," I retorted cheerfully enough. We hurried to our separate flights, still largely in the dark about the wider details of 1MDB's multi-billion dollar losses but certain that we now had 1MDB on the run.

15. HOW THEY DID IT

IHAD my window seat and a space beside me and time, at last, to go through those files. Lift-off was around midnight and I was exhausted. But, as I started opening up the documents one by one, I knew I would not sleep until I had gone right through every one.

Xavier had pulled out the emails he regarded as most significant from a database that spanned 2009 to 2011, the term of engagement with 1MDB. It would take months of studying the remaining documents and corroboration from other sources before I ironed out the full details. But, as the plane traced its long arc across the globe, I was able to reconstruct a broad picture of how these young men on the make had carried off their plan to defraud Malaysia.

It was an extraordinary, brazen scam, one that would have made Bernie Madoff blanch. Aided at all times by an army of willing banks and legal firms, Jho and his small group of associates had simply walked away with hundreds of millions of dollars. As Tony and I had already seen, they had made a token effort to mask their work by dressing it up in dense legalese in the agreement documents. But, stripping away all the complexity, they simply calculated that they could take hundreds of millions of pounds out of Malaysia, and swat aside any questions by invoking the involvement of Saudi Arabia and "the top boss" in Malaysia. The really remarkable thing was that they were proven right. Time and again, as I poured through the files that night and in the days to come, I would see how Jho and his friends had used the lustre and wealth of Saudi Arabia to allay the queries of those wondering why on earth so much cash was walking out the door. And then there was always Najib in the background, acting as their guarantor, should anyone still be asking further questions. The banks – which should have stopped such obvious money laundering – were putty in their hands.

The gang knew that, by telling a grand story, they could distract people and disguise their real intention. And what I had on my lap, as I hurtled west back to the UK at 30,000 feet, was effectively their manual. It was a record of how they plotted to set it all up. It showed how they invented the story, and how they worked out how it was to be told.

As Tony and I had worked out at the airport, at the heart of the entire plan was the joint venture, set up its by its parent company PetroSaudi, called 1MDB PetroSaudi. It sounded impressive, of course. As Xavier had already said to me a few months earlier, how could it not, with that word 'Saudi' promising riches to all? This was the company into which Najib was to pour the cash from 1MDB.

The first task that the conspirators set themselves was to hide the fact that 1MDB PetroSaudi – and indeed its parent company PetroSaudi – was worth virtually nothing. Even Malaysian officials might quibble at handing over hundreds of millions of dollars of taxpayers' money to an entity that offered exactly zero in return. So, how best to hide this fact?

The emails showed exactly what they decided. To begin with, the conspirators invented a fiction – they declared that 1MDB PetroSaudi had been loaded with $700 million of debt. This debt, they claimed, was because its parent company PetroSaudi had injected valuable oil assets onto its books. Thus they underpinned the first part of their story – that there were, indeed, huge assets that Malaysia would profit from if it decided to take part.

It was total nonsense. All PetroSaudi actually had at that time – all it genuinely owned – was a failing concession in Argentina (funded by a loan from investment manager Ashmore) and an option (also funded by Ashmore) to buy another concession in a disputed part of the Caspian Sea claimed by Turkmenistan. This was currently owned by a Canadian company named Buried Hill. The option was about to expire. That was pretty much it – unless you count the *Alfa Nero* boat hire.

Nevertheless, here was the plan. If the bosses at 1MDB or bankers in Malaysia started asking any questions about why so much of their money should be thrown at this venture, they had their answer. Here was a Saudi-backed business – headed by a member of the Saudi royal family no less! – offering to plug Malaysia into its asset base. What I had on the plane was the email-by-email account of how they fabricated it.

The first email that Xavier had highlighted was sent a fortnight after Najib and Jho were entertained on the *Alfa Nero* off the coast of Monaco, on 9th September 2009. The author was Patrick Mahony, the London-based financier who was to prove a driving force behind the entire plan.

Mahony's initial contact in the business had been Prince Turki's sidekick Tarek Obaid, who had been his classmate at the International School in Geneva, a city where Swiss financial folk float in awe around the ostentatious wealth of expat Saudis. Still in his early 30s, slight with dark good looks and the requisite charm, Mahony had become a darling at Ashmore, and was already known for his deal-making flamboyance. Two of his former colleagues referred to their work in emerging markets as "cowboy" antics, admitting they walked a narrow path on the ethics front (like so many, Mahony had also learnt his trade at, among other places, Goldman Sachs).

Thanks to Tarek, he had now taken on the title of Head of International Mergers & Acquisitions, PetroSaudi International Ltd – a spurious title, given the fact that, at that time, PetroSaudi was largely a shell. It was Mahony who had managed to get PetroSaudi up and running, persuading his bosses at Ashmore to invest several million dollars in the prince's new business to get it rolling.

Prince Turki was not much of a businessman: the young Saudi was given to moods and tantrums and childlike behaviour that could be endearing in the right party atmosphere but caused dismay in more formal situations. But Mahony and co knew that in the currency of access-seekers, there can be no greater contact than the Saudi royal family. Here was the world's greatest wealth resource, managed by an autocratic, secretive bloodline with unlimited enduring power. "Those Saudis don't just exist on another planet, they live in another galaxy to the rest of us," whispered one insider, who had spoken to me from Mahony's circle. "You can never touch them, they have unimaginable wealth and influence and they can do whatever they like. Don't cross them ever, they can be very, very dangerous." With Prince Turki's father then the king, it didn't really matter whether Prince Turki was a dud or not: he had the power to impress.

Mahony boarded a business class flight from Heathrow to meet Jho in New York on 7th September 2009, just prior to the meeting with Najib. Two days later, writing to Jho and his sidekick Seet Li Lin, he came up with the idea of the joint venture: "what would make sense is that we set up a joint venture where we contribute our assets and you can contribute cash to match our asset base. We can then decide where that cash goes," he wrote.

The total confidence, the sheer brazenness and staggering brass-neck of the emails is hard to take in. In further emails, Mahony casually acknowledged that PetroSaudi didn't actually own the asset in Turkmenistan which was to form the big-ticket item that it would bring to the venture. It was, he acknowledged, still owned by a Canadian company. But not actually owning it would not stop them listing it as an asset, nor ascribing a crazy value to it: "We can value the Argentinian assets at around $50-$75m and the Turkmenistan asset at around $700m pre-border dispute being resolved and at $1b-$1.5b," he declared.

In other words, Mahony was proposing that PetroSaudi over-inflate the value of an asset it didn't own, so it could then use that asset as a reason to get money out of Malaysia. Imagine asking for a re-mortgage from the bank, but instead of offering up your own home as capital, you offer up a house down the road. Then imagine telling the bank that the house you don't own is ten times its actual value. Now you're close to where this was going.

On he went. "We know there are deals you are looking at where you may want to use PSI [PetroSaudi International] as a front, we would be happy to do that. You need to let us know where… I have tried to think of deals that would be very justifiable to any investment committee… I am also thinking of structures where funds need to move a few times, which generally makes it easier for any fees we would need to pay our agents."

Fronts, complex structures, multiple money transfers, fees for agents – it wasn't hard to read the purpose between the lines.

Jho's responses displayed little interest in the specifics of PetroSaudi's investment proposals, beyond getting them to look as viable as possible as quickly as possible. He left most of the arranging to Seet Li Lin, who had followed him into his company Wynton Group from Wharton Business School and was his right-hand man. If Mahony was brazen, Seet was almost comical.

He got back to Mahony the very same day with an email entitled "Proposed Timeline for JV with PetroSaudi":

Dear Patrick, Jho has spoken to the top boss and received the following guidance:

Target to close a deal by 20th Sept where all agreements are signed and monies can be paid to PetroSaudi before end of Sept.

Arrange for official signing and meeting of dignitaries by end Sept.

By "the top boss" I assumed he meant Najib. The substance of the email made clear that PetroSaudi would get its millions, based on Mahony's musings, in just ten days' time. Jho butted into the same email trail the following day, in a characteristically brusque style, to emphasise the need for ridiculous speed: "We need to move fast n we need as much detailed info u have as fast as possible. We want to sign and pay by Sept 09. Will be emailing out a timeline."

The pair weren't even bothering to ask any further questions; the task was to shift the money out of Malaysia as fast as they could. I continued to read. Another series of emails laid out a timeline for everyone involved to keep to, so that the cash could be paid out on the last day of September. Tellingly, the actions on the 'for 1MDB' strand began only in the last week of September, days before the planned signing on the 30th and once the actions of the other two parties had been completed and "agreements finalised". The fund which Goldman Sachs was to describe as having a "robust three tier management structure free from political interference" was relegated merely to briefing its own board of directors about the billion dollar investment four days before it was due to happen; organising a special board meeting to sign the agreement and then making the payment at the end of the month. It was Jho's team (on behalf, one assumes, of the prime minister) who was in charge, ordering Mahony to deliver the valuation reports on the assets (that they didn't own).

In case Mahony had not already got the idea that Jho was serious, Tarek emailed him the morning that presentation was sent over, at 7.30am: "Dude – on doit fermer avec eux, Jho ma reveiler la, et ils sonts prets a verser un millard... D ici la fin du mois appelle quand tu te treveille je suis a londres [Dude, we need to close with them, Jho just woke me and they are ready to tip in a billion... Before the end of the month call me when you get up, I'm in London.]"

The idea was clear. The Malaysians would throw in $1 billion. Of that, $280 million (later revised up to $300 million) would stay in the new joint venture to spend on actual oil investments (what would become Xavier's responsibility). The other $720 million (later revised down to $700 million) would be used to 'repay' PetroSaudi for the assets they had sunk into 1MDB PetroSaudi (the assets which, to repeat, it didn't own and which it had therefore not loaned to anyone). Seet, as always, helpfully put things clearly. While others in emails tended euphemistically to parrot the line that the $700 million was "a repayment to PSI for loans extended to the JV company or asset", he bluntly wrote that the sum would really be "to pay Promoter" – in other words, Jho.

Mahony, who was still supposed to be working for Ashmore, now laid everything else aside to pull together the deal. He called on the services of the law firm White & Case in London to work on the template sent over by Jho's lawyer in New York, Tiffany Heah. Insiders have described a pressure-cooker atmosphere, as the London legal team worked flat out to draw up the contract in less than two weeks.

On 22nd September, a hastily constructed PowerPoint presentation, prepared by White & Case, set out the developing story. Now, rather than just having one joint venture, the plan was for PetroSaudi to set up a whole bevy of brand new, offshore subsidiaries as well: there was to be PetroSaudi International Holdings Cayman Ltd, 1MDB PetroSaudi Ltd (British Virgin Islands), PetroSaudi Ltd (Panama) and PetroSaudi Ltd (Jersey). None of these companies had or did anything. The purpose was to create the impression of a large corporate entity with money all over the globe. In this make-believe world of pretend money, the PowerPoint plan proposed that these shell companies should start issuing millions of shares to lend to one another and shuffle cash around, supposedly $3.5 billion. Crucially, PetroSaudi International Holdings Cayman Ltd would 'lend' $700 million to the new joint venture company 1MDB PetroSaudi Ltd (British Virgin Islands), which 1MDB would 'pay back' the moment it bought into this new company that already had its name on it. Confused? That, of course, was the plan.

The pressure was now on, and as the group headed towards their deadline of the end of September, they realised a key part of the story was still missing. They did actually need some kind of evidence to present to the world to suggest that the assets they didn't own were worth something.

Seet did not mince his words, emailing London: "We need to work backwards, with the objectives above in mind to produce the right valuation... Valuation report should come in to value assets at US$3.285bn."

To obtain the pre-ordained valuation of its assets, Mahony turned to an American banker pal, a former deputy secretary of state for energy, called Ed Morse. Morse was between jobs at the time, following the collapse of Lehman Brothers, where he had previously worked. Documents show that he was engaged by Mahony on behalf of the prospective joint venture group on 20th September, in order to value PetroSaudi on behalf of 1MDB.

Mahony emailed him on 23rd September to say what he needed the valuation on the Turkmenistan oil concession to come to: "We are looking for a mid-range of $2.5bn."

"OK, Got it!" Morse replied.

That was it. Morse's final valuation, based entirely on documentation sent to him by Mahony, in fact put PetroSaudi's assets at $2.9 billion, most of which constituted the supposed value of the Turkmenistan oil concession. A disclaimer in his report points out that he had not checked if the information that Mahony had sent him was correct nor whether the company actually owned the assets concerned. Morse was paid $100,000 for his troubles.

Nobody at 1MDB asked a single question. Indeed, the board at the state fund were entirely cut out of the loop. Their CEO, Shahrol Halmi, only heard about the planned joint venture when he received an order from Jho on the 15th to hook up to a conference call. Seet gave Mahony orders on how to speak to him: "Emphasize Prince Turki's role in PSI... Hint that PSI is owned indirectly by King Abdullah... Prince Turki was tasked by King Abdullah to follow up on this matter and has met PM Najib Razak to re-iterate this desire. Leaders of both countries are committed to partnership between PSI and 1MDB," he spelt out. The message to 1MDB was clear: don't worry your little heads about the money; there are big Saudi boys involved here.

Shahrol's first email to anyone from PetroSaudi on 20th September, just one week before he was to agree to inject a billion dollars into PetroSaudi, made clear he had virtually no information about the company. He emailed Tarek to ask what he could tell the media.

Mahony butted in: "I would suggest you send to me a draft of what you would like to release and we will let you know if it works for us. PSI is very press shy and usually never announces our investments (one of the main reasons governments like to work with us) but we understand you will need to make some statements."

The story was still being weaved: a media-shy Saudi firm, headed by princes close to the king, with untold billions at their disposal, now condescending to work with Malaysia – and with the Malaysian prime minister giving his support. Little wonder that 1MDB's weak executive team simply nodded their heads. On 23rd September,

Shahrol headed over to London to meet PetroSaudi to 'negotiate' the deal. The meetings were held in White & Case's conference rooms because PetroSaudi's own premises at the time consisted of a pokey hired office space in Victoria. Jho was confident about the 1MDB dupes. "They will do what they are told and sign," he emailed Mahony.

◆ ◆ ◆

So – the story was working. Here was a fabulous, Saudi-backed firm, replete with gold standard oil assets, prepared to launch a joint venture with Malaysia – and all 1MDB needed to do in order to gain entry to this Aladdin's cave was to pony up $1 billion. Nobody had yet seen through what was going on – apparently. But there was one final problem: it's all very well taking away hundreds of millions of pounds but you then have to put it somewhere. And, as the group entered the final few days before the cash was released, they were having problems.

Jho's plan, by this stage, was for $700 million of the cash to go straight to him. He had created a company called Good Star and had chosen a small private bank called BSI. He wanted to open accounts there both for Good Star and the 1MDB PetroSaudi joint venture. Sticking the cash into the same bank – albeit into two entirely separate accounts – would help to disguise what was going on.

Unfortunately, however, the compliance officers at the bank were beginning to raise some eyebrows. Anti-money laundering requirements were in place, and they were required to examine excessive payments into offshore companies. Jho's proposed transfer was therefore raising a red flag.

"Can you explain [to] us briefly where and how the money will be invested? We suppose the business plan is financing oil investments/ projects. My compliance has to give some sort of explanation on the 700 especially," wrote the bank, with one week to go until the deal was to be formally signed.

"The $700m is premium that was made in the transaction and will be used to fund future transactions in any sector (not necessarily oil and gas)," replied Mahony.

But BSI was unimpressed. It sounded as if the $700 million 'premium' was commission. And who in their right minds would pay 70 percent commission? It wrote back to demand more detail. And then it landed a bomb. With just three working days to go until the deal was due to be signed by Najib and Turki in KL, Mahony got an email:

Dear Mr. Mahony,
  The details you sent today are not sufficient to allow our Compliance Officer to give a favourable report to our Management which has to rule on the opening of accounts.
  The missing elements are listed below:
  - Precise business plan with the list of investments by type, size, place and date, the precise object of the project and what return is expected and at what date.
  - A valuation of the assets is essential to enable our Compliance Officer to form a judgment.
  - A precise list of cash flows especially those of the USD 700 million.
  - The draft contract is obscure and not precise enough for this sort of amount.
  Based on the information you have provided, a decision by our Management cannot be taken now. We await the additional necessary details. When we have these our Management will need two working days to make a decision.
  Thanks in advance for your reply.
  [translated from French]

I continued to trawl through Xavier's cache of emails. They showed Mahony working late into the night that Friday to rescue the disastrous situation. He asked his legal team to send copies of all the correspondence with the bank. But it plainly wasn't going to work. He and his lawyers from White & Case and Maples & Calder all bugged the bank during the remainder of the day for an answer on whether the account would be ready to receive money by the following Monday, the 28th.

They would have nowhere to transfer the cash to. Desperately they scrambled to find another bank. Mahony went to JP Morgan Suisse, where he and Tarek also had personal accounts. It agreed to receive the $300 million that would go into the joint venture. Meanwhile, Jho turned to another private bank, the UK Government-owned RBS Coutts to open an account to receive the larger and less easily explainable 'premium' of $700 million. I would later learn that a few weeks before, in May, Coutts's Singapore branch had helped incorporate his new offshore shell company, Good Star Limited, in the Seychelles. So they already had a relationship.

The Zurich branch was now persuaded to accept an account for Good Star that would receive the money from 1MDB. This was done largely thanks to a deliberate deceit aided and abetted by an official at 1MDB named Casey Tang, the executive director. Tang's key involvement in the affair was recorded throughout the early email trails that I was reading and it would emerge that this top official helped confirm a brand new story-line concocted by Jho to Coutts, alleging that Good Star had been appointed as an 'investment manager' by 1MDB. Tang even flew to Zurich to identify Jho and vouch for his alleged status at the bank. With 1MDB seemingly sanctioning the whole thing, Coutts obliged.

On Wednesday 30th September the deal was signed. A press release went out to the domestic newspapers, who were briefed that this was a sign of global confidence in the new Prime Minister of Malaysia: "Partnership to Spearhead the Flow of Foreign Direct Investment from the Middle East" was the prepared headline. And Najib obliged with an entirely misleading quote, suggesting that PetroSaudi had more than matched 1MDB for cash: "More or less, it will be a 50:50 venture, but for now, Malaysia will put in US$1 billion in the fund while PetroSaudi will contribute US$1.5 billion," he told a reporter from the *New Straits Times*.

"Keep it to the local press, let's hope the international media don't pick up," Mahony nervously emailed his collaborators later. "You can't call it Government to Government," Tarek's brother Nawaf had warned back from his office in the Saudi civil service, fearing any questions about whether the Saudi government had put in a single penny (answer: no). However, Najib had insisted on beefing up the 'state to state' connotations. That was his political cover for the investment of a billion dollars of public money, underwritten by himself in his dual capacity as finance minister – money which was about to disappear.

The deal had been done, but the money had still not been sent because their bankers still hadn't given the green light to the mega-transfer. Now RBS Coutts was asking questions too. "Why was it [the $700 million] being sent to a different account to the rest of the money?" asked a banking officer. At 1MDB, Tang took up the case on behalf of his friends. According to phone recordings later obtained by the FBI this is what he said: "It was repayment for a loan from PetroSaudi, there was more value in the assets that company had put in, so why should 1MDB care where PetroSaudi wanted to put the money – as far as 1MDB was concerned it could be sent to Timbuktu". Tang added that his life was getting very difficult because the finance minister-cum-prime minister was getting restless for a personal assurance that there were not going to be further hold-ups. Failure could bring consequences for himself and the bank, which had privileged interests in Malaysia. Don't upset "the big boss" in other words.

Coutts then asked to know who exactly was getting the $700 million. At 1MDB, CEO Shahrol – utterly out of his depth – replied: "Please use this address for GOOD STAR LIMITED: P.O. Box 1239, Offshore Incorporation Centre, Victoria, Mahe, Republic of Seychelles".

This was almost beyond parody. Here was the chief executive of a major sovereign fund telling a leading bank to send $700 million to an unknown offshore company with a PO box address. Surely that couldn't happen. Could it? Jho, who had been back-copied into the email trail by Mahony, who in turn had been back-copied by Shahrol, seemed confident. Early afternoon he messaged back via his Blackberry: "Shld be cleared soon. Pls update tarek."

His confidence was justified. The helpful RBS Coutts team in Singapore were clearly happy to oblige. And why not? After all, it had been sanctioned by the finance minister and prime minister in KL. And so it was that late on 2nd October 2009 the two payments were finally transferred, first to JP Morgan Zurich, which then passed the second payment of $700 million on to the Coutts Zurich account belonging to Good Star – although only the number and not the name of the destination account appeared on the transfer documents, making its identity doubly difficult to trace.

There it was: at the push of a button, $700 million belonging to the Malaysian people disappeared from under their noses. Helped by the cream of London's finance and legal establishment, Jho Low and friends – with the Prime Minister of Malaysia at a safe distance in the background – had pulled it off.

Blinking back sleep, I trawled further on. There was one further thing I was searching for: concrete proof that Good Star was indeed owned by Jho, and not PetroSaudi as claimed.

Xavier had included two further items, both hefty contracts, one called an "Investment Management Agreement" between Good Star Ltd and Mahony, the other a "brokerage fee" on the joint venture deal.

It was clear why he had put them in. The person representing Good Star in Mahony's contract was none other than Seet Li Lin, Jho's aide. He even included a Singapore phone number for the firm. If PetroSaudi owned Good Star, why was its senior officer Jho's employee, I asked myself, as the thrill of discovery coursed through my veins? And the second document nailed it. It showed Seet, on behalf of Good Star, paying $85 million to Tarek Obaid for helping the venture deal. It would hardly have made sense if Tarek owned Good Star himself. No: here were Jho and Seet using their loot to pay their fellow conspirators. (Later I would come across records of a second payment to Tarek, on the same day, of $20 million. It was pointed out by one of my helpful readers that this extra sum meant the total payment to Tarek on that day was actually $105 million, which was a nice round sum representing exactly fifteen percent of the $700 million that Jho had creamed off from the deal through Good Star!) On 20th October, Tarek emailed his contact at JP Morgan to request that $33 million be transferred into an account belonging to Mahony. Some fee!

Four days later, Mahony began discussions to set up an offshore company to buy a £6.7 million townhouse in Notting Hill, and by 12th November contracts for the house had been exchanged. The former banker created a numbered bank account in Switzerland, and all payments for the purchase were made from this account. He later confided to an estate agent: "The property I own on Ladbroke Square belongs to a company, which in turn belongs to a trust. I am the beneficiary of that trust but I am not the direct owner of the property for reasons I'm sure you'll be familiar with."

Nice work if you can get it.

◆ ◆ ◆

There is something about journalists that always makes us go the extra mile. We are programmed not to stop. The fear of getting beaten to a story compels us to keep going.

Shortly after landing in London at the crack of dawn, having had no sleep all night, and by now sick with tiredness, I took out my mobile and tapped out the Singapore number printed on the Good Star contract. If the number turned out to be good, I reasoned, it would be added proof the documents were for real. I wanted to *know*. It rang, but there was no answer. It had been worth a try, I thought, but the number was six years old. A car honked. Bleary eyed and barely conscious of where I was, I had walked out into a busy street. Suddenly the same number called me back.

"Hello?" I queried.

"Who are you, you just called?" a voice challenged me from far away.

"I am trying to reach Seet Li Lin," I stumbled, trying to think through my strategy and hear at the same time.

"That's me, who are you and what do you want?

I breathed in the fresh London air – feeling the old adrenalin back in my veins.

"Well, my name is Clare Rewcastle and I write a blog called *Sarawak Report* and I understand that you are the investment manager for the company Good Star, for which you gave this telephone number," I replied.

There was a silence at the end and then a brief response: "I don't know what you are talking about," he said, and put the phone down.

The next day the telephone no longer rang. The line had gone dead.

16. HEIST OF THE CENTURY

February 2015, London

THE story was just too damn big. I ran a small blog, kept going largely thanks to donations, with barely any resources and a limited readership. Yet now I had a story on my hands that put every other financial scandal in the world in the shade.

The scam had instantly made Jho Low one of the most cash-rich people on the planet and – as would be revealed over the coming years – triggered an orgy of spending which, even among the plutocrats and celebrities whose company he so craved, was beyond compare. Between the transfer of the cash and the following summer, it was subsequently estimated that he and his entourage spent $85 million on partying. Rooms at the Park Imperial in New York were hired at $100,000 a month. Playboy models were flown into Vegas first class to attend VIP parties in the company of the ever present Leonardo DiCaprio. On one night alone, Jho lost $2 million gambling in Vegas. And on top of the partying, Jho began acquiring the necessities of the super-rich: homes in London, LA and New York, including a $36 million condominium just off Central Park. For good measure, he also bought himself a $36 million Bombardier private jet. All this in the first year after the fraud; as detailed already, he was to keep the spending going after that too.

It was utter recklessness. But Jho's insatiable desire for status appeared to knock aside any concerns that such a high roller lifestyle might provoke questions. Perhaps it was all part of Jho's attempt to prove to his father Larry, back home in Penang, that he had indeed made the big time. No big fish in a small pond, he. Now, here was Jho – at a time when cash was short in the wake of the crash – spending money like no other; truly a new King of America.

Some of this had been reported on; indeed the *New York Post* had covered Jho's extravagant Gatsby-esque lifestyle just a few weeks previously. But nobody had yet managed to join the dots back to the 1MDB cash. What I now had, in black and white, was proof that Low had taken $700 million from the fund, and had proceeded to eat through it. I decided I needed a bigger platform to get the news out there. So after a bit of sleep, I once again called up the *Sunday Times*.

It was a moment of popular grievance in Malaysia. Students and others had taken to the streets over the jailing of Anwar, but the protests were being aggressively repressed. The popular cartoonist Zunar, for example, had been arrested and now faced sedition charges (up to 43 years in jail) for tweeting on the day of Anwar's sentence his criticism over the lack of judicial independence. Perhaps, the story of 1MDB – which I could now tell in full – might blow the entire edifice away.

I jumped onto the Circle Line from Victoria with my precious hard drive and was soon entering the tall glass atrium of News Corps' plush offices, opposite the Shard Building at London Bridge. Having been cleared by security I was whisked in the lift to a high floor with stunning views across the city. Two *Sunday Times* journalists, who had by now got a handle on the story, sat me down.

"Is there enough of a UK angle?" was the first, inevitable, question.

I sighed and began: there was the fact that $700 million had been laundered by the Queen's bank, Coutts, the fact that the entire joint venture deal was negotiated in London at the PetroSaudi company base; the fact that Jho's team of lawyers were from a major London company. On top of that, one of PetroSaudi's directors, Rick Haythornthwaite, was the British chairman of Centrica Gas and of Global Mastercard.

"Oh," I added. And this guy, Jho Low, he went to Harrow!"

"Is that what they teach at Harrow" the senior journalist laughed, "how to steal a billion dollars?"

We went through the nuts and bolts of the story and I passed him the pen drive containing the top 100 documents.

"There is enough here to prove the $700 million was deliberately siphoned out of the deal to this company Good Star Limited under the guise of a 'repayment' of a meaningless paper loan from PetroSaudi. There is also enough to tell you that Good Star Limited is associated not with PetroSaudi, but with Jho Low," I said.

I went home, confident that a piece in the *Sunday Times*, plus more detail in my blog, would get the story out there. But it still didn't feel enough. This, surely, was more than just a bit of corruption. It was multi-continental state-sponsored theft on an almost unimaginable scale. I already had a contact, from my days of battling Taib, in the United States Department of Justice. I emailed to say that I had acquired a "considerable body of pertinent information" and that the story was about to run in a major UK paper. I pointed out that the *New York Times* had also just run a major related story on Jho. My contact got back suggesting we should arrange a call, but after the article came out.

To get the ball rolling, I decided to put up a teaser on the *Sarawak Report* website, revealing that 1MDB had paid $1 billion of borrowed public money into a venture that already carried a $700 million debt in the form of a "loan" from PetroSaudi's parent company. To rub in the point, I reminded readers that the prime minister had stated on the day of the deal back in 2009 that it was PetroSaudi that was bringing the lion's share of the cash to the table in the venture, when in fact the company had not contributed a penny, while apparently walking off with 70 percent of the money on day one.

"It starts," I emailed my friend from Australia, who had set me onto the story more than a year earlier with *The Wolf of Wall Street* tip-off.

The *Sunday Times* was preparing to go big: a front page story and up to two inside pages with detailed break-downs of the scam. It would be a brilliant result. I also learnt that Mahathir himself was due in London the following week. Through my Malaysian contacts, I helped fix an interview with the *Sunday Times*, which I too attended in the course of the following week. It was ultra-newsworthy – presented with the information by the *Sunday Times*, the grand old man of UMNO laid in to the current leader of his party, the prime minister of a major economy, and accused him of corruption.

I had less than a week until the *Sunday Times* story was published to get my own story straight for my website. But things were getting complicated.

On a personal level my husband had discovered he had a heart complication that had started to trigger arrhythmias. It had caused a major fright at Christmas and by February he needed an operation. Much of the week was spent in and out of hospital. Meanwhile, my partners in the Far East – on both sides – were getting less enamoured of their deal. The *Edge*'s computer experts in Singapore were still struggling to decrypt the data (a whizz-kid intern at the *Sunday Times* had solved that problem with my copy) – and they didn't they have the Top 100 files either. Feeling slightly guilty, I sent some of that material over to Tong and Kay Tat to reassure them. In the end their technicians did indeed crack open their copy of the data, but by now our separate agendas were becoming hard to marry up and they were angry about the teaser story I had written. Why had I published such a very sensitive document so wantonly and how come I was directly pointing the finger at the prime minister, they had demanded, aghast?

On the other side, Xavier was getting nervous. He started texting me that nothing more at all ought to be published until Tong fulfilled his promise to pay him. I was stuck in the middle, but I also knew that it is not every day that you get the full attention of a top team at the *Sunday Times* and that this was not a publishing opportunity I was about to miss. Bluntly, I had my information and were I to be unscrupulous I could ignore them altogether. On the other hand, I did not want to see our source betrayed – a commitment had been made, a deal done and his safety also was at risk.

I suppose my journalistic impatience was partly to blame. With the story in my hands, I couldn't rest until it was out there. I had found an opening, a platform with a top paper that could draw global attention to these extraordinary crimes and start the ball rolling on the quest for the remaining missing billions from the fund. Maybe I could have held back, asked everyone to wait a month or so, and perhaps with less of a glare of publicity the deal could have been completed. But it was anathema to my journalistic instincts to sit on a story of this magnitude that I had chased for a year.

No – I knew already; it might upset Tong and might leave Xavier feeling bruised, but there was only one way to go: all in. Together, my small team and I entirely re-configured the website to put up a multi-part story. The main headline, 'Heist of the Century'.

After that I focused on the teams of foreign facilitators, from PetroSaudi itself to their banks and legal firms; Jho and his extravagant lifestyle; and Jho's shady entourage. The last section was on the political side of the story, looking at some of the material that had started to emerge concerning the extraordinarily wide area of influence and operations in which Jho and his co-conspirators were involved as part of Najib's inner circle, acting as a secret parallel civil and diplomatic service, particularly in relation to the prime minister's dealings and aspirations in the Middle East.

Working into the early hours before the Sunday deadline I had started to realise what an immense task I had set myself. One of the advantages of the lightning deal was that all the emails and documents relating to it had been exchanged over a period of little more than a week, so they were easier to track on the database. However, it was still an immense job to piece together what had taken place as the international teams of lawyers chopped and changed their plans, switched banks and managed crises. And at the time I still only had snapshots of the action with the full picture only being filled in over the following months.

I had no idea what the *Sunday Times* was writing or had further dug out, but I laid out in detail what I had worked out so far and embellished the story with details of Jho's outrageous lifestyle and super-spending. Amy had meanwhile traced the revealing Facebook postings of Seet Li Lin as the deal had progressed and then closed that September 2009. Lin had provided a series of comments on Facebook during this period of deal-making.

On 30th September, just as the money was about to be transferred from 1MDB, he gushed: "I feel the earth move under my feet..."

A friend replied: "Yes, I felt it too...lol'"

Then, ten days later, with the money securely transferred, he and his friends were celebrating: "in vegas, bring a jacket cos its raining cristal haha!"

◆ ◆ ◆

My plan was to publish my own more detailed version of events on the same day as the *Sunday Times*. But Jho and his team were not giving in yet. Contact with the team at London Bridge had started to diminish towards the end of the week. Then on Saturday afternoon, hours before the deadline, they called to say that much of the story was being pulled. "I have only worked on one previous story that attracted as much legal backlash," my contact at the paper told me, "six major law firms all hammering at us representing the different parties."

A lot has been done by well-meaning politicians to 'curb abuses by the press' in the decade since I began working in a major newsroom. Many investigative journalists have confirmed to me that it has played into the hands not of those vulnerable individuals the regulations are intended to protect, but of rich big shots who can afford argumentative lawyers. The reforms mean newspapers now have to provide considerable detail of what they intend to publish to subjects before they go public. And, as 'rights' and 'protections' have been extended and the issue of privacy enhanced, so have the hurdles to getting any story out. Now a newspaper can be found legally liable not just for getting the story wrong, but for not going through endless hoops of engagement, even if they have the story right. Wealthy and often criminal targets of exposés exploit this, with the aid of specialist lawyers who have developed an industry around producing extremely lengthy letters in which they will happily argue simultaneously contradictory points, secure in the knowledge that if a newspaper refuses to engage in the process they could face censure in a later court action, whether the story is correct or not.

As an individual who can't afford full-time legal support I had often ignored similar attempts at legal harassment – "another one filed in the bin" had become my mantra when legal letters arrived at my house. However, under the present regulatory system a mainstream paper cannot. It all costs money, which newspapers are running out of, and it costs time, when staff are being pared down. Faced with the legal onslaught around Jho and PetroSaudi, management at the *Sunday Times* had plainly started questioning if these wealthy foreigners were worth the hassle.

"They've decided to put it on Foreign and it's pretty much reduced," one of the journalists told me bitterly, before disappearing for what was doubtless a much needed break. It was very disappointing, given the work and enthusiasm put in by the excellent team at the *Sunday Times*; they had got to grips with a major cache of material.

It could have been a lot worse. The *Sunday Times* had not backed down entirely, by a long chalk, and the coverage, though minimised to a profile of "Harrow playboy" Jho Low, managed to get in the most important points on what had happened: the article gave the lie to Jho's declared non-involvement in 1MDB; substantiated my earlier story about the $700 million siphoned out of the PetroSaudi joint venture; noted the money had been supposedly passed to an investment company managed by Jho; backed up my claims to have a trove of accurate data on the deal; played up the ridiculous nature of later excuses about where the money had gone; and drew attention to the ostentatious spending of Jho and his support for Riza's movie *The Wolf of Wall Street*. To crown it all they had brought UMNO's towering figure, Mahathir, onto the international stage publicly acknowledging that the goings on at 1MDB stank something rotten.

The paper had further extracted a key statement from the Malaysian prime minister himself, who was still sanctimoniously pretending to have no real involvement in the fund. But at least he did concede that "if any wrongdoing is proven, the law will be enforced without exception". That public statement was to force the prime minister in coming days to set up various key enquiries, which he doubtless hoped to control, but which would open a can of worms that would irreparably damage him.

As the *Sunday Times* story went live, I sat at my laptop at home in

Victoria, read my own copy one more time, and pressed 'publish'. The scandal of 1MDB was out there.

17. IN COME THE FEDS

EVEN from 6000 miles away in London, it was possible to feel the reverberations in Southeast Asia.

The *Sunday Times* story went on to score the top number of internet hits for the newspaper that week, bringing the highest number of subscription sign-ups to the paper. The power of the 1MDB story to attract popular attention, especially in Asia, was to prove itself many times subsequently.

My version – containing far more than used by the *Sunday Times* – landed like a nuclear missile. Among the first reactions I got was from Kay Tat in Singapore. "You even picked the bare bones," he said, tersely, clearly angry that the *Edge* (which was, after all, the one supposed to be paying for all the data) had been beaten to the punch. (Later I think he forgave me readily enough – the *Edge* produced its own scoops on 1MDB and the attendant backlash affected all of us.)

By Monday evening, my site began registering massive hits (half a million reads by the end of the week); tweets started mushrooming; Malaysian Facebook then went viral on the story. It was like watching an explosion in the distance before the sound and wind catch up.

It was fortuitous that the Federal Parliament was sitting at that time – It meant that questions could be asked and make the news. The *Edge* also moved immediately on the story with a major headline on the Monday: "Jho Low Accused of Siphoning US$700 Million from 1MDB". The respected *Asia Sentinel*, run by the *Wall Street Journal's* former KL correspondent, John Berthelsen, was also in like a whippet: "In December of last year, the controversial fund 1MDB abruptly called in all of its computers, employee laptops and servers and wiped them clean. It was too late. The reason has become embarrassingly clear with a report by Clare Rewcastle Brown, the indefatigable blogger who edits *Sarawak Report…*"

These were rapidly followed up by online media such as *Malaysiakini*, *Free Malaysia Today* and *Malaysian Insider* (the latter also owned by Tong), who were all soon on to me for feedback and the next day were producing reports.

Eric Ellis, a business writer for *Euromoney*, who had just obtained agreement from Jho for a rare interview in Hong Kong, also emailed me: "I must say, this latest of yours is one of the most comprehensive gotchas I've seen in 25 years in this biz..." he generously stated. In fact, Ellis's subsequent interview was also to prove highly revelatory, taking place just as recriminations were beginning to surface between the different parties who had been caught in the spotlight.

With Najib distancing himself from any direct involvement in the scandal, Jho gave Ellis a long and self-pitying interview in which he complained that he was effectively being made the scapegoat for 1MDB's ills: "It's so frustrating. I've never faced this kind of attack from all directions. It's just crazy, and these UMNO guys are spin-masters, they know all this sort of nonsense." The heavy implication was that Najib's men were hanging him out to dry and stoking racial prejudice against him as a Malaysian Chinese.

He then went further, pointing the finger pretty clearly at Najib:

> Guys, it's very simple, there's a board, who's the shareholder? Have you ever seen one statement from anyone that talks about the simple governance of a company? Are you telling me the prime minister doesn't make his own decisions? That the ministry, the minister of finance, who is the prime minister ... just signed without evaluating it? No one seems to ask the question, who is the ultimate decision-maker on 1MDB? No one asks that. No one ever asks about the shareholder's role.

Then there was a further self-pitying outburst, in which Jho complained of being blamed for such gross thievery when he could see everyone else around him getting away with it: "There are so many other people who get away with ridiculous billions and billions and billions' worth of projects. But every single time there seems to be a political attack, wow, suddenly Jho is there again."

Jho was to return to the same theme a week later in a series of interviews attempting to get himself off the hook. The man who could tell all hinted that investigators should examine who was really in charge at 1MDB – who was the shareholder and who could sign off deals, before they pointed the finger at him, the frontman. Indeed, information would later emerge to show that the articles of association of 1MDB had been deliberately altered to give the prime minister an extraordinary sole authority over the fund. At the time we didn't have that proof, but no one had really assumed other than that Jho was acting as a nominee for his 'Big Boss' in 1MDB matters. That was the point of flushing out the role he had so long denied he held.

Then, after a few days of media interviews, Jho went as quiet as a tomb. It looked like his silence had been bought with an understanding. In an interview with the *South China Morning Post* he had protested: "If the Malaysian authorities ask me to assist with their investigations, I'm happy to cooperate. I've nothing to hide. I believe in the rule of law." However, it became increasingly apparent that there was no will whatsoever on the part of the Malaysian authorities to ask him questions. Yes, the Central Bank, the auditor general, the Public Accounts Committee and the Malaysian Anti-Corruption Commission all wanted to speak to him, but no warrant was to be issued to assist them in so doing. By contrast, my growing band of sources were telling me that over the coming months, Jho and Najib and Rosmah conducted a series of private meetings in places such as Turkey, Bangkok and Singapore. A compact had clearly been reached with him and indeed all the main players at 1MDB (CEO Shahrol Halmi, Nik Faisal, Casey Tang and Jasmine Loo) that they would be protected if they stayed quiet.

They were not going to go down without a fight. Indeed, such was their hubris, they didn't think there was any danger of their having to go down at all. Instead, they began to fight back. And long before Donald Trump arrived at the White House, before Vladimir Putin would be fingered for interfering in the US elections of 2016, they began to use the art of online misinformation and smear tactics to get their way. In short: if you don't like the message, shoot the messenger.

UMNO's heavily resourced New Media Unit, the so-called 'cyber troopers', together with a team of the prime minister's key spokesmen, began trying to spread doubt about the authenticity of the allegations. *Sarawak Report* was "notorious", waded in one key UMNO blogger going by the name of 'Rocky's Bru', for its "to hell-with-your-ethics way of going about" criticising corruption. Apparently, I relied on "a lot of half truths and dubious spins", which was why "professional scribes" (like himself) didn't "waste time" on my "so-called *exposés*". However, in a comment which I took as a backhanded compliment, he regretted that after this latest story "Suddenly, those who didn't give a damn about *Sarawak Report* are quoting from it, eating out of Ms Brown's hands."

The *Rakyat Post* was a relatively new outfit that also set to work, accusing me of having "fabricated" the emails and implying that it too had been sent *the Sunday Times* material, but had risen above being taken in. The website, under the headline, 'PetroSaudi slams 'malicious and slanderous' claims about 1MDB monies', claimed the company had lodged a complaint with the "City of London Police Action Fraud Unit".

At the same time, Najib tried to kick the entire issue into the long grass. Even his docile Cabinet were now raising questions about what had happened to all this money. Najib organised for 1MDB's own auditors, Deloitte, to be brought to Cabinet to answer questions on the fund. Following their presentation, the prime minister's office issued a media statement to say that the "Cabinet expressed confidence that no wrong-doing has been committed within 1MDB, and their desire is for the company to be allowed to implement the proposed outcomes of its strategic review." The statement concluded with an attempt to shift any blame onto PetroSaudi: "Cabinet was told that the recent allegations directed at 1MDB have nothing to do with the finance ministry owned firm, but relate to transactions undertaken by third parties such as PetroSaudi, not 1MDB."

So, in two hours, 1MDB had been given a clean bill of health. It was, as Tony Pua pointed out the following day, utterly absurd. The fear was, however, that Najib's tactics would work. The international media would move on. His total control over government would enable him to lock the story down. And, from somewhere else in government or from among his billionaire cronies, he'd find the money to keep the whole show on the road.

This was the game that Najib had played his whole life. He had been implicated in massive corruption as defence secretary over the purchase of two French submarines – and escaped the net. He had been linked to the murder of a translator involved in that deal – and walked away scot-free. He had always been able to rely on his political connections, on the power of money, and on the institutional system in Malaysia which managed to keep corruption and money politics out of the public eye. Read out a few catchy slogans about the importance of multi-culturalism to an inattentive international media, cultivate the image of a pious and devoted religious man to the people at home, and hope that – as it had done for the last 50 years – Malaysian governance would pass under the radar. Sometimes it's good to be small: your crimes don't get spotted.

The trail went quiet. The slurs against me and the international media continued. The same old populist appeals were trotted out: foreigners like me and other international media organisations were trying to talk Malaysia down. Malaysians wouldn't be dictated to by these outsiders with agendas of their own. What did we know? Who were we to pass judgment?

I began to wonder if, just like the $700 million itself, the story would simply vanish into thin air. But then, in March 2015, I travelled to Switzerland to organise funding for our *Radio Free Sarawak* station which, having been taken off air for a few months, was now going to return to the air waves. I was on the train after arriving when, in the middle of a noisy carriage, my mobile rang. It was a call from the United States. My contact in the DOJ Kleptocracy Asset Recovery Unit had decided to call me back.

They had read the coverage, they said, and had a team listening in on the line: was this a reasonable moment for a conference call? For the next hour, sandwiched between carriages, then travelling by cab and then finally whilst settling into my destination, I spelt out to some apparently very interested transatlantic law enforcers the gist of the information that I now possessed. I was on my way out east to sort out my project, I explained. How about they come to London to meet me at the end of the month, they suggested? After I'd switched off the phone I literally jumped in the air.

It was a moment of massive importance. Najib was clearly going to fight this one out, secure in his control of Malaysia. But if the United States of America's law enforcers were now on to him he had his work cut out. He, together with Jho and the boys from 1MDB, had made a cardinal error by conducting their thefts in dollars and then channelling much of the proceeds into the United States. It not only meant that every single dollar transaction (including the payment to Good Star) had passed through the US clearing system and was traceable as such, but the proceeds of the crime could be seized under US anti-money laundering regulations.

Now it wasn't just a tiny website gunning for Najib and Jho: the Feds were coming.

18. THE PLAYBOY PRINCE OF ABU DHABI

March 2015, Istanbul

I REALLY only know one way to go as a journalist: forward, on the attack. I was all the more determined to keep digging. Sure, Najib's spin operation would continue to try and discredit me and my sources and claim he was the victim of a vendetta. That was obvious. To take the argument on would be a mistake – it would only legitimize his propaganda. No: the best thing to do was to wade back into the documentation I had at my disposal, and carefully chip away at absurdities and evasions with the one thing he and Jho really feared: facts.

I had pretty much sucked Xavier's top 100 emails dry by this point. But there was so, so much more. I had the full 300,000 emails on Xavier's hard disk. I began to trawl my way through them.

Xavier had mentioned to me when we met that, after the $700 million theft, a further $500 million had followed. Sure enough, the emails revealed that they had followed up their first scam a few weeks later by persuading two Malaysian banks to lend them the cash. Much of it was used to buy UBG over in Sarawak (as I've previously mentioned), helping Taib and Jho get out of their difficulties there.

'PetroSaudi International Limited makes RM1.4 Billion Foreign Direct Investment On its Own to Reaffirm Its Confidence And Commitment To The Economic Prospects Of Malaysia.' declared Jho's release in the wake of the deal. The Malaysian media fell for it. The *Star's* reporter Wong Chun Wai was specially flown to London. His reports will not go down as journalism's finest hour. "Posh PetroSaudi office at Curzon St London. Cash rich. Met some powerful Saudi guys", he declared on Twitter after arriving.

His article that followed explained to readers: "Saudi sources said Tarek, a partner of Renault F1 team, had a positive impression of Malaysia with support from the Saudi royal family, whose relationship with Prime Minister Datuk Seri Najib Tun Razak is at an all-time high… In Kuala Lumpur, analysts say the US$2bn from PetroSaudi International Ltd is expected to provide a boost to the domestic economy."

What $2 billion? It didn't exist. PetroSaudi had coughed up precisely nothing as part of its deal with 1MDB. The cash had been one way only – out of Malaysia and into the pockets of the PetroSaudi conspirators.

◆ ◆ ◆

I've mentioned already how *Sarawak Report* snowballed. Whistle-blowers were drawn to us secure in the knowledge that we would take their information seriously and, if it stood up, publish it. But then *Sarawak Report* was about to get its biggest call-in yet.

The first week of March 2015, I was due to fly out east to get the radio station underway again when a short email reached me. It had gone to the wrong address at *Radio Free Sarawak* and I was lucky it had been picked up by a colleague: "To Mrs Rewcastle Brown, I have got very important information to disclose. I need to be in touch with her as soon as possible… she can call me on this number… She will understand very quickly that I have the other side of the coin."

It could have been a crank – but then given the surreal nature of the 1MDB scandal so far, nothing seemed out of bounds. I rang the number and got through straight away to a nervous sounding man, who clearly wanted to talk.

The other side of the coin was, perhaps, the wrong metaphor. Rather the source had information for me which would show that everything I had discovered so far was the tip of the iceberg. He suggested we meet at Istanbul airport. There I would discover that there was far more going on which, up till now, had been hidden beneath the waves. Incredibly, it was to transpire that Jho's dealings in 2009 were just his starter. With the support of the ever helpful bankers at Goldman Sachs, the main course was coming.

Nine months earlier, I had been in Bangkok, nervously awaiting a meeting with an unknown source, Xavier. Now, here I was in another city, meeting yet another anonymous figure, prepared to divulge more information about Jho and Najib's games.

The airport was one of the region's busiest. I had found a relatively quiet corner. The source arrived (I am still keeping his identity secret for his own personal safety) wielding a large sheaf of documents. I wondered how many I would be able to see and, more importantly, to keep. What he had come to discuss was not 1MDB directly, but a sovereign fund in Abu Dhabi, named Aabar.

Aabar was a subsidiary of the multi-billion Abu Dhabi public company IPIC (International Petroleum Investment Company), the state's own mega sovereign wealth fund. It made 1MDB look like child's play, with billions and billions of the country's oil wealth at its disposal. After the PetroSaudi deals concluded in 2009, Aabar had floated in as 1MDB's new partner. The arrangement was slightly different to the PetroSaudi joint venture. 1MDB had never raised money on the open market and therefore had a problem convincing investors it was legitimate. So Aabar had been brought to guarantee any debt it issued would be repaid. Goldman Sachs had arranged two bond issues in May and October 2012, totalling $3.5 billion. The following March, a further $3 billion bond was arranged too. As already described, the first $3.5 billion was intended to help 1MDB buy two big power stations in Malaysia. The second $3 billion was for a new 'Strategic Development Initiative' with Aabar that was supposed to fund development of KL's proposed 'Tun Razak Exchange' business district.

That project had been announced with full official pomp in the presence of Najib and the Crown Prince of Abu Dhabi on 12th March 2013 just before the general election. It had been trumpeted as yet more evidence of Middle East inward investment and confidence in the Malaysian finance minister.

When I had broken the PetroSaudi side of the story, there had been some regret that Xavier's email cache ended in 2011. Ho Kay Tat, the editor of the *Edge* had told me then that we would find some of the worst scandals took place over that money linked with Aabar. He would turn out to be absolutely correct.

"You know who is the key man behind the whole of Aabar?" my source in Istanbul challenged me as we settled down to coffee and sweetmeats. It all felt very reminiscent of my first meeting with Xavier in Singapore: once again, here I was being handed a new facet to the story on a plate.

I didn't know.

"He is KAQ," my source said.

"Who?"

"Khadem al-Qubaisi. This is the most powerful man. He is the chairman of Aabar and he is the CEO of the parent fund IPIC. He is the right-hand man of Sheikh Mansour himself."

The Middle East was not my patch, but a bit of quick research before our meeting had given me some of the basics. Sheikh Mansour was the youthful fourth brother of the Emir of Abu Dhabi, and held a key economic role in the emirate. He had come forward in 2008 to bail out Barclays and made such a killing from that short-term investment that he had celebrated by buying Manchester City Football Club.

Al-Qubaisi – or KAQ as he seemed to be known by just about everybody – was Mansour's fix-it man. He was to become one of the key figures in the 1MDB scandal. Like Jho, he was brash, bold and utterly brazen. Like Jho, he had a global reputation for soliciting and taking kickbacks. And, also like Jho, he had a love of the high life – including a collection of high-end cars (embossed with his initials) and luxury properties across Europe. My new source was about to spell out just how lustful for wealth and glamour he really was.

"Khadem, he organised the Barclays deal for Mansour. That was where he made his first hundred million – nothing too substantial, his kickback reward. Afterwards though, especially with this 1MDB, he has made hundreds of millions."

I replied that I thought a hundred million 'kickback reward' sounded like quite a lot of money.

My contact spluttered. "Ha! but now he has taken billions. He has learnt all the dirty tricks and has become so powerful, spending money everywhere. You cannot imagine the spending everywhere. Huge!"

I looked at a bank statement he had passed to me, relating to something called the Vasco Trust, owned by al-Qubaisi, as an attached embossed, letter-headed note from the bank confirmed. The statement, from the Edmond de Rothschild private bank in Luxembourg, showed large monthly payments, of sums between six and eight million euros to an outfit named OCEANCO for 'Topaz'. *Topaz* was the world's fifth largest private yacht, widely considered to be owned by Sheikh Mansour, manufactured by the ship builder Oceanco. It seemed that in fact the payments were being covered by al-Qubaisi.

I recalled that Amy had pulled up stories of how Jho and his pal DiCaprio had partied with friends on that very same yacht off the coast of Brazil during the World Cup in 2014. A connection... So where had al-Qubaisi's cash all come from?

"These are the payments that should most interest you, my friend," he then murmured, passing over a separate list, also provided by the bank. "You see, $20.75 million dollars paid from Good Star Limited to KAQ's account. Look at the date, 20th February 2013. This was why I knew to make contact. We have a common story."

It was an extraordinary connection. Jho, the owner of Good Star, was paying Khadem al-Qubaisi, the powerful aide to Sheikh Mansour. Why? I couldn't help but notice that the date of the payment came just before the last of the multi-billion dollar bond deals involving Aabar and 1MDB. Was it another kickback?

And there were other, even more substantial, payments into the same account around the same period. Just under half a billion dollars had passed in a series of massive multi-million dollar transactions from the end of 2012 into 2013. They were all registered as coming from a company called Blackstone Asia Real Estate Partners, which had an account at Standard Chartered Bank in Singapore. Last on the list, there was a payment of $24 million (to be precise, $23,999,977) from an individual named Prince Faisal bin Turkey bin Bandar al-Saud, made on 26th April 2013.

What was going on, I asked?

My source shrugged: "What I do know that this was all connected to 1MDB. That was the big deal that KAQ made at that time – it was so huge that he was scared of all the money coming in at once. He wanted it bit by bit. There was nothing that he was doing that could make him so much money except this at that time. But why it came in through this Blackstone subsidiary I don't know. It is simply amazing if a major company like this could be a conduit for such illegal cash."

We wondered, appalled, if somehow America's private equity giant Blackstone was involved in all this deceit? It was only later that we discovered 'Blackstone Asia Real Estate Partners' had nothing to do with the actual Blackstone back in America. It belonged to Jho, and had been deliberately given that name to muddy the waters. It was something he would do repeatedly during the 1MDB scandal, ensuring that inattentive bankers, auditors and board members would feel reassured by an apparently legitimate brand. In other words, Jho's business model was the financial equivalent of a dodgy market stall selling fake branded watches.

Our forward flight times approached. "Here," my companion flicked open his mobile phone, "look at these pictures. Remember all those ceremonies with KAQ and Najib signing all those agreements – all in white robes, looking so pure? Now, see this. This is the real Khadem al-Qubaisi!". Before me was a small album of pictures of the fund manager in lewd poses in various nightclubs, jiving in front of naked women, quaffing alcohol, and dressed in t-shirts displaying more lewd pictures. "They won't like that in Abu Dhabi, believe me," my companion said.

"The truth is he is a fraud. He is obsessed with drugs, gambling, women and fast cars. He has splashed all this stolen money everywhere. Pink Bugattis, blue Bugattis, dozens of top sports cars. He has three huge villas in South of France – San Tropez. He has been buying jets, properties… after he made that money with 1MDB he went mad. He has been stealing from everywhere since and spending all over. There is a $50 million New York penthouse he bought straight after the Blackstone money came in, here are the lawyers who did it all for him. Look, they knew, all these documents here prove they were helping him to hide and to avoid tax.

"And the other big fish you need to catch: Edmond de Rothschild Bank in Luxembourg. They are caught up in all this and here is the proof. The chief executive was working together with KAQ in all his private companies and helping him to invest it all – his name is Marc Ambroisien. See this transcript of a recorded conversation where he warns KAQ that any other bank would have frozen the Blackstone money coming in. And here, these are the papers for the Aston Martin KAQ bought Ambroisien as a gift to thank him."

I was struggling to take it all in. It was sensational stuff. Here we had a character to rival Jho himself in terms of debauchery and ostentation (and a 'strict Muslim' to boot), a major New York law firm helping to funnel the money, and one of Europe's most prestigious private banks caught up to their neck in the skulduggery.

Publishing it all would require a major exercise and I would need to keep hold of some of the evidence. What would he let me have, I asked? There was a pause. "Take it all, these are copies, but we need to be careful to work together on how you publish this". We shook hands and the following day when I arrived in Singapore I found the undignified photographs of al-Qubaisi in my email inbox.

I wondered what to do next. I could try to interest the mainstream media, although that had proven only a limited success with the *Sunday Times*. Or I could follow my own instincts. Not for the first time I decided, to hell with it, just publish and ask some legitimate questions. And so, a few days later, I ran a story on *Sarawak Report* which led on the $20 million payment then summarised the Aabar/1MDB relationship and connections I had spotted between Aabar and Jho's own private ventures. I also went to town on the contrasting public and private images of the powerful Abu Dhabi sovereign wealth fund boss, presented as a sober business partner to the public, whilst spending his spare time partying in the 'sin bins' of the West. Not for the first time, it provoked tuts and accusations of 'tabloid tactics' on my part. So be it – hypocrites ought to be exposed.

◆ ◆ ◆

I didn't have all the details then, but in revealing al-Qubaisi's links to Jho, I had struck an entire fresh line of enquiry which would put the PetroSaudi scandal in the shade. Kay Tat had been bang on the mark: while Xavier's data had given us *prima facie* evidence of criminality, it was really only Jho's warm up act. As it would soon transpire, it was the Aabar deal, organised and advanced at every turn by Goldman Sachs, which would turn out to be Jho's most audacious and lucrative scam of all. In total, once the dust settled, we would discover that the deal allowed Jho and al-Qubaisi between them to divert $1.4 billion into their own personal accounts. It would fund a yacht for Mansour, diamonds for Rosmah and a movie for DiCaprio.

I was now beginning to get to the heart of the 1MDB affair. Across Southeast Asia, the Middle East and in London, some very powerful and wealthy people were beginning to feel threatened. They weren't happy that their plans were being exposed by some upstart hack from London. They were angry: I and others were about to discover just how angry.

PART THREE

THE BACKLASH

19. MOVE ON, THERE'S NOTHING TO SEE

Spring 2015, London

A few weeks after my story on al-Qubaisi and his connection to 1MDB appeared, a contact who was connected to my source on Aabar was driving through Paris, near the Champs Elysées. Suddenly, a car and a motorbike – one behind, one in front – tried to corner him in the middle of a major road, in broad daylight. He was forced to stop. Men emerged from the cars. Without thinking, my contact drove across the central reservation on the road and sped straight to the nearest airport. He hid for the next eighteen months, terrified for his life.

It was a shocking episode. After that point, over the following weeks, I could not help but wonder if I too might be a target for an 'unfortunate street incident'? I found myself stepping back from the curb and retreating from the edge of tube platforms – it seemed ridiculous in London, but I realised I was threatening powerful and criminal interests.

The attacks were carried out electronically too. I received an email from a reader saying he was looking for the al-Qubaisi story on *Sarawak Report* and could not find it any longer. Wearily I searched for the story so I could send our supporter the link – but I couldn't find it either. I rang Christian, our IT guy. Any thoughts as to why this particular story had disappeared? He looked into it and got back to me. Someone had got into a 'back door' of our site, he had discovered, and plucked out the story.

They had then gone to some considerable effort sweeping around our system to wipe all record of it. We had got used to DDOS attacks and other cyber hits to put the website out of action, but to sneak in and remove just one story was extraordinary – and rather obviously suggestive of the culprit. Not only that, we realised later, these operators had gone into our Google settings to wipe out our preferences and make us hard to search via normal methods. *Sarawak Report* had been high up the first page of results of any Google search for 'Sarawak' for several years, but now we had disappeared for casual browsers.

Later, I established through French sources that al-Qubaisi had hired an expensive outfit linked to former senior French secret service operatives to conduct the attack. He was that worried. I was going to learn over the coming weeks just how hard I had hit them – and how hard they were prepared to strike back.

◆ ◆ ◆

Over in Malaysia, Najib was getting very angry indeed. Up till then, spring 2015, he had managed to keep the scandal out of the mainstream media and present it, especially to the less informed rural populations, as a complex financial matter that was being misinterpreted. But people everywhere were at last getting the message that thievery in high places had occurred.

My source Din got in touch: "1MDB is what they talk about in the market and in the back of taxis all over. People are furious. This is what they had always suspected and now they know it's true."

The fact that $700 million from the beleaguered and indebted fund had now been traced to the account of a known close associate of the prime minister, whose links could not be denied, was fuelling daily headlines in all the online media and dominated local Facebook. What's more, it dominated the opposition agenda in Parliament. The story developed by the day with accusations and counter-accusations. Why hadn't Najib and Jho sued *Sarawak Report* and the *Sunday Times* if we were lying, people were asking?

Najib's personal popularity was plunging. He had just implemented a hike in Malaysia's goods tax. And this all came as news and pictures were leaked of the absurdly extravagant series of six separate wedding celebrations to mark the union of Najib and Rosmah's daughter to a member of the Kazakh political royalty. These were jewel- and flower-bedecked extravaganzas in Malaysia and Kazakhstan, the like of which had never previously been seen even on royal occasions.

Desperate to keep a lid on it, wedding invitations instructed guests not to post photographs – we know this because photographs of the invitation were leaked too. Anonymous guests jested that the garlands were of such proportions they had been fearful of getting lost in them.

Across Malaysia, people were mobilising. 1MDB was just a part of it; ordinary voters were sick and tired of the widespread corruption and malpractice. There was the cover-up over Altantuya's murder, the buying of the election, the graft and corruption everywhere. For so long, politicians like Najib had been able to rely complacently on people nodding their heads. No longer: increasingly, Malaysians weren't having it.

It was clear the prime minister's office was beginning to panic – and resorted to ever more heavy-handed tactics to keep everything under control.

Najib struck at the very end of March when police arrested three editors of the *Malaysian Insider* for alleged 'sedition', relating to a report about the rejection by a government council of a proposal to introduce Islamic law. Najib in his earlier, 'reformist' days had pledged to abolish this outdated law along with a number of others permitting arbitrary arrests. Now he was employing it in a transparently spurious manner. The following day Ho Kay Tat and one of his colleagues at the *Edge* were also arrested and detained on vague, unspecified grounds. They were eventually set free and charges dropped, but the authorities had sent an unambiguous message that journalists who pursued the 1MDB scandal could expect to be targeted. It was a harbinger of things to come, as Najib moved to create a whole new category of crimes and punishments and executive powers to crack down on the media and opposition and protect himself and his circle.

Then, shockingly, Najib introduced a new 'Prevention of Terrorism Act' – a tactic that has become standard for oppressive legislation that ought to be debated long and hard. It enabled the authorities to detain 'terror suspects' without trial for a period of two years.

POTA, as it was immediately known, was rightly criticised for being a reincarnation of the Internal Security Act, revoked in 2012.

The opposition leader Anwar Ibrahim, meanwhile, was still in jail. His daughter Nurul Izzah told me that Najib and Rosmah were personally insisting he be treated poorly. "They are refusing him books, writing materials and they are refusing him company. He is an older man now and they are denying him a mattress. He is lying on the floor. It is very difficult to arrange any visits or to keep in touch."

It was at this point that the FBI appeared. Having called me on the train in Switzerland, they flew into London to meet me. A team of three, including a lawyer from the DOJ, had come to shake me down. Over several hours, I laid out the details of the PetroSaudi scam.

"There is just one more thing," I said, having handed them a copy of the data I'd received from Xavier. "I have just picked up a whole lot of new material, which is all related to this Aabar sovereign wealth fund. I don't know much about that side of the story at the moment, but my feeling is that it could turn out to be even bigger than the rest of it." They looked rather unenthusiastic. We were all exhausted.

"Well, I don't think we can afford to go off on a tangent and we probably should remain focused," one of them ventured.

"Yes, but it is clearly all part of the same fraud and the sums are even more enormous," I gently persisted. We agreed it might be worth their copying the documents I had received from my source the previous week. And that was it. The FBI made clear that they were very interested in what I had to say, but that whatever they did would take time and it would be one-way traffic only. I was an informant not a partner. I understood their position perfectly. I also knew they would be wary because I was a journalist. Though I kept the meeting with them to myself, they must have known that I would not be letting go of this particular affair.

◆ ◆ ◆

And nor did I. I simply ploughed on. Din had been back in touch asking if I wanted to meet yet another new source back in Singapore. In a six-star hotel suite in the city I was passed documents from Malaysia's Central Bank setting out its investigation into 1MDB. They also contained letters from the Suspicious Transactions Reporting Office at Singapore Commercial Affairs Department. Those papers, dated just four weeks earlier, 13th March, showed that Singapore had uncovered another part of Jho's money trail. It transpired that Jho had loads of accounts at BSI bank in Singapore. One of these, in the name his company the Abu Dhabi Kuwait Malaysia Investment Corporation, had received $529 million from his Good Star account at Coutts Zurich. ADKMIC (another of Jho's imaginatively titled companies) was the very same company that he had used to invest in Sarawak's UBG, I remembered.

Curled up in my own cramped hotel room looking out over the tower blocks of Singapore, I realised it was yet another devastating piece of evidence of Jho's staggering money flows. And it showed that Singapore was now on the case.

There was another bombshell document. 1MDB's management was claiming they had walked away from the PetroSaudi joint partnership with a handsome profit and BSI Singapore was the bank they said they were keeping this cash in – to assuage pressure from opposition politicians demanding to know where the money was. But a letter from the Singapore financial cops made clear their claim was false. Coupled with the information that BSI was where Jho banked and that he had accounts bursting at the seams there reinforced the picture of an unholy overlap between Jho's and 1MDB's affairs. If the money had actually found its way to Jho, how on earth could 1MDB have it as well? The claim that 1MDB had got any cash out of PetroSaudi was just a complete lie.

Up went the story. In response, Najib urged people to wait for official inquiries to be complete. Everyone should just be patient until that was done and dusted, rather than rely on the reporting of scurrilous journalists like me:

> When concerns began to be raised, I wanted a detailed explanation, so I ordered the Auditor General and PAC [Public Accounts Committee] to investigate 1MDB's books. Anyone found guilty of embezzlement or misappropriation will be brought to justice … In the meantime, please do not speculate and form conclusions … If we are sincere in finding out the truth behind those allegations, we need to get the information from legitimate sources and not third-party news portals or online blogs that might have hidden agendas.

he bemoaned in an extensive statement on his own blog that May.

But the thing about scurrilous journalists is that we don't like waiting. By mid-May 2015 I had published the rest of the detail from Singapore about Jho's accounts with BSI bank. Going through the documents, I next discovered that, in 2011, another huge sum of $330 million had been paid straight from 1MDB to Good Star, once again to the account at Coutts Zurich. This information came from an investigation being led by Malaysia's Central Bank into the payments it had authorised for the fund. Purporting to be an investment, the "lending", their documents declared, "had been approved by Minister of Finance (Najib) and the Board of Directors of 1MDB."

With story after story, I piled the evidence higher and higher. As did the *Edge*. After Aabar agreed temporarily to bail out 1MDB with a $1 billion loan in June, the newspaper began to dig into this odd relationship. As previously stated, Aabar had agreed to guarantee the bonds sold by 1MDB. 1MBD used this borrowed cash to pay for the two power stations in Malaysia. But it also declared in its accounts that, as a payment for the guarantee, Aabar had received around $1.4 billion. That in itself was bizarre. Yet the *Edge* had found that there was nothing recorded whatsoever in Aabar (or its parent company IPIC)'s own accounts to indicate such money had been received. Where the hell was it?

Now, finally, the international media woke up. The *Wall Street Journal* published its own scoop on this story, revealing that Aabar chairman, al-Qubaisi, and its CEO, Mohamed al-Husseiny, had set up a separate bogus company, 'Aabar Investments PJS Limited', the name almost identical to an actual subsidiary called Aabar Investments PJS. The bogus version was incorporated in the British Virgin Islands, but was not part of the Aabar group, despite the deliberately deceptive name – a classic Jho Low signature ruse. It appeared that 1MDB's billions hadn't gone to the joint partnership with Aabar, they had been siphoned off into something else altogether.

By July, the new managing director of IPIC was writing to Najib in his capacity as Malaysia's finance minister expressing "some concerns". His fund was not aware of any payments made for its 'guarantees' and he wanted to know why the sums 1MDB claimed to have paid Aabar had not been received. Najib apparently ignored those letters. But by August I had another major development to report – Aabar's boss al-Husseiny had been sacked.

To the wider Malaysian population, much of this passed them by. They could hardly be blamed; the details were tough to comprehend, involving bafflingly complex corporate structures and transfers of impossible to grasp sums of money in faraway places. But that May, a story broke that felt much closer to home. The Muslim Pilgrimage Fund (Tabung Haji), a government-sponsored savings fund to support pilgrimages to Mecca, had been pushed by Najib to buy land in KL from 1MDB. It was land his Ministry of Finance had earlier given to 1MDB for peanuts. And Najib wasn't just demanding that the Muslim Pilgrimage Fund buy the land, but that they do so at a ludicrous mark-up.

Here was the pious Muslim leader using the savings of trusting believers to bail out his corrupt state fund. The price that the Muslim Pilgrimage Fund was forced to pay conveniently amounted to almost the exact sum that 1MDB was owing in an upcoming debt repayment later in the month. The head of the fund was a spectacularly under-qualified fellow named Abdul Azeez, who boasted a degree from a Pakistani diploma mill named Preston University (to sound like Princeton). Azeez had been appointed by Najib and was known to be obedient to Rosmah.

Of all the pillaging from Malaysia's public funds, this perhaps provoked the most instant public outrage. No one could match Najib when it came to protestations of personal piety and he constantly claimed to be helping pilgrims pay for their trips to Mecca. Yet here he was conducting a blatant raid on people's savings for that very trip, in order to pay off the debts incurred by his earlier thefts from 1MDB.

I took the opportunity to remind people of my earlier *exposés* concerning similar raids on Islamic savings funds by politicians in Sarawak. Yet, staggeringly, Najib simply brazened it out. He announced, after several days of awkward headlines, that he had actually done the Muslim Pilgrimage Fund a favour by selling it the land 'cheap'. He had now advised Azeez to sell the land on for a profit, claiming there were no fewer than three prospective buyers already queuing for the chance to buy it. The land would be sold within a month, he told a press conference. Unsurprisingly, the Muslim Pilgrimage Fund has still not found its buyer four years on. With his powerful government leaning on the press and television, Najib was able to deflect the story and move on.

It began to feel surreal. The evidence of corruption around Najib and Jho was now overwhelming. But they were still being largely ignored internationally and protected domestically. Deprived of a free press, and failed by a judicial system and a parliament that had been systematically enfeebled by years of overweening executive power, someone in Najib's position could, it seemed, get away with what he wanted, in spite of the widespread anger at his behaviour in Malaysian homes, online portals and private WhatsApp groups. In public, he appeared calm and steady, a figure of stability in a wider region beset by political uncertainty and even violence. In private, it was all a little different. I was informed that Najib had decided to stick it out not least because Rosmah's witchdoctors, or *bomohs*, had advised that if they could cling to power till the end of July, they would be invincible. Those who do not believe in black magic (which ought to include good Muslims) tend to respond with bemusement over the addiction of certain top Malaysians to 'voodoo' beliefs. But Rosmah was known to have an obsessive belief and fascination in spells and their *bomoh* practitioners. She kept a permanent entourage of them, burning magical concoctions, and wailing incantations.

Yet whatever weird stuff Najib and Rosmah were getting up to in private, they seemed to be keeping their stranglehold on power. They were not expecting one thing however – the remarkable return of Malaysia's most famous octogenarian.

20. THE RETURN OF DR M

May 2015, KL

MAHATHIR was supposed to be enjoying his retirement. But he wasn't one to subside gently into his dotage. This controversial politician was not done yet. As 2015 went on, it was becoming clear that, aged 89, he was contemplating a comeback.

I had met the grand old man of Southeast Asian politics once, more than a year earlier, while I was still looking for someone prepared to pay for Xavier's documents. On a visit to Singapore, Din had casually suggested that I speak to him.

I had been nervous about going: I was risking arrest going into Malaysia given my reporting. But Din had friends in high places able to remove, at least temporarily, the alert beside my name on the border control computers, and the immigration officer at the airport merely placed my passport in his scanner, glanced at me and let me through.

A few hours later, I was in Putrajaya being ushered into the presence of the man people referred to as 'Dr M'. We greeted each other with a somewhat prickly, formal politeness. This was a man whom I had long regarded as a dictatorial, ruthless and corrupt leader and to him I was doubtless a tiresome activist journalist.

Despite his age, he was still a fired-up, anti-colonial warrior who regarded me personally as having a record in that department. The interview had been granted on the understanding I would ask mostly about Sarawak. Quickly, I was getting the usual post-colonial lecture: Europe had chopped down its own trees a thousand years before; it was some cheek now to demand the developing world desist. Were there not better options than mega-dams, I countered? Wasn't the potential of the rainforests to combat global warming relevant?

"Well, if you want us not to cut our trees you should pay for that!" he barked.

We talked more about Sarawak – where he was due to go the following day. Our time was coming to an end: if I was to raise Najib's finances with him, I needed to do so now.

"Dr Mahathir, before I go," I finally said, as I snapped my recorder shut, "I believe you are aware that I have viewed some extremely revealing information on the subject of the missing money from 1MDB."

"Hmmm." I faced a sphinx.

"Well, it is obviously valuable information and this seems a critical time to get the full perspective on the matter… I think I need to be put in touch with someone who would be in a position to.. er.. persuade the holder of this information to produce it."

"Hmmm…"

Then finally and in a low mumble, he said, "You know, I am an UMNO man. This is my party. I would not want to help unleash something which could cause destruction." Then he blinked, his eyelids lowering like those of a frog, and was silent.

I left and hurried back out of the country before Najib and his cronies got wind of my presence.

Now, in mid-2015, my soundings told me that Mahathir still reckoned he could 'reform UMNO from within', by getting rid of the bad apple at the top. He felt he still had it in him. But even for his supporters, it felt like wishful thinking. A party that had held power for six decades through entrenched corrupt practice, packed with venal and incompetent yes-men, who looked only to what privileges and perks they could vie for, was in no position to reform itself. If merely Najib was replaced, Malaysia would go on as before.

Nevertheless, Mahathir's attacks on Najib were a positive development. If the Mahathir lobby succeeded in rupturing the UMNO monolith then the anti-Najib elements might in the end have to turn to the more reform-minded opposition parties to get the numbers in Parliament to boot him out.

Dr M was certainly on startling form: he remained one of the veteran political fighters in Malaysia. He went on the stump, held rallies and thundered daily on his influential blog, countering each and every weasel explanation of Najib's with rock hard reasoning and good sense. Another notable warhorse from the previous era who was also speaking out was Lim Kit Siang, leader of the opposition party DAP, whose son was now chief minister of the opposition-run state of Penang. Both father and son had been jailed in their day under Mahathir – now all three were singing to the same tune thanks to 1MDB.

Mahathir was also meeting people behind the scenes, I gathered, building a party within a party to oust Najib. He was still a frequent traveller and I would hear inklings of foreign meetings, away from watching eyes, where liaisons were being forged. In particular, a crucial meeting was said to have taken place in Milan on 10th May attended by several UMNO power-brokers, including the highly dubious former finance minister, Daim Zanuddin. These 'plotters' were said to want to replace Najib with his deputy and UMNO second-in-command, Muhyiddin Yassin.

Within days, news of the meeting got out, prompting Najib to accuse Mahathir of seeking to return to a position of influence within the party in order to promote the leadership pretensions of his own son. Mahathir was not plotting, he shot back, he was openly criticising a failed prime minister who should have resigned already. And if he had been planning a succession for his son, then why had he not put such provisions into place when he still held the power and position to do so? The son in question, Mukhriz, had in fact quite recently secured a powerful regional post as the Chief Minister of Kedah, a power-base which Najib would soon move to undermine as part of his battle with the father.

For Malaysians used to a monolithic single party it was a political drama the like of which had not been seen in decades. The previous grand battle had been between Mahathir and rivals led by MP Tunku Razali, who was also now being resurrected as a potential compromise candidate to bring UMNO and the opposition together in a coalition government. There were many who were dismayed that the main figure emerging against Najib was none other than Mahathir. But without him, I doubted whether the 1MDB scandal, huge and blatant as it had now become, would have achieved any more than a whimper in the local press, let alone recognition worldwide.

As it was, every story in the Malaysian news at that time concerned some aspect of the 1MDB scandal and the unfolding political fall-out. There were signs that Najib was losing the support of his deputy, Muhyiddin, and Home Minister Zahid Hamidi over 1MDB, which was confirmed on 21st May when a video was circulated online showing Muhyiddin confiding to a smallish group of UMNO figures, including key players Zahid and Deputy Finance Minister Ahmad Maslan, that the situation had to be dealt with and the first step had to be the sacking of the 1MDB board (something that would not actually happen for another year):

"We have to take action. Never mind 'give it a bit more time', no!... I told the prime minister, sack all those guys. They should be sacked since because of them the prime minister has to shoulder the burden. Yet they have not been sacked," said Muhyiddin. It was clear he was exasperated by Najib and fearful of the repercussions of the scandal on his and his fellow politicians' positions: "[If] the company is mine and I wake up in the morning and read reports that the CEO had borrowed up to RM10 billion... what do you do? You not only sack the CEO, you call the police to investigate... if not, this will be a burden and will bring our downfall." The deputy prime minister's words were blasted across the nation.

Amidst this unprecedented political situation, Najib simply cleared his throat and, like a Malaysian Comical Ali, declared 'business as usual'. He went to Parliament to make a long-scheduled speech on his new 'grand economic strategy', the so-called '11th Malaysia Plan'. His formidable wife and newly-wed daughter with her Kazakh husband made a rare visit to Parliament to support him. Rosmah, with her entourage, seated herself in the opposition section of the public gallery, to hear her husband, stony-faced and gimlet-eyed.

As always with Najib, however, farce was never far away from the surface. At the start of June, he pledged to take part in a televised 'Tell All Session' on 1MDB, open to the press and public. The event had been set up by an UMNO-leaning NGO and Najib had agreed to participate. He had been clearly misled, intentionally or otherwise, into understanding that this would be a staged PR event for him to lay out his case in a friendly and supportive context.

It turned out to be a trap. On his way to the event in his car, he learnt that Mahathir was waiting in the audience to ask questions. There could be no doubt as to who would steal the show and who stood to lose the argument. Najib bolted: the prime ministerial cavalcade spun 180 degrees and shot home. The public could see that he had run away and his credibility plummeted further in Malaysia.

Arriving back in Singapore at the end of that heady month, after a trip to put the last elements in place to restart Radio Free Sarawak (we had found a new way round jamming antics being employed by the Sarawak state government), I texted Din in a state of amazement: "It's an absolute political theatre out here. Dr M hero of the resistance and Najib running for cover!"

Nevertheless, the debacle also revealed what cards the PM still held – he still controlled the agencies of the state. At the televised event, Mahathir had tried to use Najib's no-show to seize the spotlight. But within moments a gang of embarrassed police officers arrived to halt proceedings. As the cameras rolled these officers, although halting, shamefaced and polite, told Malaysia's veteran politician that if he didn't cease speaking they would arrest him. Mahathir bowed and left the stage, maintaining his dignity.

Najib could run, but he was finding it harder and harder to hide. It was soon confirmed – for the first time – that, under 1MDB's constitution, it was the finance minister (aka Najib) who had complete control over decision making, appointments and removal of staff (as well as being the sole official shareholder of the fund). His persistent stance up until then, that it was nothing to do with him, was smashed.

By now even Najib's own family was openly turning against him. Najib's influential banker brother Nazir stated on Instagram that he was disgusted at the unavailability of the heads of 1MDB to speak to the PAC, which had opened its investigation: "Your company has triggered a national crisis and you can be too busy to face Parliament? Unacceptable," he wrote. It caused a ruckus, made worse when photos emerged and circulated online of Shahrol Halmi's successor as CEO of 1MDB, Arul Kanda, two days later spending hours in conversation in a KL hotel bar with Najib's trusted British PR man, Paul Stadlen, and the Barisan Nasional Backbenchers' Club president, Shahrir Samad.

Back in 2015 in fact, this could be seen as one of the first major political dramas conducted primarily through new media – blogs, Facebook and Twitter – where political discourses and controversies developed that would then be reported in the mainstream media. It was fascinating to watch.

In later months, when, eventually, the PAC got to question key 1MDB figures, the impact of 1MDB's constitutional arrangements, i.e. Najib's total control, would become clearer still. The successive CEOs acknowledged to the committee that the set-up made it clear that the PM's word over-ruled that of the board. This was why, time and again, board instructions and qualms relating to investments such as PetroSaudi had been over-ruled. All that mattered were the commands of the sole shareholder and signatory of 1MDB: Najib Razak.

◆ ◆ ◆

Thanks to Mahathir's campaigning, the net was closing. Still Najib maintained that he was the innocent victim in the affair, not the key conspirator. Everything was at fever pitch and the stakes couldn't have been higher.

It was exhilarating to watch and report on. But one thing was worrying me enormously. Xavier had not been paid. And he was contacting me every day feeling ever more outraged and cheated. I felt badly for Xavier, because hands had been shaken on an agreement and he had played his part and acted in good faith, parting with the material. But I did not want to get involved any more than the *Edge* did.

I explored options with various lawyers. A donation to *Sarawak*

Report that could be passed on, for example. But it would provide ammunition to a growing band of malicious pro-Najib attackers, who were longing for an excuse to brand me a mercenary, liar, plotter and all the rest. I could not jeopardise *Sarawak Report*'s credibility by handling such a large sum of money. So Xavier remained unpaid.

Then I heard alarming news from Xavier. PetroSaudi had taken legal action against him in Geneva, accusing him of stealing documents, and demanding his bank accounts be frozen. I was only to learn much later that Xavier had spent years in bitter dispute with his former colleagues and had already threatened them that he had the wherewithal to sink them. The moment I had published my Good Star story they had realised exactly who had shopped them. At that time I still didn't appreciate how much they knew and the danger he was in.

For all the players involved in this story, and for Malaysia itself, everything was now on the line. Either Najib would be ruined, and this wonderful Southeast Asian nation would face a new future, or else he would ruin his accusers, and send his country careering further down a path of corruption and dictatorial rule. Both sides were about to play their big cards – and I would find myself at the centre of it, once again.

21. FALCON

June 2015, London

O N 18th June I was speeding down the Gatwick approach from London to pick up my father from the airport. The phone buzzed – Din was back from travels. I pushed loudspeaker on the hands-free:

"So, who do you reckon took $680 MILLION into their own private account just before the 2013 General Election?" He was sounding jubilant.

Najib.

"'Which account, where?" I asked back.

"AmBank KL. I told you he had big money in an account there with two junior people who were having to manage all those figures and keep it quiet. They've now been sacked."

"Are they talking?"

"Listen, his NAME was on the account!"

"He had his NAME on an account that took in $680 million dollars? Najib? That's extraordinary!"

"There were two payments," he was reading from notes now, I could tell, and I was frantically wishing that I too had my notebook to hand to do the same. "The first payment came in 21st March 2013 for $620 million then the second on 23rd March for $61 million, more or less. It came from Singapore. The account that sent it was called Tanore Finance Corporation."

"I will have to call you back to go through these details," I replied, swinging round a roundabout heading into the airport.

"Wait," he was enjoying himself, "I haven't told you the best bit. Guess where this Tanore kept its account in Singapore."

"BSI Bank?"

"No, Falcon Bank."

"Who?"

"F-A-L-C-O-N Bank."

"So? Never heard of them."

"Small, boutique bank. They have an office the size of a cupboard in Singapore I hear. Guess who owns them?"

I was tired of guessing and trying to find the parking.

"The owner of Falcon Bank is Aabar Investments PJS. It's Khadem al-Qubaisi's handy private bank. They bought it from AIG after the crash killed them off in 2009. It's Swiss-based, Abu Dhabi-owned, a subsidiary of Aabar and IPIC."

When something huge happens, a big bang moment, you remember your surroundings and how it felt when other details of time and connection fall away. I was in a grey car park at Gatwick Airport, heading to the arrivals hall, laptop under my arm as I finished that call. From that day on, multi-storey parking lots would always be associated in my mind with momentous scoops.

◆ ◆ ◆

In the preceding days everything had seemed to drift as Malaysia's political establishment failed to take Najib to task for his evident responsibility over 1MDB. Part of the lull was due to Ramadan, putting politics on hold and giving Najib a massive break. He took advantage of the Hari Raya festive holiday to hold big parties for thousands of people, who were always happy to accept free food without asking rude questions like: where did the money come from?

Now there was a huge smoking gun, it seemed. For months, I had been asking a question: what was in all this for Najib? It was Jho, not the PM, who seemed to have benefited the most from the looting. And while he had clearly been using large parts of his cash to pay for Rosmah's diamonds and Riza's movie career, there had been no direct evidence yet that the PM himself had benefited. Now – I tried to breathe and process what I had been told – it appeared he had received a bung worth $680 million. And to think we in the UK got steamed up about MPs claiming expenses for duck houses.

The significance of this information (if true) was astonishing. Quite apart from anything, it must have been among the largest personal accounts in the world. And all the cash had gone in in one go. How could Najib have been so stupid?

"Do you have documentary evidence of all this?" I had asked, knowing that without concrete proof I would be nowhere with all this tantalising information.

Din replied: "Not yet. I took down those details over the phone. But soon there is an opportunity to have the real thing. The material will be with us soon."

I guessed that the source Din had introduced me to in Singapore had gained more information from the Malaysian investigations. He rang off and I walked with a somewhat wobbly step into the arrivals lounge.

I presumed the information must have leaked from the 'Joint Task Force' inquiry into 1MDB (comprising investigators from the MACC, the police, the Central Bank and the attorney general's chambers) which Najib, under pressure, had reluctantly allowed to be opened in Malaysia. It would therefore be quite widely known within the reasonably large body of officials now liaising on their enquiries. It could hardly stay quiet for long, unless Najib got wind and clamped down hard.

I texted my trusty two colleagues, Amy and Christian: "Looks like we should be able to eventually slay the big beast... talk later.."

Like just about everything in the 1MDB scandal, it seemed an utterly preposterous revelation. What kind of politician in their right mind would put a $1 million bung in their own bank account, never mind one for $680 million? Like Jho's spending orgy, al-Qubaisi's greed, Rosmah's lust for handbags, everyone in this story seemed to have lost their minds.

In the minutes waiting for my father to emerge, I propped up my laptop against a barrier and browsed for information on this Falcon Bank, of which I had never previously heard. It was revelatory. Falcon Bank was founded in Zurich in 1965 as Überseebank, renamed AIG Private Bank and purchased from AIG in 2009 by Aabar Investments PJS, Abu Dhabi. The chief executive was Eduardo Leeman, a Swiss citizen, ex-Goldman Sachs. Meanwhile, the LinkedIn CV of Khadem al-Qubaisi confirmed that he described himself as chairman of the bank from 2009 "till present", although he was not listed as such on the bank's own website.

Delving further, internet archive sites showed that al-Qubaisi had been chairman of the board for a short period after the purchase of the bank and then passed on that role to his trusty right-hand man Mohammed al-Husseiny. During the period of the transfer to Najib in March 2013 he had indeed been the chairman of the board. Al-Husseiny was no longer chairman of Falcon, but, having left it for several months, had just come back on the board.

The implications of this new information were ringing out like hammers in my head by the time I was heading back to London.

Days of family visits, a birthday, tracking the progress of Radio Free Sarawak as it started broadcasting again (we were the subject of a police report almost immediately, placed by a Barisan Nasional party worker, who considered our content to be "seditious") all kept me busy. On 22nd June there was disruption to our online operation that lasted all day. Was it deliberate? We could not be sure.

Anyhow, I was in an optimistic mood. This latest outrageous revelation might be our chance finally to bang Najib to rights. I had not, however, counted on how utterly ruthless and tenacious he and his associates would be. Mid-afternoon on 23rd June a news story popped up on my phone: Xavier Justo had been arrested in Thailand.

◆ ◆ ◆

I would learn later what had happened. He had been expecting a visit from local government authorities to sort out paperwork for his plans to open a hotel on the beautiful island of Koh Samui. Instead, his offices had been raided by a squad of armed Thai police. He was bundled to the ground and cuffed so tightly his wrists bled on the floor. The police quickly moved into his office, ripping out the computers and emptying the filing cabinets. Two days later, he was flown to Bangkok and paraded before the media – still wearing shorts and flip-flops – flanked by four machine gun-toting commandos. The message from the Thai authorities was clear: Xavier, charged with blackmail, was being set up as some kind of criminal mastermind.

The UMNO-controlled newspaper, the *New Straits Times*, had the 'scoop' on events – as if dictated from Najib's office: "A former IT Executive at PetroSaudi International has been arrested for blackmail and extortion," the story declared. There followed a smug statement from PetroSaudi: "We are relieved that Mr Justo will now face justice through the courts. We have been the victims of a regrettable crime that has unfortunately been politicised in Malaysia. We are happy that the Courts will now address this matter, and we apologise to the Malaysian people for the harm caused to them."

Here, then, was Najib's counter-attack – and the reason, perhaps, why he and Rosmah had been so blasé about the allegations they were facing: to blame a lone foreigner for having tried to blackmail and extort the Malaysian people. For many Malaysians, bombarded with propaganda, how much easier would this be to believe, than the fact their own leader had been ripping them off? The report revealed that Xavier's laptop had been seized. In the hands of these people, there was no knowing how they would attempt to distort the facts.

I was by myself and sorely limited as to what I could do. My family were away. Amy was also away, helping with the radio for the month, and Christian was dealing with the battered website off base. All I could do was to start ringing and emailing everyone I could think of: the Swiss Embassy in Thailand, the Consulate, the Foreign Ministry in Bern. None were in the least bit helpful or prepared to say anything to me.

By now, the *New Straits Times* was dripping out further details. They had no hesitation accusing Xavier of being the leak for the material on 1MDB at PetroSaudi. And they published the photograph of Xavier at the scene of his arrest; handcuffed and surrounded by a battalion of heavily armed, menacing-looking police, along with a line-up of what were described as police chiefs and generals, Xavier had been made to look every inch the dangerous criminal. It was also an extraordinary show of force.

I read the rest of the article, my jaw clenched over every embellished and highly spun piece of detail it came up with:

> Two years after he was dismissed from the company, Justo allegedly attempted to blackmail and extort PetroSaudi for as much as 2.5 million Swiss Francs (approximately RM10 million). Justo had allegedly threatened to release confidential business information, purportedly stolen from the company, if his demands were not met. In a statement issued in Riyadh, PetroSaudi said it welcomed the arrest of Justo and that it would fully cooperate with the Thai authorities. It also said it was considering further legal action in other jurisdictions. In addition to the ongoing case in Thailand, PetroSaudi is believed to be preparing to file a claim against Justo with the London police in respect of blackmail and computer misuse offences, and is commencing proceedings in Switzerland for numerous breaches of contract.

I had not known about this history of communications between Xavier and his former colleagues after he had left the company. If I had it would have been obvious to me that his former colleagues would have deduced he was the source – and that he must get out of Thailand. There was no way they would have dared to try and frame him in the UK or Switzerland. But in Thailand, like Malaysia, power and money trump the law.

There was more: "Following the attempted blackmail, various emails and documents appeared on a politically-motivated blog *Sarawak Report*, sparking a wave of allegations against 1MDB." So there it was. Just as in 2009, when I had sought to report in Sarawak, I was being smeared as part of a foreign conspiracy: a colonial intruder, out to exploit the Malay people once more. I read on. PetroSaudi, the report continued, had brought their own 'cyber-experts' from a company called PGI to Bangkok. According to a spokesman from this company, *Sarawak Report* had not only "received stolen data" but had allegedly "tampered" with it:

> The stolen data sets are incomplete, and underwent an editing process after they were removed from PetroSaudi's systems, and before they were published on the Internet … There are many inconsistencies between the published data and the data which still exists on files within PetroSaudi relating to that period of time. Simply put, it is incomplete data, creatively selected and edited to fit a desired narrative … the information [relating to this issue] published on the Internet should be considered unsafe and unreliable.

The audacity of it was breathtaking. They reckoned they could pull the rug from under their accusers. Backed by newspapers and paid 'experts' their lies might sound so credible to people in Malaysia. And I felt very worried too: this was an attack that had been planned and carried out with meticulous ruthlessness. What else were they preparing?

Meanwhile I had a source in jail at the apparent mercy of the people he had exposed. I needed to help him. It was one of those times when it feels like each minute matters and there are no hands on deck. I had to get the information out in Switzerland and to try and mobilise support to get Xavier out. For the rest of the day I tried to identify and contact, by phone and email, newspapers in Switzerland, and emailed them a press release on the plight of their national. I also tried what contacts I had in Switzerland to take the matter up wherever I could. Yet, by nightfall I was feeling that I had made very little headway. There was a general lack of interest. I tried the Swiss Consulate in Bangkok again. They tersely informed me that Xavier was being attended to by staff and that he was receiving the best advice of lawyers and that was all they could say. It later turned out they were barely attending to him at all.

It was awful. I realised I should have given Xavier better advice, as I gave up trying anything further that night. He had told me over the past couple of weeks that PetroSaudi was moving against him in Switzerland, trying, through court action, to freeze his bank accounts, he said, over some dispute he had had. But he had still been evasive over what was going on. He had decided not to join his family's trip to Switzerland, because of all these issues, was all he had said. Ironically, he had felt safer in Thailand.

I texted Kay Tat. All the more good reason for not paying him, was his response. The *Edge* the next day did what most in their shoes would have done and made clear they had performed a public service by tricking the material out of Xavier and providing the information about 1MDB's lost billions to the public. But it left Xavier horribly isolated in jail in Bangkok.

It would, undoubtedly, have been so much cleaner if he had not insisted on the money. Then he would have been invulnerable to the smears and criticisms, which enabled his reputation to be trashed over the coming months. Not that paying for stories automatically invalidates them. The UK media pay for 'public interest' stories on a regular basis – for example, the £375,000 paid by the *Telegraph* for the MPs' expenses claim story.

The following few days were dreadful. Xavier hadn't deleted a series of WhatsApp messages between the two of us, in which I sought to mediate on his behalf with Tong over the unpaid data. These texts were to provide perfect material for PetroSaudi, who got their hands on them at once thanks to their obvious close collaboration with the Thai police. Editing them to suit their own purposes, they were used to further 'prove' that I had ulterior motives.

Meanwhile UMNO politicians and their client media declared that the entire development was proof there had been no wrongdoing by 1MDB, PetroSaudi or Jho Low, and that the incriminating documents were all forgeries. Home Minister Zahid Hamidi was claiming that, during interrogation, Xavier had already implicated several Malaysians who allegedly asked him to manipulate the leaked information, which was passed to *Sarawak Report*.

One UMNO bigwig named Sayed Ali (soon to be promoted to minister in apparent reward) claimed (without explaining why) that the arrest of Xavier "proved" we had doctored all the evidence condemning 1MDB: "1MDB is being used as a weapon to bring down the prime minister and tarnish the Barisan Nasional government's image," he said. "They [*Sarawak Report*] received wrong information but they have published it widely, with the aim to put pressure on the prime minister. It is now proven that the slander thrown at the prime minister, linking him with 1MDB, is unfounded."

At least this was a variation on the theme that I had doctored the documents myself.

Youth and Sports Minister Khairy Jamaluddin also had his say: "Justo used distorted facts on 1MDB to blackmail it, probably for his own financial gain. News reports revealed that he lived a luxurious lifestyle."

Ironically, the *New Straits Times* then went about its own bit of doctoring, altering a picture of Xavier in order to make him look as sleazy as possible. Xavier had immersed himself in his new Southeast Asian lifestyle with enthusiasm, getting some local tattoos, and had posed without his shirt by the sea in a Facebook picture together with his wife and baby. This was meat for the *NST*, who referred to him as "heavily-tattooed" and cropped his family out of the picture to make him look as thuggish as possible.

As the story went wild in Malaysia, I was deluged with requests for comment from online media. With no information about what was going on in Bangkok, there was little I could say except to deny the allegations.

◆ ◆ ◆

Then late morning, a different sort of email landed in my inbox. The subject was "URGENT HELP FOR XAVIER JUSTO" and the sender was 'Laura Winkler'. It read: "Hello, I need help from you … Could you please ask Mrs Clare Rewcastle Brown to contact me asap it's very urgent." There was a Swiss number to call, which I did immediately.

Laura Winkler: aka, Mrs Justo.

22. CLICKING IS A SIN

June 2015, Geneva

IT was the first time I had been in touch with Xavier's wife, although he had frequently spoken about her and their new baby boy. So, we both felt we already knew quite a bit about the other. Laura told me that her husband had been kept at the local lock-up overnight, allowed to make only one telephone call to warn his family, then flown the next day to Bangkok where the staged press conference had taken place. They had used handcuffs which had cut his skin. Beyond that, it was plain she was almost as short of information as I was and needed all the support that she could get. She was in Geneva and I told her I would book a flight the next morning and be with her by midday June 25th – four full days after Xavier had been arrested.

The following day, I arrived at a pleasant, modest block of flats in a quiet neighbourhood, where Laura was staying with her parents. She and her mother and child were at the door as I arrived. Tall, slender, olive-skinned and a very bright and beautiful young woman, she was tense and tearful. I wouldn't have blamed her for holding me at least partially responsible for what had happened, but she didn't. She just wanted help.

I had arrived with a clear plan in mind: my view was that she should go public and immediately shout blue murder. As the wife of a wrongfully imprisoned man, Laura could get publicity for the case. This is what Xavier needed – for the case to be on the Swiss radar. I would be willing to do anything I could to help her. But she was anxious not to second guess her husband's judgement and had had little chance to communicate with him or anyone else close to the situation. She was getting little out of the Embassy and Foreign Ministry. There was a government-appointed lawyer, so far unhelpful and uncommunicative. She was relying on close friends locally, who were trying to visit Xavier and see if they could do anything to help.

So, to begin with, we just talked. Her mother was Scottish, like my husband, which accounted for Laura's fluent English. We found much common territory. She told me how she had met her husband, having taken a job with his company back in the mid 2000s. Xavier's business, which he had originally used to help Tarek's enterprises (even to the extent of lending him the start-up money for PetroSaudi) had tanked in the crash of 2008 and he had cashed out and headed with Laura, now his girlfriend, to Thailand.

When they came back to London after PetroSaudi clinched the joint venture, it was already clear that Tarek and Mahony were now enjoying the fruits of their new wealth. An unofficial part of Laura's job had been to collect substantial sums of cash from the bank to pay a certain Dave Thomas, who 'fixed' things for Tarek and his friends – things that you might not wish to pay for openly on a credit card, she said. Dave Thomas was a British ex-soldier who ran a company called Spy Games and another called Marleymanor, described on his LinkedIn page as "A unique Concierge Service providing highly confidential and discreet services and solutions for high profile clients".

By 2010 Tarek's lifestyle of parties, women, alcohol and drugs had become out of control and character-changing, said Laura. Xavier was left to manage the business, but lived in constant fear of raging tantrums, insults and irrational behaviour from Tarek.

Stories of Tarek's unstable moods had come to me from other sources: for example, shortly after he had invested in a Formula One team (a must now he was so super-rich) he had appalled his partners by launching into a screaming tirade at a business contact in public on the side of the piste. "He is a madman," his new colleagues at Renault had told a confidant. Within six months the partnership ended.

This was the type of behaviour Xavier was having to deal with, Laura explained, as he worked on building up of the Venezuela business and raising more investment money. "We were living in this amazing flat in Mayfair and it was a great life for a few months. But, it became impossible. Tarek became impossible. They weren't covering the bills or travel… There was a growing pile of expenses being owed to Xavier and it was becoming hard to extract them."

Their former friend had become debauched, arrogant, bullying, ungrateful and mean – they were falling out beyond repair. When finally Xavier told Tarek he couldn't stand it anymore and was leaving, Tarek didn't believe him. When he realised Xavier was serious, he saw him as a deserter. As his severance pay, Xavier wanted his outstanding expenses covered and a settlement. Initially they agreed on a very handsome six million Swiss francs, however Tarek later unilaterally reduced it to four million.

I had booked my night's stay at the airport budget hotel and we agreed to reconvene the next day, by which time she hoped to have heard from Thailand. As good as her word she picked me up the following morning. But there had clearly been some developments, which brought problems for our relationship. Before picking me up she had texted me, "Please don't do anything for the moment have some news… Can't make any statement for the moment…" I assured her (as I had already promised) that I would not publicise anything without her consent.

Suddenly, everything was different. When we met she was nervous and constrained. It was all a marked contrast to the day before. Now she told me that she feared speaking out while certain delicate negotiations were, apparently, underway. In fact, she had big news, something that sounded exciting. Xavier had just been visited by UK Scotland Yard detectives, who had come to Thailand. According to her intermediaries, these officials had been allowed in to see her husband by the Thai authorities and were offering to help him in return for his turning Queen's evidence on the PetroSaudi story.

I was gobsmacked and, to my shame, was also taken in. Could it be that the British authorities, for all their apparent inertia and lack of interest when I had raised this matter with them, had actually moved like lightning to pick up this valuable new witness?

"They are working with the Thais," Laura added. "But they just need Xavier to make a small confession, so they can process this all through quickly. He will have to spend a little time, maybe a couple of weeks inside, a slap on the wrist. Then they can get him home."

That seemed odd. I couldn't understand it. "Why does he have to confess to anything?" I remember asking.

"Well, he wrote some angry emails when he was in Thailand. He says sorry for that and that satisfies the pride of the Thais. Then he is released and he can come back to the UK to give evidence."

When I pressed Laura for further details she seemed as confused as I. And there was another matter – the message to her, alongside all this positive development, was that there must be no press whatsoever. Typical officialdom, I thought. As a journalist champing to do the story and aware that publicity is normally a whistle-blower's best hope in a case like this, I became more troubled by the minute.

We talked a little further and then Laura took a decision. She would keep me in the loop but not speak on the record to the media. We did an interview under the guise of speaking not to her but to "close friends" in Switzerland.

◆ ◆ ◆

The article I wrote then was my chance to hit back at the naked lies that were still pouring out about Xavier in the Malaysian media. The previous day the *New Straits Times* had published yet another outrageous character assassination, which had the fingerprints of PetroSaudi all over it.

Meanwhile, the government-controlled TV3 went to town with a four-minute rant by a government flunkey, Tunku Abdul Aziz Ibrahim, who spoke as if PetroSaudi's accusations amounted to a conviction by a credible court after a lengthy investigation and trial. The narrative was telling: "All the allegations against 1MDB are proven to be part of an evil plot to bring down the government and tarnish the country's image," intoned the announcer in his introduction to the star guest, "and, says Tunku Abdul Aziz Ibrahim, the people behind the evil plot in Malaysia must be also tracked down." At which point the report cut to Tunku Ibrahim accusing

Xavier of being a "blackmailer". Publications like *Sarawak Report* and *the Edge* were, he declared, "publishing lies". Threateningly, he continued: "These people should be held accountable, you cannot just destroy people's reputation and that of Malaysia."

On it went. 'Don't be 'keyboard warriors' on 1MDB, Muslims told', was the headline of one report. Apparently, simply reading a blog like mine was un-Islamic. Minister in the prime minister's office, Jamil Khir Baharom reminded Muslims not to abuse social media by "spreading slander" on the issue of 1MDB: "Such actions would reduce the deeds gained from fasting and even clicking on a 'like' would also receive a sin," Jamil told reporters after handing out Hari Raya Aidilfitri festival gifts to patients at The Army Hospital in KL.

A slew of blogs repeated all this stuff, including a newly created 'NGO', Citizens for Accountable Governance, Malaysia, who produced "4 facts" to show how my "articles were used by unscrupulous individuals". Another 'expert', Datuk Huan Cheng Guan (a retired air force officer), was featured in the *Rakyat Post* saying that his examinations of my various articles revealed that they could not have all been written by the same person:

> Who are the real writers for *Sarawak Report* over an international conspiracy to damn 1MDB to oust the prime minister? The website had fooled the nation with a series of articles based on stolen material. For sure, posts in *Sarawak Report* attacking 1MDB are written by different people. If indeed it was Claire Rewcastle-Brown's writing, she wouldn't have written in such a manner

he rambled, concluding that I was in fact a "group of people, ranging from powerful persons to professionals".

"They think I am a one woman army!" I messaged Tony Pua.

"Aren't you??!" Tony messaged back.

The smear campaign culminated in the middle of the summer when the government-controlled, Ananda Krishnan-owned satellite TV station *Astra* even produced a three-part documentary series explaining my evil character and motives over 1MDB.

I felt utterly embattled. On social media, the prime minister's well-funded cyber-warfare department was circulating slurs and cartoons in Malay, which likewise vilified Xavier, the *Edge* and me (at one point, depicting me as a money-grabbing witch with a pointy hat and shoes). All I could do was try to hit back. I published the article I had prepared with Laura entitled 'It's All Lies About Xavier', together with the uncropped picture of Xavier and Laura together. Rather than the *New Straits Times*'s "heavily-tattooed foreigner" (cut out from the couple's Facebook page) it showed him leaning fondly against his lovely wife, who was holding their new baby in delight. The tattoos no longer appeared threatening, just a tribute to local culture picked up in Thailand.

I headed back to London, taking comfort from Laura's information that the British authorities were now on the case. But Laura herself had suddenly become curt. Several days passed and Xavier was still in jail – with nothing happening. On 16th July, I lost my patience and texted Laura: "Laura what is going on and how long are you going to refuse to speak to me? How can it be helpful to Xavier to have this media blackout in Europe while the guys in Asia say what they like and they are keeping him in jail for no legal possible reason? … I am really concerned he is still being held." She fobbed me off again, declaring she couldn't communicate.

But every action has a reaction. Mahathir was among those who declared that Xavier's arrest was "suspicious". And Najib had underestimated who he was dealing with. I was not going to be bullied off a story by anyone. It hadn't worked when I was a TV reporter door-stepping criminals in London and it wasn't going to work now either. The only way I could answer them was with more facts. And luckily, they were all about to emerge.

23. LIVING IN A MOVIE

July 2015, London

WHILE Najib and his cronies had thrown people off the scent with the arrest of Xavier, the smell was still there. I had been keeping in touch with Din the whole time, remembering the allegations he had told me about over the phone concerning Najib. Now, midsummer, it was all to come to a head.

Din had told me that the proof for the material he had mentioned would be in his possession shortly. "There are bank transfer statements and charts that show the task force investigators have established that the accounts belonged to Najib," he told me "It is yours to run."

But at this point, I was reluctant. Having been slandered in the Malaysian press, and with my relatively tiny online presence, I felt we needed a recognised title to get the story out properly. Din left it up to me. I opted for the *Wall Street Journal*. I told Din they would require more than just Din's documents to be persuaded they could get the story past their lawyers. They would need one of Din's sources to verify them too. Din, in turn, was reluctant. There were real concerns about personal safety for people prepared to speak out about this. A few days later, however, while I was having coffee with Kay Tat in a London breakfast bar, he called to say he had arranged a meeting.

I had already been in touch with the *Wall Street Journal's* Southeast Asian correspondent Tom Wright, even putting him in contact with sources like Din himself to try to encourage further coverage of the PetroSaudi deal in particular. I hadn't been overly impressed with the level of coverage they had given to the scandal but the advantage of getting America's biggest financial paper on board would be hard to overstate. I called Wright again, promising him new 'explosive' information. I suggested the meeting could be held by one of his colleagues in London.

Wright bit my hand off after I outlined the details in a call. So it was on the following Tuesday morning, 30th June, that I picked up one of the *Wall Street Journal's* London-based correspondents on an agreed street corner in my battered Vauxhall Corsa. Simon Clarke turned out to be an enthusiastic journalist with an active interest in many of the issues I was writing about and we soon had a rapport going. He even knew about my blog, owing to a palm oil story he had been investigating. We didn't have to go far to reach the location in Central London where we had arranged to meet the source.

"Aren't you coming in too?" Simon asked, after we parked round the corner from the agreed RV next to a coffee shop where I planned to wait. I shook my head, warning him I might get noticed by any watching Malaysian special branch.

Simon nodded and headed off. His job was to ask the source if he could answer for the documents that Din was about to show us. If the answer was yes, then he could be assured the material was genuine. I had only just settled with my laptop barely opened before Simon was back. Far too soon, I anxiously thought, as, flushed in his suit in the summer heat, he burst through the door and made a beeline towards me in my corner at the back. Had everything gone wrong?

"Blimey. It's like living in a movie, is your life like this all the time?" he challenged me as he came up.

"Did it work?"

"Absolutely. Like clockwork. Actually, we had quite a talk."

"Really?"

"They said if they or any of their family get killed I should let it be known that all the relevant information is already with people in a safe place away from Malaysia and there are instructions to publish everything. *That is what they told me. It was surreal.*"

"Put yourself in their shoes," I replied. "Did they verify the documents you are about to be shown?"

"Absolutely," he confirmed.

So, with stage one sorted, we climbed back into my cramped

little car, looking over our shoulders as we did, and headed out of London. As we drove, I filled Simon in on the background to the story. He made a good listener. Eventually we reached the entrance of a very stately building, which was where the person who had been entrusted with the documents had left them with Din. We were waved past the guarded gatehouse. Living in a movie, Simon had put it: he wasn't wrong.

The building was set in cedared lawns in the traditional style of a country pile. It now was owned as part of a business and someone had kindly lent it for the meeting. We were shown to an enormous, silent board room to wait. Not for long.

Din appeared clutching a sheaf of paper. He laid them on the board room table. Together we sat down to consider the documents, prized out from the Malaysian Joint Task Force investigations into 1MDB, which finally led all the way to Najib himself.

"The big boss" had been a shadowy presence in the background for so long. It was on his orders that Jho had been working, on his authority the entire 1MDB looting had been agreed. Now, here he was, in black and white.

On no condition should the actual documents be published, we were told, as it would jeopardise the source. However, we could quote all the details. There were offers of coffee and telephones rang. Together Simon and I got down to work. There were plenty of papers from the Joint Task Force itself. But perhaps the most damning papers of all were the copies of the bank transfer notes, most particularly through the US dollar clearing system.

Din had told me about major transfers from March 2013. Here they were – from Falcon via Standard Chartered, to be cleared by Wells Fargo, New York, before funnelling into an AmBank personal account of Najib in KL.

The sheaf of papers also included the Singapore reports which I had already written about, and, almost as an afterthought, some extraordinary documents relating to Rosmah Mansor, including a bank account that was receiving bags of cash (literally) on a regular basis, brought in by one of her aides who was registered on the account for that purpose. The account had received RM2 million in cash payments over just the last two months. We took photocopies and headed off. Once again, it felt utterly surreal. Here we were, holding evidence of unprecedented corruption by a national leader on the other side of the world. It was a scandal beyond anything I had ever seen before.

First and foremost in my mind, however, was the need to get back into town and attend my younger son's school leaving ceremony. I dropped Simon at the station and rushed home to scrub up before dashing to join my family on the green at Westminster's Dean's Yard to hear the speeches and final congratulations – after seven years at the same school our family was moving on to a new phase of life. "Never thought we would reach this day, look how tall they are," we mothers trilled to one another.

It had been a significant day.

◆ ◆ ◆

As was the next one. In fact 1st July 2015 is etched in my mind. It had been three months exactly since I had published the PetroSaudi story, detailing how $700 million had been siphoned out of Malaysia and straight into Jho's hands. I thought that had been big. It turned out to be just a starter.

I was up early. Word came back to me from the *Wall Street Journal* that they planned to move fast – there was top-level support within the paper to run the story, possibly as soon as the very next day. It was time to write. First, I went over the documents again. Despite everything I had seen over the previous few months, they were easily the most staggering pieces of source material I had ever come across.

There, on a bank statement dated 21st March 2013, was the figure: a sum of $619,999,988 had been paid into an AmBank account in KL in the personal name of Najib Razak from an account at Falcon Bank in Singapore of an organisation called Tanore Finance Corporation. Four days later a further $60,999,998 had been paid in via the same route. Adding them together, a total of just shy of

$681 million had been dumped in Najib's personal account. The similarity to the $700 million filched by Good Star back in 2009 was eerie but since, as Din had first told me, Falcon Bank was owned by Aabar, the bank's involvement betrayed the more likely link to 1MDB's later deals with Aabar. And the date was significant too: the third of the three bonds issued in conjunction with Aabar (through the good offices of Goldman Sachs) had been completed on 19th March 2013. So it was only two days later that Najib had got his cash – and just before the announcement by Najib of the Malaysian general election. Coincidence? I didn't think so.

Apart from this $681 million there were details of another series of payments of lesser, but still enormous, sums, into two further accounts owned by Najib at AmBank. Three payments were made in December 2014 and February 2015, according to this data, totalling RM42 million. Diagrams drawn by the investigators illustrated the cash flow on all the various payments, showing, devastatingly, that the latter ringgit payments which had been made into Najib's accounts had come (via two intermediary accounts to muddy the waters) from a company called SRC International. SRC was a subsidiary of 1MDB which had been established back in 2011 with a single loan from the Malaysian civil service pension fund.

What the money trails from the documents showed was that the money from SRC went first into the account of a private company named Gandingan Menteri, then to another private company called Ihsan Perdana and then straight on within another couple of days into the prime minister's account. Ihsan Perdana was a company supposed to be providing corporate and social responsibility programmes for 1MDB. Domestic transfer documents included in the papers showed that the payment to Najib was described as part of a 'Corporate Social Responsibility payment' for 1MDB.

I sat back wondering where to start. Should I go with the $681 million that had been paid into Najib's account from Falcon bank? Or with the smaller ringgit payments which the evidence showed had passed to the PM's account from SRC, the 1MDB subsidiary? I decided to go with the latter on the grounds that there could be no doubting where the cash had come from.

There was another document in our dossier that made the SRC link especially damning: a letter to AmBank showing that the chief executive of SRC had been made an 'Authorised Person' with authority to make "urgent cash payments" into those accounts (the letter concerned the fact he was delegating that authority to another person, given he was so often travelling abroad.) That chief executive was none other than Nik Faisal, a lieutenant of Jho's at UBG who had moved to 1MDB to manage the 'PetroSaudi' buyout of the former.

So, Jho's placeman at 1MDB was also the man managing these personal accounts for the prime minister. In addition, the documents also showed that he was the director of Gandingan Menteri, the first intermediary company. He therefore managed both the issuing of this cash and its transition through companies linked to 1MDB, as well as its receipt in the acceptor account belonging to Najib in his capacity as authorised person on the account. What a tight circle of thieves I mused. This was public pension money – it was outrageous.

As ever, I knew that my blog had one big advantage as a news source over a major newspaper (apart from being free) which was that I could go into far greater detail, whereas the mainstream news story would necessarily be constricted by the column inches assigned to it. My Malaysian readers, particularly local news outfits and politicians, would want to know the fullest amount of detail I could provide to chase the story further. Furthermore, while the fact the *Wall Street Journal* had decided to run the story was already extremely strong substantiation, the further depth of detail would sweep aside any serious attempts to dismiss the matter as innuendo. I was determined to lay out all the bank account numbers, dates and information available on the transactions. I would then challenge Najib's people to prove any of them wrong.

I also knew that the *Wall Street Journal* would not delve at that time into Falcon Bank's connection with Aabar. So I spelt it out – and hinted that the most likely source of the $681 million was the 1MDB bond issue. I made the point that the attorney general, Abdul

Gani Patail, had all this information on his desk – and that it was now his job to move and issue charges. Having seen his reluctance to move against UMNO cronies like Taib Mahmud or Musa Aman in corruption scandals I had exposed earlier, I decried "the notorious and longstanding refusal of the attorney general... to ever prosecute cases involving senior member of UMNO." I was soon to regret that jibe as unfair. And finally, I emphasised the role played by the banks. It was global brand names which had overseen these transactions into the bank account of a major public figure, despite all the anti-money laundering regulations which should have raised a red flag. How did it all get through, I demanded? I wrote more in hope than expectation – given the lack of movement following my PetroSaudi story, I had grown cynical. Perhaps, though, the impact of this stunning information from Malaysia's own investigations, splashed by a major US news organisation, might get things moving.

The *Wall Street Journal* confirmed its story would be published the following morning. I went to bed, rose early, pressed 'publish' and sat back. I was seven hours ahead. It would be a few hours yet before Malaysia woke up to the news that their prime minister had received hundreds of millions of dollars into his private bank accounts days before announcing an election he had been expected to lose in 2013.

I then flew to spend time with my father in Spain.

24. PERSONAL GAIN

W E caught them absolutely unawares.

Thanks to Xavier's arrest, Najib's team had been getting increasingly cocky. They all felt that their attempts to discredit me and other independent media sources were working. And with Malaysia's opposition alliance, led by Anwar Ibrahim from jail, in a state of total disarray, Najib's selling point, as a beacon of stability, held weight. Then, on the morning of 2nd July, he – like everyone else – woke to my and the *WSJ*'s scoop.

To begin with, he tried to laugh it off. Would a prime minister really be so daft as to take $681 million into his private account, he asked at a rally on Sunday the 5th? "Surely, If I wanted to steal, it wouldn't make sense that I would place that money into accounts in Malaysia?" he quipped. He would be consulting his lawyers, he added. They would advise him on what steps to take.

No legal steps were taken, however. And, as the stir caused by the story didn't die, but grew into a clamour, the laughing stopped. A day or so later, the spin operation reverted back to shooting the messenger. I had a "track record of fabrication and lies", declared one UMNO crony who described my "typical British tabloid" style. The material was "unreliable", intoned the head of the data management company PGI – which had been paid by the Malaysian government to offer allegedly expert analysis of the documents. Yet, even thousands of miles away in London, I could feel the story hitting home, and hitting where it hurt. His two most senior cabinet members, Deputy PM Muhyiddin Yassin and Vice President Shafie Apdal, publicly urged the PM "to take legal action against the *WSJ*, if the report is untrue."

Meanwhile, Najib's line subtly changed. No longer did he deny the cash being in his account. Instead, he stressed that "I have never taken 1MDB funds for personal gain." It was a dead give-away to even a moderately savvy reader. Their PM knew the game was up and was fishing for an excuse.

A few days later, much against my wishes, the *WSJ*, under pressure to prove its story, published all the documents online. It was, as far as I was concerned, a massive breach of trust, putting our source in danger. It was also a chance for the paper to claim the story for itself – and I was forced to watch on as their Asia desk boss strutted through the TV studios explaining his policy on the documents and standing up for his brave investigative journalists, all heroes of the hour.

I was angry with them and concerned for the source. Within hours several of the source's colleagues were rounded up and questioned. Luckily nothing stuck. Meanwhile, astonishingly, my one-woman website clocked a million hits within a few days of the story breaking. From one laptop in West London, to the world. It was a powerful feeling. A couple of weeks later, John Berthelsen, the veteran editor of the *Asia Sentinel* jokingly emailed me, "congratulations, you seem to have singlehandedly sunk Najib. People seem to be counting the hours."

It wouldn't be the end of it, of course. I had already seen what happened to people who had taken on Najib and his cronies. Some like Xavier had been arrested. Some like me were simply slandered. I braced myself and waited for the inevitable.

The attacks varied from the sinister to the ridiculous. A Walter Mitty character called Lester Melanyi, claiming to be a former writer at *Sarawak Report*, lodged a police report against me, telling a packed press conference that he had worked with me "for years" as an "editor of *Sarawak Report*", watching on as I filled up my day forging documents and fabricating evidence (in fact he had done a few weeks as a volunteer on the radio station back in 2010.) I was "a very rich lady", Lester claimed to a room full of journalists. (His allegations were subsequently to crumble when he attempted to 'out' my web designer as one James Steward Stephen. He seemed to have pulled the name out of the blue. A person of that name was tracked down as the manager of an East of England bus company. Their spokesman issued a firm denial that he was a forger or had anything to do with Malaysia.)

On 18th July, the plug was pulled. I woke to a string of messages from friends telling me that my site was no longer accessible in Malaysia. The Malaysian Communications and Multimedia Commission had put me on the banned list on the grounds that the site "may undermine the stability of the country."

Then I suddenly realised that I was now being followed. I had noticed, as summer reached its height, that there appeared to be some unusual activity in my quiet little backstreet in Westminster, which sees little through traffic and provides virtually no street parking for non-residents. Various neighbours began to remark on it too. "There's that man in the black car sitting outside again," people in my block started to say. Meanwhile, the eerie sense that that someone was looking over my shoulder as I worked at my laptop in my local coffee shops was getting stronger. Stocky, white toughs with crew cuts seemed always to be sitting just a table or two away from me, staring fixedly into their iPads – even though they didn't look like readers. Their ears seemed pricked whenever I received a call. What might have been written off as paranoia was confirmed when, later that month, I had coffee with a senior Malaysian law enforcer, whom I had met once before and who had a place in London. He was waiting at a table inside looking out through the vast picture-windowed frontage, looked nervous. "You realise you are being followed?" he said to me.

"Really? Who by? And why?"

"To find out about you meeting me, for example!"

He nodded outside. "That guy you can see walking past again now. He followed you the other way before. I can tell you he will come back again in a minute. He is going to and fro."

I turned and spotted another version of the sheer shorn types, who had been sitting too close in my local coffee shop, sloping past the window, from right to left.

I glanced around the café. There was only one other table

occupied besides our own at this quiet time of mid-morning, by three chatty girls, who seemed like Asian tourists. We carried on chatting – mostly small talk. The girls then got up and headed to the door. My eyes drifted lazily after them and I observed that, as they continued to chat and gossip right outside the plate glass window, they had been joined by another Asiatic looking young man, who was making out as if he was taking snaps of the girls on his mobile phone. Then it dawned on my partially engaged mind that the girls were taking no notice of the apparent photo-shoot and that he was in fact pointing that lens not at them but over their shoulders and through the glass – straight at me, in fact. He was filming us.

I was furious. And before I had stopped to think, I found myself leaping to my feet and running out at him through the door, just as the girls were leaving altogether. The young man seemed stunned. Stupidly, he continued his pose of snapping through the window, even though by then I was standing right beside him. "Stop that now, it's bloody rude!" I yelled and had the satisfaction of watching him pull up, panic and run off. I immediately berated myself for not having got a shot of him.

Not surprisingly, my contact decided now was the time to go – and suggested leaving through the back, which he did. Still enraged, however, I strode defiantly out of the front of the café and down the road towards my parked car. They would hardly do me harm in broad daylight in Hyde Park, I judged. There was no sign of the bald guy anymore. But, as I drove back along the south of the park towards Park Lane, I felt again that I was being tagged, this time by a large black Mercedes, much like the one sitting outside my flat.

I made my way round Hyde Park Corner and decided to indicate left, as if about to turn down the side of Buckingham Palace, but then at the last moment I swerved back into the Victoria-bound lane. The black car, which was still behind me, did exactly the same, zigzagging on my tail. I phoned a contact on my mobile and told them what was going on. The traffic had slowed to a halt. If they were trying to intimidate me, I thought, two could play at that game. I wound down my window, leaned out and looked in an exaggerated fashion at the number plate of the offending car and read its details into the phone. I then raised my eyes as if to examine the driver, who responded by pulling a sudden right and darting across the traffic into Wilton Street and then away.

Later, my nervous companion texted me that he had been followed home on foot. The character who had been filming us through the window and who I concluded must be a Chinese Malay Special Branch operative (there are said to be no fewer than 90 such personnel engaged by the High Commission here in London) had been waiting for him outside the back door. He and the bald guy had openly tailed him to Knightsbridge and he had had to adopt tactics to shake them off before returning home.

I mentioned it to my husband when he came home. "There is another of those black cars outside right now, actually. I noticed it as I came in," he replied glumly. Not for the first time I was feeling somewhat guilty about the pressure on my family. Earlier my six foot four teenage son had complained he was feeling frightened by the whole business. Perhaps a little harshly, I had meanly barked that he should "man up" and remember I was half his size.

◆ ◆ ◆

And I was angry for other reasons too. Xavier was still being held. And it appeared he was preparing to confess to anything in order to get out. For example, an alarming article had appeared in the relatively independent Singapore *Straits Times*, entitled 'Justo Names 10 over Plot to Tarnish Najib'. Quoting a "top Thai policeman" it declared that he had "confessed everything", selling the data he had taken from PetroSaudi to a group of ten people, including media figures, a member of the prime minister's own party and "a Malaysia-born woman who had moved to Britain."

"She has a news blog," the policeman continued. Asked if the blog was the *Sarawak Report* website, he said: "Maybe. I didn't name it, you named it." *He* went on: "The website tampered with the data to discredit the PM." It was a straight up libel. I was later to learn from Laura that the policeman, a Lt Gen Prawuth, was described by employees of PetroSaudi as being in their pay. He was to be sacked and arrested on separate charges of malfeasance the following year. For now, however, I had to watch as the Malaysian client media gloated over who the "plotters" might be in this alleged ring against the prime minister. The names of all Najib's enemies were thrown into the pot, along with business people I had never heard of, but who were said to be paying me millions to fund my "lavish lifestyle" and "media operation".

The surveillance, meanwhile, was becoming obvious. I had had enough. Sitting in the café where I regularly worked near Victoria, I spotted yet another prickly-haired, thick-set man sitting near me gazing unconvincingly into his tablet just as I read in the Malaysian online media that I had been "spotted" in Hyde Park holding a "secret meeting" with my contact now treated as a suspect (proof if we had needed it that we were indeed being spied on by Malaysians.) I picked up my stuff and walked straight down through Victoria to Belgravia Police Station, ringing my husband and my father on the way who agreed that this was the most sensible thing to do.

The officer at the desk clearly considered me mad, even though one of my sons had joined me to vouch that I was not just a crazy middle-aged female blogger. As I tried to explain how I could now prove that I was the victim of a team of stalkers his brow began to furrow. People behind me in the queue politely tried not to listen. "It sounds complicated, Madam," he said, "If it's Malaysian I don't think it can be to do with us." As always, however, I persisted. And whether it was this, or the fact that I had confronted them, the stalking suddenly stopped. "She is manipulative," Mahony was later to text, "she has got herself protection."

25. IT ALL KICKS OFF

End of July 2015

NOTWITHSTANDING the fact I'd hit Najib hard, I was also focusing a lot of my efforts on Rosmah at this time. Thanks to a leak, I had established that one of her aides, one Roslan Sohari, had deposited a total of $551,000 in cash in her bank account in a series of transactions at the start of the year. I envisaged the scene as the young man entered the bank time and again with a suitcase stuffed with notes. Keen to dig further, I headed to Hong Kong to chase down another tantalising angle, namely her extravagant shopping habits and some particularly huge diamond purchases she had made there.

At which point, everything in Malaysia went completely crazy. Investigators trying to dig their way through the scam made progress – and at the end of July, two bank accounts in Singapore related to 1MDB were frozen. I assumed that these were Najib's and Tanore at Falcon Bank.

Then Najib suddenly acted in an extraordinary show of blunt political force. First, he moved to silence his critics. After publishing a brave and comprehensive article setting out the money flows detailed in the PetroSaudi data, the *Edge* was served by the government with a three-month suspension, The government also announced that any publication which used my material would be similarly punished. Another target of the retaliation was Tony Pua. On 21st July, he was prevented from leaving the country on a planned speaking trip to Indonesia and had his passport arbitrarily confiscated, despite his role as a duly elected representative of the people. Then, as I scouted around Hong Kong, collecting evidence of Rosmah's staggering greed, I discovered that the home minister, Zahid Hamidi, together with the Foreign Ministry, might pursue an extradition request against me, "were the police to find *prima facie* evidence" of my "meddling in Malaysian affairs" (perhaps Zahid had been emboldened by the tin-eared announcement by Prime Minister David Cameron that he would soon be visiting Najib.)

A few days later, on 28th July, Najib moved. After openly criticising Najib, Deputy Prime Minister Yassin Muhyiddin was sacked – along with half the ministers in his team. And it was announced that the attorney general had suddenly "retired on health grounds", to be replaced by one of Najib's favourite judges (a man who, previously, had ruled in court that Christians must be banned from using the word 'Allah' in their bibles.)

It was, effectively, a coup against his own government. Later, the truth of what had happened came out. The heads of the task forces investigating 1MDB had requested a meeting with the Agong (the Malaysian king) to propose a full investigation into Najib. Their view was that it was time to press charges and for a royal order demanding he step aside.

The Agong agreed and signed off the warrant. Yassin was pencilled in to take over as caretaker leader. But overnight, Najib had got to work. When Attorney General Abdul Gani Patail arrived at his office the following morning, nervously intending to put in effect the order for the removal of Najib, he found a squad of Special Branch operatives waiting for him, fully armed. They bundled him back home where he was placed under house arrest. At the same time his office was raided and many documents taken away. The 'retired' attorney general (who did have a chronic kidney complaint and had been due to leave office in October) went silent as a grave and stayed within his home for months, speaking to no one.

The removal of the country's chief law officer at gunpoint, a man who under the constitution can only be sacked by the king himself, signified the desperate lawlessness of Najib's coup that day. He decided simply to shatter the investigations into 1MDB, which his own government had set in motion. The following day a mysterious fire broke out on the 10th floor of the Bukit Aman Central Police Station in KL; there were shocking pictures of the flames and black smoke billowing out of the windows. This just happened to be the floor of the fraud investigation squad, where the task force into 1MDB had operated. Too bad then; any papers relating to that investigation could now be said to have been consumed by flames.

To his eternal shame, this was the day that UK Prime Minister David Cameron decided to visit Malaysia. It was a PR gift to Najib, giving him just the foreign power affirmation he needed for his own domestic news purposes in the middle of this crisis.

◆ ◆ ◆

But, once again, Malaysia would not be cowed. As 29th July drew to a close, I received an anonymous email sent late Malaysia time. Fortunately, I forwarded it to another account because a couple of days later I was to be targeted in a hacking attack and the correspondence related to this email was methodically erased. The email read as follows: "I can't quite let you know who I am, or my sources, so I suppose you may need to evaluate yourself as to how genuine these are… This is the reason why Gani Patail was removed as AG."

Attached were two photographs of what were clearly official documents in buff folders. They were in Malay but Google Translate was on hand. They were headed: "in the sessions court of Kuala Lumpur, arrest for criminal case No.… There were then the words: "draft of the first charge". And then "The State Prosecution versus". Then there were two names:

Dato' Seri Mohd Najib Bin Tun Abdul Razak
Dato' Shamsul Anuar Bin Sulaiman [the director of Ihsan Perdana, the company responsible for 1MDB's Corporate Social Responsibility]

It was a charge sheet, laying criminal charges against the prime minister.

The documents looked like drafts. But they also looked genuine. And here, it seemed, was the reason for Najib's ruthless strike at his cabinet and the attorney general – he was about to get charged.

Of course, it's one thing believing that something is genuine and another thing deciding you can print it. I ran it past a Malaysian criminal barrister friend who agreed the documents were genuine. I emailed the contact to ask for more. He was just a "technical person", he said, who had been passed the papers by a contact. He had also spent time in London, accounting for his colloquial English. "There is currently a civil war of sorts going on within the civil service. There are those trying to protect Najib and those who've had enough of getting shafted. I am not sure which side will win." Later, he continued: "The police continue to be rather aggressive in trying to uncover the sources of the leaks. And not actually trying to nab the lunatic on top of the pyramid, running this country to the ground just so his arse his saved."

I had asked for more documents, but he couldn't provide any. Screw it, I thought. I decided to publish.

◆ ◆ ◆

'ARREST WARRANT FOR THE PRIME MINISTER! – The Real Reason The Attorney General Was Fired – EXCLUSIVE!' ran my headline. I detailed the charges for corruption Najib had faced (including the possible punishment of up to twenty years' imprisonment), the dramatic sackings of the past 48 hours, and the latest outrageous development, which was the cancellation by Najib of the following day's meeting of the UMNO Supreme Council.

The story exploded into Malaysia and went viral. One of my persistent Malaysian critics Ramesh Rao didn't like it – "Fuck Off! stay Away From Malaysia! Who The Fuck Are You To Interfere In Malaysia Affairs? Stupid White Bitch", he tweeted, charmingly. The new attorney general was pressed for comment. At first he tried to obfuscate; he hadn't seen the report and didn't want to comment. "I am very tired, so can I take a rest? Thank you," he told reporters. Then (presumably after political pressure) he declared that the documents were false.

But, in truth, by now Najib and his team appeared no longer to care if people thought the documents were false, nor if the evidence of his theft stacked up. They had left shame behind a long way back. Najib and his acolytes simply declared that none of it mattered.

The idiocy continued. A newly appointed Communications and Multimedia Minister named Salleh Said Keruak made the first of his trademark loyal yet blindingly stupid statements in defence of his new boss, demanding action be taken against *Sarawak Report* "for publishing a hoax meant to trigger unrest in the country." I stood guilty, he declared, of making allegations that will "definitely upset many people." Clumsily delivered, Najib's team were deploying the tactics of authoritarians everywhere, since time began: nobody must be allowed to disturb 'the peace'. Worse, they played the religion card too. It appeared to be OK under Islam for leaders to steal from the people but to criticise the fact, declared the Malaysian Islamic Development Department, risked "maligning and insulting Malaysia and its leaders". Those who do so, it added, "could be seen as victims of foreign powers who are trying to tarnish Malaysia's dignity and prestige." Orwell would have recognised the discourse.

And who were these foreign powers? Well, me. By now, I was public enemy number one. And it was quite clear that it was seriously bugging Najib that he couldn't get his hands on me. Privately, he was raging against my material. Indeed, footage emerged of a speech he made to UMNO followers: "Everything is being exposed in the *Sarawak Report* as if foreigners are deciding how we should run the country. What's their right? Ladies and gentlemen, I cannot allow this to continue. I cannot allow the white people to determine our future."

The racist vitriol appeared to go down well with the delegates. There were cries of *"hidup Melayu"* (long live Malays). He also stressed, as the explicit theme of the speech, that he valued loyalty above all, rather than intelligence, an oblique reference to the sacking of Muhyiddin Yassin. And he reiterated furiously: "Everything has been blown up in the *Sarawak Report*."

It was shocking rhetoric; the kind of language that would only inflame hatred and xenophobia. But it was, of course, also a huge badge of honour for me as a journalist. Furthermore, I took it as a sign that Najib was cracking up. The modernising reformer he had pretended to be at the start of his regime had now died a death. In its place, as panic and paranoia swept through his offices, a full-blown authoritarian had emerged. He began to float the idea of tighter laws to stop online criticism. Alleged leakers who were fingered for having spread information about him were sacked. And then, on 4th August, I found myself being charged. My alleged offences were under Section 124B and 124I of the Penal code, for "activity detrimental to parliamentary democracy" and "dissemination of false reports". Apparently they carried sentences of up to twenty years in prison. Malaysian police were applying to put me on the ASEANAPOL wanted list and obtain an INTERPOL Red Notice (designed to catch terrorists) in order to seek my arrest and extradition from any country that was a member of INTERPOL. Crikey, I thought – not bad for a mum from London.

Najib could not have done more to ensure that his crimes received major international coverage and to offer me a platform to talk about them. I did my best to sock it to him. Exhausted, I had made my usual plans to go up to Scotland with my family. We rented a house and got in in plenty of hill-walking. Not for the first time, it all felt rather odd: here I was, on my holidays in Scotland, apparently now an international criminal on the run.

26. ALL OUT WAR

Summer 2015, Scotland

THE Scottish Highlands are a long, long way from the tropical heat of Malaysia, even in summer. Perhaps the only thing they share is a problem with flying insects: midges in Scotland, mosquitos in Malaysia. But that holiday, as on previous holidays, I found I could simply not get Malaysia out of my mind. The story was everything. Plus my family were gleefully taking the mickey, asking when I would be arrested and sent to jail. I later learnt that Najib's cyber warriors had even tracked me here, having hacked the email address I used to make travel bookings.

I was safe in Scotland, and with my husband and boys once again shrugging their shoulders, I continued in the only way I knew how. Ducking out of fringe theatre shows and into coffee shops, laptop in hand, as I continued to lob rockets.

'Was Aabar's Khadem Al-Qubaisi Connected To Your Secret 'Donation', Prime Minister?' I asked in a blogpost. I had been joining some dots. The $681 million payments from Aabar-owned Falcon Bank into Najib's account had started to arrive just two days after Goldman Sachs had completed a hurried bond issue for $3 billion on behalf of 1MDB on 19th March 2013. That in turn had been organised just a week after al-Qubaisi had signed a joint venture with 1MDB on 12th March which, it had been claimed, was a 50:50 agreement to invest cash in KL's new financial zone. As with PetroSaudi, it stank to high heaven: where was the evidence that the cash had been used to build anything? The area identified was still a waste ground.

Then, five weeks after the original story – which Najib first laughed off, then derided, then accused me of conspiring in a foreign plot, then racially abused me – his team finally settled on an explanation for the $681 million. Sure, they now appeared to acknowledge, the money going into the account was a fact. But the $681 million was a 'donation from the Saudis'. Azalina Ottman, a new minister in the Prime Minister's Department, insouciantly declared: "The RM2.6 billion [$681 million] is not a big issue. There is nothing wrong if a person receives the gift of money as long as it is with the consent of the recipients." The information was released via the Malaysian Anti-Corruption Commission. It declared it could not reveal the identity of the donor though he (or she?) was from the Middle East. The MACC was continuing investigations into the separate and smaller funds which had come from the SRC, it added.

You had to laugh. The idea that somebody would 'donate' $700 million to the personal account of a prime minister was self-evidently deranged. That, however, was now Najib's line. On 8th August Najib explained himself, using the MACC as if it had cleared him: "The MACC had said that the RM2.6 billion was not corruption and not 1MDB funds… All funds received is only for the benefit of the party and rakyat [ordinary citizen]," he announced on his Facebook page. So: here was his line. All this was being done for the benefit of ordinary poor Malaysians.

◆ ◆ ◆

Privately, I picked up that he had started calling in all the key UMNO leaders and telling them the brutal facts: yes, he had received the money, but how else did they think he – and they – had managed to win the 2013 election against the odds? They owed their seats to the 'donation', he told them, cleverly fostering a sense of complicity. Bundles of cash had been handed to them and their acolytes to buy votes. Did they think it came from thin air? It was notable that he did not bother to try to explain the source of the money, only its use – essentially to buy the election. It was a gobsmacking attitude, designed to go down with UMNO mentality, which had come to view political corruption as not only normal but justified. After all, UMNO maintaining its grip on power was justification in itself.

Meanwhile, his client media breathlessly declared that Malaysia's Inspector-General of Police Khalid Abu Bakar had been in discussion with the German Secretary-General of INTERPOL Jurgen Stock and was confident he would soon obtain the Red Notice authorising my arrest in any of INTERPOL's 190 member countries. I was still in the Highlands at the time. I wondered if the local Scottish constabulary might be dragged in.

It all just made me more determined. It was clear I had Najib on the run. *Sarawak Report* was successfully getting round the internet block and scoring plenty of hits. I had to keep going. I started flinging out information as it came in with slightly more abandon. I had heard from reliable sources that shortly after the election Najib had closed his AmBank account down and returned the remaining cash to the same Tanore account in Singapore Falcon Bank. I had not been given the documents for this transfer, but the original source was the same and I had an exact date, 30th August 2013, and a figure – over $650 million (RM2 billion).

It was easy to assume (and many did on the limited information at the time) that this implied Najib had only handed out a paltry $30 million or so for the election after all. In fact, as later became clear, there had been a great deal more in the account than just the money transfers of early March. Najib took full advantage of the false assumption and even started putting it about that he had returned the bulk of the cash to his kind donor, having not needed it for the election after all. It was Mahathir who observed that if there was anything less believable than a Middle Eastern donor offering Najib $681 million, it was that Najib might hand it back.

I ploughed on. I had also received information – again correct but only verbal – as to the names of some of the UMNO bigwigs to whom Najib had handed cheques, so I decided to publish that as well. They included the UMNO Back Bench Chairman Shahrir Abdul Samad, who received RM1 million after the election and the Deputy Finance Minister Ahman Maslan, who got a cheque for RM2 million. I named and shamed them and they stayed silent. And then I revealed that the stolen money from SRC had been used to pay off Najib's massive credit card bills of over $1 million run up during his summer holiday in Europe following the election. So much for the money not being used for personal purposes. Again the information was passed to me verbally – later the Visa and Mastercard bills would come into my hands.

There had never been a story like it in Malaysia. Not a day would go by without some development in the multi-faceted tale that had been unleashed – whatever steps Najib took to attempt to put a lid on it. For the moment, he concentrated on complaining he had been treated unfairly. His Facebook page was full of recriminations. He was, he said, "boiling with anger" at the way he was being targeted. "I was made a target for no reason," he wrote, "The spread of false facts and allegations are at the tip of our fingers… That's why we need to mobilise a larger number of our own keyboard warriors to counter false allegations and to correct the people's false perceptions of the government." It was through the looking-glass stuff. Najib's allies even tried to claim that putting money in a personal account was evidence of "transparency".

Sources told me that Najib's 'cyber-warfare unit' was being managed with a large budget directly from the prime minister's office under the management of one of his key cronies, Habibul Rahman, soon to be popped onto the board of Petronas as well. This was a full year before the Trump machine got going in the States; Najib was an early purveyor of 'post-truth' politics. There were no depths they wouldn't sink to. Najib's new education minister, one Mahdzir Khalid, set the tone with an accusation that *Sarawak Report*'s reporting was "an attempt by Christians and Jews to split Muslims":

The Jews and the Christians have pledged that as long as there is the moon and the stars, as long as the end of the world is not here yet, they will decide that Muhammad's followers will be confused and split among themselves. This is the pledge of the Jews and Christians. And today, those who do things to us are not only from within the country, but from outside the country like *Sarawak Report*.

◆ ◆ ◆

And traps lay everywhere. Xavier's trial was scheduled for 17th August. There had been further confessional interviews given to newspapers by Xavier, incriminating himself and slandering me. I sent Laura a text offering my support on the 13th. Since the end of July she had broken off contact with me. But now, she replied immediately: "I went to see him!.. I just came back! It's horrible! Nobody can help!! He will be judged tomorrow and the only thing I can do now is pray! I can't believe he will have to stay in jail! I feel so helpless… it's so unfair!!!"

I replied, and along with sympathetic words, added:

> I only wish you could have let me in because being able to bring the press and other agencies to fight for him would have helped hugely. I still don't know the extent of what he has admitted, but the mitigating side was the genuine crime of the others who accused him. Their vicious deceit should be made plain. Mahony should be exposed. I have reported Mahony to the police here. By refusing to fight you are letting them have a field day… he has allowed certain interviews that make him sound only like a mercenary… It's not being managed at all well.

Then, uncharacteristically, she wrote back immediately, "We should talk.. I need to do something as doing nothing as I was told to do hasn't helped until now!"

We arranged that she would ring me that evening. It was a strange phone call, in which Laura, in a somewhat provocative tone, wanted to talk mainly about the negotiations for the payment of Xavier, and my supposed involvement in potential money transfers, and not much about her own husband's situation and prospects for release.

I would later learn that this phone call was recorded and the entire conversation was a set-up, orchestrated by Patrick Mahony, who wanted to have my voice recorded discussing all these matters to that he could selectively edit it to distort the meaning and attach it to a video to circulate anonymously online attacking me 'using my own words'. Laura had been given a script; even the story about seeing her husband wasn't true, she was still in Geneva. I put down the phone dissatisfied.

I was being played. Laura had got sucked into a plan to get her husband out of jail – something that had been cooked up while I was in Geneva. The story that the British authorities had got involved was nonsense, although at first she hadn't realised it. The couple had decided they had no choice but to play ball with Mahony and his co-conspirators at PetroSaudi in a propaganda battle against me to get them and 1MDB off the hook.

But Laura was being played, too. She had been told cooperation would ensure Xavier would get off lightly, maybe freed at once. Instead, when the trial came the following day, Xavier was convicted, immediately, to six years in prison, reduced to three. The conviction was purely on the basis of the confession that had been drawn up for him by his so-called advisers. His own lawyer, who had participated in this manipulation and had been paid for by PetroSaudi, did not even turn up in court.

Xavier made clear he was completely taken by surprise at the outcome of the trial. He had expected a light sentence, because he thought a deal had been done. His evident shock was widely reported.

I immediately messaged Laura and told her that there was an international journalist currently in Bangkok interested in following up the story: "You have to fight now. It's the only way. Look what they did to you by shutting you up. Please get to him asap and tell him to start getting his story out. You need to pick yourself up and use [the media] to help you fight before they go away."

She replied: "I can't believe the sentence!!!!! I'm in shock... I will let you know asap". But, instead she went silent again.

We were getting ready to leave the Highlands and head back down to London when another bombshell landed. The Swiss newspaper *Le Temps* reported on 21st August that the Swiss Prosecutor's Office had confirmed that it had too had launched an official investigation into 1MDB. There were no details as yet, but for me it was a complete game-changer – like the relief at the Battle of Waterloo.

For months I had feared that there would be no official action taken: it was what Najib was counting on, so the whole scandal could be smothered. Najib may have been shutting everything down domestically, now, however, he was in the international spotlight. I had to hope that the Swiss step was the beginning of a wider unravelling – and so it turned out to be. He, meanwhile, was visibly creaking. His government was attempting to block a protest march by the pro-democracy Bersih movement in KL. On the eve of the protest, he issued a vile speech in which he sought, deliberately, to racialise the struggle he faced: "Some people say that the Malays will be defeated, beaten or fall flat on the ground but I choose the word 'bastardise'… The Malays and Muslims would lose everything if UMNO loses power."

In doing so, I felt that Najib revealed perhaps the most dangerous aspect of his mentality, which was his sense of inheritance: that somehow he was duty bound, come what may, to protect the privileges of the family, class and caste he had been born into and pass them on. "I will surely not destroy the party. My late father built this party," he exaggerated.

We had, by this point, got back down from Scotland and were back in London. I arrived to good news: an email from Interpol declaring that the red notice they had received from Malaysia, demanding my arrest, had been refused.

We got back in time for a Bersih solidarity rally the next day, which was to take place outside the Malaysian High Commission in Belgrave Square, a short step from where I live. I realised I needed something of a suitable canary yellow to wear. Luckily my sister-in-law had a clothes glut and had passed me just the item: a smart yellow top, which was pressed into valuable service for this and future Bersih occasions.

During an impromptu speech, I let the 500 or so protestors know about Interpol's decision. Back in KL it was clear that, despite all the horrible threats, a simply enormous march had gathered – 300,000 according to the local independent media, notwithstanding attempts by police to block people from reaching the city centre. Even Mahathir had turned up, attired in yellow. He addressed the crowd. It was a sign of the impending seismic rupture he would soon cause in his own party by joining the opposition. Najib's retaliation at this point was clumsy but brutal. As September rolled on, the head organiser of the march Maria Chin and six of her colleagues were duly arrested. In the face of domestic and international protests she was held without trial for several weeks, under Najib's abuse of the 'anti-terrorist' legislation called SOSMA. It was to be a harbinger of the deadly abuse of power that the establishment would now use as it sought to cling to power.

27. DEATH IN THE RUSH HOUR

September 2015, KL

ON the morning of 4th September, lawyer Kevin Morais left his Menara Buta condominium in KL to head to work at the Attorney General's Office in nearby Putrajaya. A leading prosecutor, he had recently been pulling together papers for the MACC (where he had been until recently on secondment.) He had also been liaising with the Attorney General's Office on the 1MDB investigation. I did not know him at all. But it was he who had drafted the photocopied papers I had received showing that Najib had been charged.

Driving to the office, Morais's car pulled to a halt in the fast lane after a car behind rammed into the back of him. CCTV shows what happened next. Kevin jumped out, preparing to remonstrate with the driver behind him. But he had walked into a trap: several other men jumped out of the rear vehicle. They dragged him into their own car whilst one of them hopped behind Kevin's wheel. As traffic began to move around them, the gang drove both cars away. A few days later a Proton car that matched the description of the one he was driving was found burnt out and abandoned in a field some distance from KL. Not only had the number plates been removed, but someone had scoured off the serial number from the engine as well.

Several days after that Kevin's body was found. It was encased in cement in a barrel, dumped in shallow water. Gruesome pictures, which I later received, showed his hands in front of him pushed through the cement as if he had been clawing the side of the barrel, trying to get out.

The authorities moved quickly to deliver an "open and shut case" with a gang of low-life Indian gangsters. Morais had been strangled, they claimed. They arrested an army doctor (also an ethnic Indian) who stood accused of having commissioned the murder. Kevin was the prosecutor in a case where the doctor stood accused of having inflated the price of medicines. So, it was claimed, the doctor had killed the prosecutor in order to get off the charge.

None of it made any sense at all. The police announced they would not be extending their enquiries and paraded their frightened clutch of some six 'gang members' and the doctor before the cameras. After which, the entire case moved into glacial slow motion. Despite the "open and shut" nature of the case, at the time of writing, almost four years after their arrest, none of these imprisoned accused have been brought to trial apart from one alleged assistant in the disposal of the body.

Why would a doctor attempt to murder a professional prosecutor over a bribery case? An educated man would know that the removal of one prosecutor would only result in a second one being assigned to the case. Nobody credible believed the story. "What happened to Kevin was a warning to all of us," emailed one of Kevin's colleagues, whom I had previously been in touch with, "I can't speak to you anymore." Not for the first time I was reminded that the crimes linked to 1MDB were by no means limited to theft, greed and political dishonesty – there were far darker deeds too.

Kevin had three brothers, Charles, David and Richard. Charles, a businessman based in the States, and David were both respectable figures. Richard, however, was a well-known figure in Malaysia's gangland crime world. Just before Christmas 2015, Charles called a sensational press conference in KL. He denounced the way the authorities had removed his brother's body from the hospital morgue without the knowledge, permission or presence of either himself or his brother David. Both brothers had publicly demanded a second, independent post-mortem, by doctors from Australia, given the deep concerns they had over the circumstances of Kevin's death. Yet, just as the autopsy team from Australia was boarding their plane, the news came through that an unauthorised cremation had taken place in secret hours before.

It was Richard, the underworld figure, who had sanctioned this removal of Kevin's body. He had done so in public defiance of the rest of the family, said Charles, despite the fact he had been estranged for years from Kevin and the rest of the family and had no authority to do so. Charles made his suspicions only too clear at the press conference that Richard was acting on behalf of the authorities. Then, in front of the cameras, Charles read out a statutory declaration. He testified that his brother had confirmed to him before he died that he had been working on the investigation into Najib over the appropriation of money from SRC, something that had been vehemently denied by the authorities from the moment Kevin disappeared. Charles went on to say that his brother had been hugely troubled by the investigation and had mentioned that he was working with another officer, who had recently been arrested, interrogated and then sacked from her job.

Charles also revealed that he had been in touch with me about the charge sheets I had published. He also noted that I had sent him some of the emails I had received from the original sender and these had convinced him that it was indeed his brother Kevin who had been my correspondent (on this he was mistaken – the leak turned out to have been less direct.) He declared, "Kevin was killed… due to the fact that he knew too much about the criminal acts of those high up in the echelons of power in Malaysia and he needed to be silenced because of that."

Finishing with a final sensational claim, he revealed he had received a pen drive of information from his brother and that he had forwarded this to an individual in the United States, who had instructions to publish its contents should anything happen to him. Later that day I received a call from Charles himself.

"Where are you?" I immediately asked, stunned and appalled by the danger he had put himself in over such a public defiance of Najib. He was still in KL, but making his way out, he told me. All I could do was urge him to hurry, which he did. That night he dashed for the border, escaping back to America via Singapore, before anyone laid their hands on him.

Once in America he passed me information about the pressure he and his brother David had been put under by Kevin's former employers at the Attorney General's Office. They had demanded that the brothers agree to an immediate cremation of the body – for reasons that were not explained. Charles said he had been rung by them at least ten times about it, and sent numerous text messages to skip the autopsy and cremate his brother.

These principally emanated from someone called Mabel Muttiah, who had been promoted to the position of special assistant by the new Attorney General Apandi soon after taking up his post. Muttiah affected to have been a close friend, as well as colleague, of Kevin's, although Charles said that Kevin had never given him the impression that he felt close to Mabel when he was alive. In one of her grotesquely mawkish, insensitive and pestering texts, thinly disguised in a presumed friendship, she tried to encourage Charles to organise an immediate cremation by suggesting the musical programme for it:

I wd have named the funeral programme as A HERO'S JOURNEY BACK TO HOME SWEET HOME ... Bring the remains to Nirvana – hve the wake for that particular night and next day in a chapel setting hve the svs with the priest ... singing they hymns and his favourite Amazing Grace.. followed by the reading of the scriptures and the message ... a multi media show... eulogies and his final hour would be the coffin dripped in the AGC and Malaysian flag – then the cremation

When this and other tactics, including an offer to David of a meeting with Apandi, who "will give you and Charles all the explanations needed," failed, she tried to persuade Charles and David to take a 'golden handshake' offered by the Attorney General's Office. They offered the three brothers a substantial sum of money, RM580,000 to be divided amongst them. In return, the AG's officials made plain they wanted the three brothers to sign a 'declaration' – presumably buying their cooperation and silence.

Charles and David refused the money, not least because legally it belonged to Kevin's estate and not them. Richard, on the other hand, was desperate they should accept it. "From the beginning," Charles told me, "Richard was anxious to cooperate with the authorities in their wish to avoid a second post mortem after Kevin's death." It had become a divisive issue – Richard had at times become aggressive and violent over the matter. Richard had long been believed to have high level links with establishment figures – Rosmah was said to be one of his contacts. In the end, with the connivance of the AG's office, Richard had simply taken the body and cremated it behind his brothers' backs. The question was, why?

I pointed out something that had been admitted by one of Najib's own key ministers, Rahman Dahlan earlier that summer. In an interview in the *Star* newspaper, he had made clear that when Najib had executed his coup to prevent himself being arrested earlier in the summer, he needed to "take out people" after the charge sheet had been published. That was the only way, he added, to return matters to "normalcy".

After the press conference, a series of vicious attacks against Charles began immediately. He was described as a business failure and a dishonest operator. Most sinister were the public threats by the head of the police, Khaled Abu Bakar, who declared Charles was under investigation for "withholding information and sabotage". His self-professed gangster brother was soon wading in as well, denouncing Charles and backing Najib.

◆ ◆ ◆

Was Morais's murder linked to his investigation into 1MDB? I couldn't prove it, but the obvious suspicion was there. Plus, it wasn't the only one. A few months earlier, Hussain Najadi, the retired founder of AmBank, had been shot dead in cold blood in broad daylight in the middle of KL. No attempt was made to investigate the shooting. As with Morais, a lowly gun for hire had been picked up. And that was that.

But just as with Morais' case, Najadi's family were insistent something else was going on. Najadi had been reporting his concerns about corruption at the bank relating to certain large, politically connected accounts. He had made a personal representation to the Central Bank and in the days before he died he had also filed a police report, according to Pascal, his son. His father had not provided details at the time but had told his son he was deeply troubled by evidence of serious misdemeanours involving powerful people.

Within 24 hours of the shooting, he had been buried. Najadi's family – who were based in Switzerland – had been called by a local lawyer informing them of the matter. He had insisted "local customs" had to be followed. That man just so happened to be Najib's closest legal adviser and confidant, a lawyer called Shafee Abdullah. "I didn't know that at the time. Neither I nor my mother knew who he was. Who appointed him or why he was taking charge, we still don't know – we just accepted the advice at the time," said Pascal later.

Pascal was pretty certain his father was assassinated because of his voluble concerns about Najib's bloated accounts at the bank he had founded. Even more damning was the fact that his father had been lured to the scene of his death by a call from none other than Richard Morais. The pretext was that he was involved in a planning dispute connected to temple property and had called him to come and help. Had the gangland figure been used to set up Najadi so he could be shot at the appointed time and place? It was another question left unanswered. And it was another reminder that those of us challenging Najib were playing for the highest stakes.

28. HERE IS THE FAKE NEWS

Autumn 2015

MORAIS'S death and the growing brutality of the Malaysian government's response made it clear beyond doubt that they were determined to crush all opposition. But, living in London, I was protected more than some. I decided to up the pace. What else could I do? The story was still growing before me – and I had to follow it through.

I focused more of my time on the plundering that had taken place at Abu Dhabi's Aabar and its playboy head Khadem al-Qubaisi. With new contacts now providing me with a welter of information, I was able to dig further into his criminality. He had been spending on an astonishing scale. And his love of luxury put him on a par with, if not outstripping, the flamboyance of Jho himself. His investments included a $45 million mansion in Beverly Hills, the most expensive in LA, the Hakkasan nightclub in Las Vegas, the most expensive nightclub ever built, and celebrities on tap. Calvin Harris had been paid a reputed $400,000 a night to perform at the Omnia Club, one of the Vegas nightclubs bought by Hakkasan. On another occasion, Britney Spears was hired to perform 'Happy Birthday' Monroe-style for al-Qubaisi.

The excesses displayed by these characters were grotesque. We were continuing to follow the trail of partying that had followed the various 1MDB deals. Yet, despite the increased scrutiny, they showed no sign of stopping. That autumn I received a tip-off that Jho was planning yet another major birthday bash to celebrate his November birthday. This extravaganza was to be held on his enormous multi-millions pound yacht *Equanimity*, the latest luxury he had bought with his stolen cash. If nothing else, the purchase confirmed what we had suspected and reported, which was that Jho did indeed own or at least control this brand new blue whale of a boat, the 34th largest in the world.

The journey in itself had made an epic story, as the monster super-yacht had crossed over from the Atlantic into the waters of the South China Sea via the North Pole, taking advantage of its melting waters (super-yachts are the single most gas guzzling extravagance on the planet.) It was the 200th vessel ever to make the path through.

We soon stood up the story, thanks again to social media. On the day before the event we picked up excited tweeting from Jho's pet rapper Jamie Foxx and his entourage as they were flown over from the United States to Incheon, South Korea where the yacht hovered off the coast. Jho, I learnt, would be flying up from Taiwan (where he appeared to be taking refuge) by helicopter, since the yacht was one of the few in the world equipped with a special landing pad. Other guests were to be the local Korean star Psy and another favourite Jho contact, the bikini model-cum-movie actress Kate Upton.

But the real story of this event lay with other guests entirely. Trawling the internet, Amy had discovered that Jho's all-important birthday party had been sanctimoniously couched as an event to support the UN Foundation. Since I had been writing to and goading this outfit all year to watch out over their association with the dubious Jho, I was simply amazed that they had allowed themselves to be used in this way and I could only wonder at how much they must have received to get involved?

They were not, of course, replying to let me know, but there was no doubting whatsoever that the joint event had taken place, because we unearthed, on the website of its proud designer, a fancy booklet prepared for the occasion. The gushing text promoted Jho's amazing philanthropy to the UN, but also more importantly established his new narrative about being a third generation billionaire, with much fawning coverage about his super-rich Dad and grand Dad.

The moment I published the story the designer pulled down the page on their site – he must have received a hell of a blasting. Jho and his UN Foundation friends plainly didn't enjoy the exposure.

◆ ◆ ◆

Pity poor Malaysia, I had written, which had raised so many billions for its supposed development fund, raided for such excess. Yet Najib was doing nothing to hunt down or punish these hedonists, he was just going after the critics.

His latest victim was the renegade UMNO politician Khairuddin Hassan, who had been travelling round the globe noisily seeking action on 1MDB. Khairuddin came to London, where he also looked me up. Najib had him arrested on his return. When his lawyer Matthias Chang protested on behalf of his client Najib had him locked up as well. This was all done under the arbitrary powers of arrest he had pushed through Parliament under the so-called Security Offences and Special Measures Act (SOSMA), supposedly targeting terrorism. Chang bravely went on hunger strike.

It was now October. I accepted a kind invitation to the Conference for Investigative Journalism in Lillehammer where I met a number of Swiss journalists. Some had interviewed Xavier in jail. He, and they, were blaming me for his arrest and incarceration. It was clear to me that he was now part of a wider propaganda war designed to discredit Najib's tormenters.

As I wandered around the conference, mulling what on earth was going on and how I was going to fight back against this, my email suddenly started pinging. I started to receive messages with documents attached. The documents were excerpts from the crucial and until then secret minutes of the 1MDB board meetings at the time of the PetroSaudi deals back in 2009 – which took place, in accordance with the timeline drawn up by Seet Li Lin, just days before the signing, in order to ratify 1MDB's acceptance.

These documents were being investigated by both the auditor general and the Public Accounts Committee, which had now restarted its enquiries after all the disruption in July and was calling in key witnesses, such as the original Chairman Bakke Salleh, who had resigned shortly after the PetroSaudi deal. I was soon spending most of my time outside the conference hall, trying to work out the order and significance of the excerpts I had been sent.

First, there was a minute from a 1MDB board meeting from

earlier that year. It confirmed that the then CEO, Arul Kanda, had lied to the board about the fund's assets. They were in hard cash, he declared (the word also employed by Najib in Parliament). This, we had ascertained, was nonsense: they were mere worthless 'units' in shady investment funds, an attempt to hide the disappearance of the money.

I moved on with the trove of revelations from the minutes I had been sent – most of which dated back to 2009 and the original signing of the PetroSaudi deal. The documents were fascinating, because for the first time I could see the other end of the negotiations that had been driven through in London and New York. They fully confirmed all our suspicions that the management had been working for the conspirators, and the board had been kept totally in the dark until almost the minute they signed the deal off. And when they did, belatedly, start telling the board about the deal, they misled them – informing them, just ten days before it was signed, that PetroSaudi was owned by King Abdullah. The joint venture was signed while the board were still demanding further assurances. Then, after it was completed, 1MDB directors went berserk. They discovered that $700 million of the $1 billion had not gone into the main joint venture account. At that point, the documents showed, they began demanding that the money should be handed back. It was a matter of record that the chairman of the Board, Mohd Bakke Salleh, one of Malaysia's most senior corporate figures, resigned shortly after this episode, along with another Director, Azlan Mohd Zainol. Now we knew why. As the minutes stated, the board "was not consulted on the change of plans to remit $700m to PSI."

And then there was a final golden nugget. The documents I had been sent confirmed that Jho had been formally hired as an "official adviser" to 1MDB in April 2009, which was exactly the date he'd said he had ceased to have anything to do with the fund. I subsequently heard from my sources that, as these bizarre and angry board meetings continued during the summer and autumn, he not only attended the meetings, but sat talking on the phone to Najib throughout, passing back instructions. This was verified by former board members when they gave evidence to investigators.

There could now be little doubt at all what had been going on, even to loyalists. 1MDB had been used firstly as a personal bank account for Jho, Rosmah and Najib and secondly as the prime minister's political slush fund – a billion dollar hole in the wall for use for their own personal entertainment and for the handing out of bribes and kickbacks. It had paid for all their unbelievable excesses in the previous five years. And it had helped Najib get through the 2013 election still in power. Now, despite admitting that $700 million had been sent directly to his personal account, he was simply prepared to brazen it out, and crack down ruthlessly on anyone who sought to ask difficult questions.

◆ ◆ ◆

Over the coming year, Malaysia's democratic institutions began to erode under his authoritarian crackdown. His new attorney general did what he was told. A compliant new Cabinet did likewise. And, in Parliament, the Speaker of the House was co-opted too, blocking a motion of no confidence in Najib through lame 'procedural' excuses.

Najib announced there would be a new "urgent anti-terrorism bill" to counter "threats". We knew exactly what that meant – it wasn't terrorists that Najib viewed as a threat, it was his internal critics. He intended to use the cover of a largely non-existent terrorist threat to silence people. A 145-page report by Human Rights Watch summed up his threats in devastating detail. It accused the Malaysian government of creating a "culture of fear" and of "criminalising freedom of expression in Malaysia." The Sedition Act, the Printing Presses and Publications Act, the Communications and Multimedia Act, the Peaceful Assembly Act and the Penal Code had all over the course of 2014 to 2015 handed the state huge powers to crack down on internal dissent. Legal process was now being abused, said Human Rights Watch, in the form of "late night arrests, unjustifiable remands and a pattern of selective prosecution".

And, boy, did they go for me. They couldn't arrest me, of course –

not while I was safely staying put in London. So they simply carried on, relentlessly, systematically and professionally, trying to rip my reputation to shreds. A series of Facebook sites were set up dedicated to defaming me. And a raft of videos appeared online, all well-produced, all designed to destroy my motives. Behind me, I had a "history of failed journalism". My husband was dragged in and I was accused of being paid millions by just about any opposition figure or businessman that Najib had ever fallen out with "to write lies".

The various sites, with names like *Open Source Communications*, *The Real Clare Rewcastle Brown* and *The Real Sarawak Report*, churned out their anonymous articles, which would then be enthusiastically fielded by Najib's web of paid bloggers, like Raja Petra Kamaruddin (known as RPK), based in the UK, and then blasted out to Malaysia again.

The videos were promoted on Facebook using its 'sponsored content' facility. In other words, the makers, clearly professional PR teams, were paying Facebook to promote their product, boosting the links to these stories to thousands of Facebook users in Malaysia – many of whom were getting back in touch with *Sarawak Report* to warn me of the fact.

They were doing the same on Twitter. A small army of fake accounts suddenly appeared, most of whom seemed to be attractive women. They appropriated people's identities, purporting to be independent. They then tweeted and posted Clare Rewcastle Brown hate mail to one another and onto as many people as possible.

One bevy of girls, for example, with names like Deeanna, Elisheba, Delma, Yun, Dolores, seemed to have developed a sudden and highly unconvincing interest in Malaysia, together with a passionate loathing of me.

"Falsify documents, lie & get caught. The truth about @ RewcastleBrown is revealed", Elisheba retweeted from Dolores.

"Clare Brown is a lying, cheating, payed journalist! Finally got caught in bed with #Tony Pua and #Mahthir Mohamad… #ClareBrownLiar", thundered someone called Suranayaka Ewing.

"Sarawak report's founder, Clare Rewcastle Brown has falsified documents on the 1MDB affair #IMDB #Falsifieddocuments #ClareBrownLiar", retorted Deeanna Warsaw.

"Whatsapp conversations showed her true colours", confirmed Elisheba Marsden.

"Exposed @Sarawak_Report's CLARE CRIMINAL CONTACTS – SOLID DATA", said a Krisna Mukerjee.

And a very blonde and pretty teenaged Cristi Osterhoudt tweeted from some snowy ski resort: "Manipulative liars, authorities have proof @sarawak_report @tony up @suara_generasi @ theedgemarkets have falsified documents # ClareBrownLiar"

Her doe-eyed pal Lesha Sagar re-tweeted it and their friend Lucy Goetle replied, "The truth is out".

And so on. All these accounts had been created around 23rd October and the characters appeared to have no past profile. In fact, reverse imaging tools soon proved they had been created using stolen photographs snatched from the web.

Najib had made no secret of his engagement of cyber-troopers to "wage cyber-warfare". Indeed, he was given to statements about the need to counter the "dangerous freedom of the internet" with such units and this was their obvious activity. He appeared to think that fighting truth with deception was perfectly acceptable.

Dismayed that such abuse could take place, I tried to contact Facebook, only to discover that their customer services are non-existent unless you can trigger an algorithm that focuses on indecency or racism. Libel? Forget it. The outrageous refusal of Facebook and also Twitter, which was similarly being paid to promote hatred against me, alerted me to the almost total lack of accountability of the two most profitable media behemoths in the world, whilst lesser organisations, like fact-based newspapers, are tied up in knots by legislative controls, copyright, privacy, rights to reply and all the rest. I had become caught up in a major issue, that was only beginning to come up on the radar of regulators and politicians, but which has affected thousands of victims.

Since I couldn't afford a lawyer to fight a multi-million pound libel case against the likes of Facebook, I took my situation to the UK media. The *Independent* was interested in the issue and was suitably astounded at the level and viciousness of the attacks I was facing. It was plain that the failure of these two mega-businesses to address fake accounts was allowing a professional defamation industry to build up around them – a defamation industry being secretly conducted by covert wings of some of the PR industry's biggest names, as I had already encountered.

The *Independent* led on the story with a front page splash. They had found that some of the fake identities were using photos and names of people who had been in the newspapers because they had died tragically. Naturally, bereaved family members were appalled. Within hours of the story breaking, *The Real Clare Rewcastle* had scurried offline. Over the coming months a movement would begin to get going to address this vile problem and to put pressure on the unresponsive management of Facebook, as they raked in their billions.

Astonishingly, it was then, in late November 2015, that President Obama chose to meet Najib in Malaysia as part of his hopes for bringing Malaysia into his Trans Pacific Partnership. Najib was, of course, delighted to host him. Far too many Western diplomats and politicians seemed happy to support the suave, Western-educated Najib cling to power. So he was a crook, but he was our crook, seemed to be the prevailing view. "He seems to have things pretty much under control," summarised one Foreign Office mandarin, far too smugly, as opposition party members raised the issue of Anwar's incarceration in my presence.

Obama's visit went ahead with all the usual diplomatic courtesies. Off stage statements were made as a sop to the civil rights protestors about the need for Najib to respect rights, free Anwar and try not to be so blatantly corrupt. However, none of that was reported in the mainstream media and it had all been a huge and much needed boost to the beleaguered PM. All for the benefit of a trade agreement that the president's own Congress would eventually put a stop to anyway.

29. "CLARE, WE ENJOY READING YOUR BLOG."

November 2015

TOWARDS the end of November 2015, I made another trip to catch up with my Dad who was wintering again in Switzerland. It had been an unbelievable few months. But it was still not over. My phone rang one day while I was there. On the other end of the line were the FBI. Sorry they had not been in touch earlier, they said. But they were calling to let me know that their team in the department had been very busy on the 1MDB case since we had last met. They would like to question me again, if that was possible, in the near future? We arranged for another meeting back in London in the first week of December. I clicked off the phone and once again leapt about four feet into the air. It felt a bit like the Americans coming into World War II.

I met again with the team from the FBI, again at a Central London location of their choosing. One of them I had met on the previous occasion, the other was new, a third had been detained on other business. I was soon bringing them up to speed on what I had been up to, but once more it was clearly going to be one-way traffic on information.

I chatted about my latest little scoop, which was that Riza's movie company Red Granite was planning to make a blockbuster biopic of the nation's founding father George Washington – Leo DiCaprio had yet again agreed to take on the starring role in his pals' production. His participation meant this actor turned eco-campaigner was turning a blind eye to activities which had gone far beyond a financial scandal, I pointed out.

At the start of December Najib had bulldozed the 'National Security Act' through Parliament, causing outrage among civil society and human rights organisations in Malaysia and throughout the world. It gave him the right to declare emergency rule without parliamentary approval or the approval of the sovereign and even without giving any reason. The law specifically gave forces under the command of his council of five (including his cousin, the defence minister, and his crony, the police chief) the right to kill with legal immunity.

One group that protested was the Malaysian Bar Council, declaring it unnecessary and contrary to Malaysia's constitution. Najib was to respond to the Malaysian Bar Association in a matter of weeks, by bringing in new legislation to end their independence and to force a government-appointed chairman and a panoply of rules and regulations upon them that would prevent any future statements that the PM didn't like to hear being made.

And that very morning I had published a brand new story, about the fact that I now had been passed evidence from the Seychelles company register that confirmed, contrary to all the denials by 1MDB and PetroSaudi, that Jho was the sole beneficial owner of Good Star Limited.

The papers also showed that Good Star had been dissolved in the Seychelles on 2nd May 2014, shortly after Jho's BSI Singapore bank account (which received the $528,956,027 from Good Star's Coutts Zurich account) was itself closed that February.

I had shared the information with a major newspaper, but they had been too nervous to publish it, as no official body was corroborating it. I decided to publish and be damned. The FBI agents looked knowing and said nothing.

It all put further pressure on the bank RBS Coutts, I said, because the documentation from the Seychelles revealed that Coutts was listed as being Good Star's banker at the time it was incorporated, just weeks before the 1MDB heist in May. What the FBI knew, but I did not, was how 1MDB's Casey Tang had helped Jho persuade the Zurich branch that he had been appointed as an investment manager to the fund, which was at least a partial excuse for allowing a red flag transaction involving a PEP (politically exposed person).

At the time, the FBI investigators were not letting on anything about this to me. I just sat there regaling the two very straight-backed, chiselled-chinned official-looking chaps with what I knew, whilst they smiled back inscrutably, looking frequently over my shoulder to check if anyone was listening in. I was wondering what they really wanted from me. "So, generally how have I been doing on the story then?" I asked brightly. "I hope I haven't gone too far wrong on anything."

"Clare," one of them replied with a smile "we enjoy reading your blog religiously when we come into work each day and so far we haven't seen any major mistakes." That made my day.

They had been quietly investigating for months, they were able to tell me, but so far had not opened the data supplied by Xavier. Legal niceties meant that these would have to be scrutinised by a third party first to avoid the danger of their stumbling across privileged information. The expense and slowdown that such strictures must cause is mind-boggling for such investigations. "But we can read anything that you put up on your site, of course," they observed wryly.

The investigators had therefore put their case together from different resources entirely, I realised. The transactions by banks had to be made available to them and, once the alarm had been raised by my articles, these practised financial investigators had been able to access every dollar movement made by Jho and his collaborators across the globe. This did not apply to movements within banks in foreign currencies, which was why it was important that there was cooperation taking place between the US, Switzerland and Singapore.

Getting any details out of these guys was going to be harder than squeezing blood from a stone, so I didn't even try. However, I got an inkling that the complexity of the transactions had been far greater than I had imagined, with numerous big and small transactions going into those accounts like Tanore and then on to Najib. After a while I realised what they wanted: they were interested in my contacts and witnesses, and finding out if they might come forward. They were there to be approached, was the message.

They also made it plain that I would have to accept this process would move much more slowly than someone like myself was likely to understand. Their operations were like getting a big ship going and they had to be exhaustively thorough to avoid mistakes that could be exploited by highly paid lawyers. But, once they had decided to launch this level of investigation they would, they assured me, follow it through to the end. "If someone goes ahead and decides to pillage his country and his own people and then launder it through the United States then they need to understand there will be consequences," was a phrase that stuck in my head.

Remembering these assurances did help as the months passed waiting for action. Whilst others feared (or in some cases hoped) that nothing was happening any more, that the investigation had ground to a halt, squashed, perhaps, by political interference, I took heart that I had been told that this was how the financial investigators would stalk their prey: slowly but thoroughly.

They plainly had other business to attend to in London. As we politely said our goodbyes, there was one further issue I wanted to ask them about, which was Xavier. Could anyone help him? They were doing what they could, they said, but it was difficult. They had in fact decided not to see Xavier, because they knew if they interviewed him the conversation would not be private. They said they would try harder to see if anything could be done on the matter. I left it that I would certainly do what I could to reach out to people who might be useful for them to speak to. And, it is entirely possible that on occasion over the coming months I might have helped put some people in touch with the FBI.

As 2015 drew to a close, my initial fears that this scandal would be swept under the carpet thanks to the combined forces of the powers that be, deliberate blindness by regulators and lack of media interest had been overcome. The FBI was on the case. As one fellow journalist who had taken up the story told me, the genie was out of the bottle on this one and there was no way that Najib was going to push it back.

In Malaysia a largely terrified population was wondering how this wounded rogue elephant was to be contained. Yet campaigners, students and many others were risking everything to speak out and demand reform. The population had long been used to corruption at every level of the government but now life in Malaysia was taking a more sinister turn. If the attorney general could be marched out of office at gunpoint, what help was there for anyone else?

And the wider world had got the measure of the beast too. No longer was anyone gulled by the 'Nice Mr Moderate' and 'progressive democrat' PR he had been putting about. 2015 ended with Najib firmly confirmed in the world's mind as a kleptocrat of outrageous proportions and a man who was driving a coach and horses through the liberties of his subjects. I reckoned I had won a major victory in that respect, in that through my revelations and coverage I had utterly altered perceptions about the people I was set upon exposing.

Now there just remained the question about whether I could help finish them off.

PART FOUR

DOWNFALL

30. A TIGHTENING NOOSE

Early 2016

NAJIB may have been successful in repressing dissent at home, but his writ did not run outside his borders. For so long I felt I had been ploughing a lone furrow. But as 2016 began, I began to hear something comforting: the hooves of the cavalry arriving. The 1MDB affair was about to go global.

Two vital sea-changes of opinion were neatly laid out in two crucial documents, first a declaration by the European Parliament on Malaysia that winter and then, in March, a US State Department statement on Malaysia. In its statement, the European Parliament declared that it "deplores the deteriorating human rights situation in Malaysia and in particular the crackdown on civil society activists, academics, media and political activists. In March 2016, the US State Department declared that "the United States is very concerned by the Government of Malaysia's recent actions to restrict access to domestic and international reporting on Malaysian current affairs." It was a sign that Najib's attempts to portray himself as the safe, reliable old hand in Malaysia were falling to pieces.

There was only one thing for it from my perspective: keep going full throttle. Mid-January I decided to finally run a scoop which I had known about for some time thanks again to the verbal leaks coming my way by then. Another company that had also paid large sums of money into Najib's AmBank account – earlier than the $681 million payment in 2013 – was an outfit called Blackstone Asia Real Estate Partners Limited (BVI). That was the same firm that had appeared on the bank statements of the trust owned by Aabar's al-Qubaisi.

BAREPL, as it became known, had funnelled just under half a billion dollars to al-Qubaisi around the time of the power purchase loans to 1MDB in 2012. It had also transferred $170 million into

Najib's account in KL in 2011 and then made further payments later on. When I was first passed the name I had practically dropped the phone as I raced over to my papers to check that the names really matched. So, this was no subsidiary of the major company, as we were clearly supposed to believe (when questioned Blackstone denied it had any link to the BVI company), it was obviously related to Good Star and a mysterious 'Prince Bandar', who were the only other payees into the account.

To me this was all beginning to sound suspiciously like Jho's calling card – bogus offshore companies that sounded as if they were linked to a global group, thereby making it less odd to see hundreds of millions passing through the accounts. And there was now very compelling evidence tying al-Qubaisi's money to his dealings with Najib.

The icing on the cake was a separate tip-off I had received about Blackstone: its named investment manager was once again Jho's man, Seet Li Lin – in the very same role he performed for Good Star.

It was all incredibly complicated and difficult to comprehend. That was the point. But here was further evidence of hundreds of millions of pounds sloshing through various bank accounts, and ending up with Najib, al-Qubaisi and Jho – and all just after huge bond issues had given enormous sums of money to 1MDB.

Of course, the blatant lying continued. Najib's new attorney general, Apandi Ali, staged a press conference at which he informed the stunned media that he fully accepted Najib's claim that the $681 million dollars had been a Saudi royal donation and he also accepted the prime minister's explanation that he had been under the impression that the RM42 million that had come into his accounts from SRC had been part of that donation money. He therefore could not be blamed for the fact that the money was stolen from SRC. No one else was apparently being blamed either. Therefore, Apandi went on to assure the media, he could happily now confirm that there was absolutely no case to answer over 1MDB, that there was no evidence of any wrongdoing or misappropriated cash and that he was consequently closing the case and calling off all the task force investigations with immediate effect.

It was a laughable move that flew in the face of all the evidence. Small matters like the fact Najib had spent large sums of the SRC money on private credit card payments and luxury goods, despite insisting he had only taken the 'royally donated' cash for party political use, were ignored. So was the issue that the cash should surely be returned to SRC. The local press were astonished and disbelieving, but had no choice but to report the official finding of the chief law officer of the land.

What most shocked and annoyed me, however was the craven and superficial treatment of this ridiculous charade by much of the foreign press. Even those who knew the story in some depth took the easy option with headlines such as 'Malaysian Prime Minister Cleared' and '1MDB Case Closed'. In article after article the same parroted narrative was that this was the end of the whole affair and that Najib was now plainly off the hook, since the Malaysian investigations had concluded there was no case to answer.

Najib's British communications advisor, Paul Stadlen, who had clearly been spinning like mad in advance of this move, must have been jubilant. The next day he was referring the foreign media to "well-informed" articles by the BBC and the *Telegraph,* which he said explained how Najib had really come by his money so entirely innocently, and separately from 1MDB. Both pieces were particularly egregious examples of swallowing the Malaysian government line. The BBC article, by their well-regarded Middle East Defence Correspondent Frank Gardner, read:

So how unusual is it for the Saudi royal family to hand over this amount of cash in a personal donation? Not at all, said the Saudi insider, adding that Jordan, Morocco, Egypt and Sudan have all been beneficiaries of multi-$100m donations from the Saudi royal purse.

"There is nothing unusual about this donation to Malaysia," he said. "It is very similar to how the Saudis operate in a number of countries."

The piece by the *Telegraph's* Con Coughlin was on similar lines. His "senior Saudi source" told him: "It is not unusual for Saudi Arabia to make donations like this. It happens all the time to help moderate Muslim governments to remain in power so that they can provide regional security to tackle the extremist threat."

Really? I was incensed. This was plainly clap-trap (particularly since Gardner had described Christian Sarawak as one area where money needed to be spent to counter Islamic extremism) and I and plenty of other journalists had a very good idea as to the identity of this single 'Saudi source' upon whom Gardner and Coughlin were relying: Nawaf Obaid, the garrulous brother of Tarek, who had set himself up as a one-man strategic analyst for the press on matters to do with Saudi Arabia.

The BBC and *Telegraph* articles were gold-dust for Najib's camp in the propaganda war they were waging. Cartoons circulated online depicting "Frank of the celebrated *BBC*" and "Coughlin of the noble *Telegraph*" pitched against "untrustworthy failed blogger Clare Rewcastle Brown of the banned *Sarawak Report*" and so forth. I sent these to Gardner and Coughlin, along with warnings they had been duped. Coughlin refused to respond and Gardner got back to me weeks later with a response that implied he still had faith in the line spun by the Malaysian government.

But I had hope that the investigations ongoing outside Malaysia would nail the facts. "Najib's eventual problem may turn out to be that other countries retain the rule of law and that his reputation can no longer be covered up merely by appointing his own officials to 'clear' him in Malaysia." I wrote on 29th January 2016.

On cue, and just three days after the whitewash report by the attorney general, my prediction and hope about further foreign action was fulfilled. In a public "request for mutual assistance", Switzerland's normally low key attorney general, Michael Lauber, made the shattering announcement that the Swiss now calculated that $4 billion had been stolen from 1MDB.

The Swiss AG did not mince his words. He referred to a "systematic course of action by means of complex financial structures" by the alleged perpetrators of the crimes against 1MDB and made clear his impatience that despite this looting of billions from Malaysia's public companies "the Malaysian companies concerned have made no comment on the losses they are believed to have incurred." The people identified as being responsible were "various former Malaysian public officials and both former and current public officials from the United Arabic Emirates" and "foreign public officials" suspected of being bribed. He further revealed that Swiss criminal proceedings were underway against two former officials of 1MDB (which had not previously been publicised).

There could have been no more devastating riposte to the claim that no wrongdoing had occurred: the narrative that "1MDB was a closed case" had lasted less than 72 hours and I had been publicly vindicated by a credible official institution.

The following day, Singapore piled in, too. Its Commercial Affairs Department (CAD) and the Monetary Authority of Singapore (MAS) declared they were now carrying out investigations into possible money laundering in its territory and seeking information from "several financial institutions". A "large number" of bank accounts had been seized as well – ones we all took to belong to Najib himself. Then, within hours, it was confirmed that Singapore would host their own first court case into 1MDB, too. An aide to Jho, one Yak Yew Chee, was going to court to demand his bank accounts be unfrozen. He, my PetroSaudi data confirmed, had helped Jho in paying for one of Rosmah's diamond purchases in Hong Kong.

It felt, suddenly, as if the whole edifice was falling apart. Over in Abu Dhabi. Aabar was showing signs of financial strain as it emerged that it was seeking to re-finance its own massive debts. Al-Qubaisi and al-Husseiny's swansong billion dollar bail-out of 1MDB had left it with nothing to cover a loan coming due in April. And it appeared that, after years of excess, Jho was finally going from buying to selling. His bank accounts in Singapore had now been frozen. His behaviour was being investigated in Hong Kong. Word reached me that he was now auctioning his collection of Monets, Picassos and Basquiat paintings, all at a massive loss – garnering 'just' $100 million according to Bloomberg.

And, despite the credulous and ignorant reporting of the affair by some, slowly but surely the scandal was being felt around the world. Heads began to roll. The Asia head of BSI bank, Hanspeter Brunner, resigned his position, perhaps aware how exposed he was in the affair. What a come down for the Asian Banker of the Year just five years earlier. I also learnt that the Aston Martin-loving Marc Ambroisien, CEO of Edmond de Rothschild Private Bank, Luxembourg – who had been such a friend of Aabar – had also quietly stepped down from that top post. The masters of the universe were going down like nine-pins.

This was followed at the end of the month by a joint scoop from *Four Corners*, the investigative programme at the Australian Broadcasting Company, and the *Wall Street Journal*, based on internal documents from the investigations (originally obtained by *Four Corners*, who passed them on to the *WSJ*) showing how Najib and Rosmah had been spending some of their stolen millions.

Rosmah had bought a Chanel watch for over a hundred thousand dollars, for example, while her husband was playing golf with Obama in Hawaii over Christmas 2014. On the same day, SRC transferred a further $9 million to the account via 1MDB's corporate social responsibility arm. The money arrived the day after Christmas. The statements showed that Rosmah had then spent hundreds of thousands more on jewellery on holiday in Italy the following summer – using the same credit cards I had earlier identified as being paid for by SRC. Money had also been spent on cars, fancy furnishings and materials. A few months later I would receive some of these documents myself, which I drew from in detail to the rapt attention of Malaysian readers – in particular the fact that Rosmah had splashed out millions of ringgit on unorthodox anti-ageing treatments, all out of that pension fund money borrowed by SRC.

Of more political significance, the news organisations detailed how money had been spent on buying the election. One company called Solar Shine, for example, received $44 million to distribute small handouts like food and stationery to voters. Ruling-party organisations and think-tanks got large amounts, and Najib had sent nearly $7 million to the private account of one of his brothers, who told the *Wall Street Journal* that it was disbursed by bank staff to politicians according to the instructions of party leaders. The following year I myself would receive far more detail on these payments enabling me to identify some of Najib's key recipients.

Najib tried desperately to brush it all aside but it was simply impossible to hide for ever. At the end of February, Mahathir announced he was leaving UMNO in protest. A few weeks late, prominent Malaysians, including Mahathir, the DAP veteran Lim Kit Siang, former PAS Deputy Mat Sabu, Muhyiddin and several civil society leaders signed a 'Citizens' Declaration' demanding the restoration of the independence of Malaysia's institutions and the removal of Najib. The non-politician signatories included Ambiga Sreenevasan, a prominent human rights lawyer who had in 2009 received a US International Women of Courage Award from Michelle Obama for her work (an irony given Barack Obama's later choice of golf partner, one Najib Razak.) It was a coalition that would have been inconceivable just a year earlier. Most remarkably of all, it heralded a potential rapprochement between Mahathir and Anwar. It was under Mahathir's prime ministership that his former protégé was first jailed on trumped up allegations of sodomy. The fact they were now preparing to work together to oust Najib was a sign of how far things had come.

Now unleashed, the (by now) nonagenarian Mahathir threw himself into leading the charge against Najib, galvanising the opposition once more. Within a couple of weeks he was exploring legal moves against Najib, specifically around the abuse of the constitution and the bypassing of the role of the king and Council of Rulers inherent in the National Security Act. On 23rd March he filed a law suit against Najib for 'corruption and misfeasance in public office' seeking a High Court order for millions in damages for obstructing investigations into 1MDB and abusing power. This suit would eventually be struck out when a High Court judge deemed, via some interesting logic, that Najib was not a public officer, and so was not subject to the relevant laws. But in the meantime it served a useful campaigning purpose and was being covered by the international media, bringing further attention to Najib's crimes.

Then on 30th March I took a call from an Abu Dhabi contact. At the time I was hot-footing my way through the new Terminal 2 at Heathrow to pick up a plane to Arizona where I had an entirely separate job to do. The news I received over the phone was hugely significant and I was soon squatting in a corner of the departure lounge taking notes. The Gulf state had decided it was not going to sweep the Aabar scandal under the carpet. Mohammed al-Husseiny had been arrested. What's more, given the dual American citizenship of the Kenyan-born banker, the US had requested his extradition to answer the mounting questions they had on 1MDB. A further call to contacts in the States ascertained the authorities were refusing to deny that story was incorrect. It was the first formal arrest followed by charges of any figure in this scandal and it had happened in perhaps the least expected place.

I discovered that al-Qubaisi had also been removed from a number of his private business positions over the past fortnight – and in the same period IPIC had mysteriously removed all reference to a number of key subsidiaries of Aabar, which were linked to him, from its websites.

The effects of the news had already caused an apparent major loss of confidence in related businesses in the United States. The previously burgeoning Las Vegas-based Hakkasan nightclub empire, owned by al-Qubaisi and fronted by its British born CEO, Neil Moffitt, had shown signs of panic, according to contacts. Rumours circulating in Las Vegas that three top executives, including Moffitt, were about to jump ship had been quashed by al-Qubaisi's New York law firm Greenberg Taurig – for now... There were also jitters in Hollywood, where al-Husseiny had – ironically, to take the heat off the company – been posing as the major investor in Red Granite. *The General*, the Scorsese biopic of George Washington, starring (of course) the Oscar-winning Leonardo DiCaprio, was just about to go into production.

To my complete bemusement, it was around this time that *Fortune* magazine decided to nominate me as one of the their 50 most powerful people on the planet. I didn't have time – or the inclination – to enjoy some backslapping however. Not when a source was still in jail. My thoughts turned again to how to get him out.

31. LAURA'S STORY

Summer 2016, Geneva

XAVIER'S continued incarceration in Thailand had never been far from my thoughts. So it was a relief when, in early summer, Laura finally got back in touch. Our reunion was to reveal to me the full brutal tactics that were being employed by the guilty men who had raked in billions, and were now taking ruthless steps in a desperate attempt to save their skin.

"I know it's been a long time, but can I call you?" she texted. We scheduled a chat for when I was back home and she duly rang. It had been almost nine months since she had stopped talking to me – I had guessed because she and Xavier had decided, desperately, to try their chances with PetroSaudi.

We were soon back on the same wavelength. I patched up the speaker so Amy, who was with me, could hear the astonishing turn of events.

"It's been like living in a movie, these whole past months," Laura said.

"Tell me about it," I answered. It had felt the same for me and I had not forgotten for a single day the awful predicament she and Xavier were in.

She was outside on the terrace of her home in Thailand by the sea, she said, with her Mum and Dad and she felt safe using their phone. She had not felt safe trying to call me on her own phone, which she knew was monitored. For the first time in months she had shed her minders and she wanted to let me know that she wanted to work with me again to try and get her husband out of jail. She hoped I didn't mind what had passed before, but she had hoped that PetroSaudi would fulfil their promises to get Xavier out if he played ball and did what was asked, namely discredit me and all the evidence on 1MDB. But, she now realised they had been played.

Of course I understood. "Actually, you realised what was going on. I could tell from the articles you have been writing." said Laura. Well, yes, I had put two and two together.

They had been blackmailed, Laura told me. The prime players were Patrick Mahony and a hired bogus 'detective' from the UK, who had masqueraded under the name of Paul Scott, but was in fact called Paul Finnegan, she later discovered. Their most loathed enemy was none other than yours truly. "You have no idea how they hate you," Laura told me bitterly. Well, I hadn't thought they loved me.

Laura's candour with me was an important development, signalling a turn in the tide. For months Najib and PetroSaudi had controlled the narrative with Xavier, using him to undermine my reporting on 1MDB and to back up their defamation against me. She had now decided enough was enough.

Laura told me that she was leaving Thailand and would be in touch the moment she got back to Europe. She and her husband had agreed that she needed to sell their property and get away to try and release him from a distance. I said I would help as much as I could and that I fully understood what had gone before. The only way to approach this awful situation was to shout loudly, I advised – no more trying to get Xavier out through the back door or shady deals. Scream injustice from the hill-tops, tell the truth, engage the media and get the story out. I was sure now that PetroSaudi reckoned they had locked Xavier successfully away. Now they thought they could throw away the key and leave their former colleague to stew out the next few years in a Bangkok jail.

Over the next few weeks we kept in touch as Laura wrestled with her administrative problems involved in the move from Thailand. It was not until June that she finally made it safely home to Geneva and I went straight to meet her there, a full year after we had first met: a year that her husband had spent in a Thai jail.

Our relations had been complicated, with Laura playing a double game at times, hoping that by complying with Xavier's persecutors she could get him out of jail, but this was all behind us now, I mulled, as I sat on the flight to Geneva. At last, we would be able to sit down and talk over exactly what had happened over all those months. She had explained quite a lot already. But, there was a year to catch up on as we met up once again at a functional airport hotel, near where she lived. I was relieved to find that we got on very easily together and understood each other very well – after all, we had both inadvertently been caught up, on different sides of the globe, battling the same powerful network. Her situation was immeasurably worse, a much younger woman with her husband in jail, but I understood the details of what had happened to them perhaps more than anyone, and knew the types of characters we were dealing with.

"You cannot imagine how much they hate you," Laura told me again.

Sometimes it is hard for a journalist to appreciate how the person they are writing about may personalise their anger. In this story I had become Tarek Obaid and Patrick Mahony's problem. If I had not gone after 1MDB and got hold of their incriminating emails, they would still be enjoying the fruits of their labour. That was how they saw it and of course I understood, but they had forgotten to blame themselves.

Laura pulled out texts written by Mahony from a sheaf of documents. "She is the cause of all our problems. She has to be discredited", read one.

"Hmmm," I observed. "That is handy evidence for any libel case I might decide to bring."

In fact, as I soon came to realise, Laura's tightly packed briefcase was bulging with neatly ordered documentation she had compiled that showed just how her husband had been manipulated and framed.

Laura gave me the whole story. Mahony and his henchmen had presented themselves to Laura and Xavier not long after his arrest. Reassuring them, they admitted that they had denounced Xavier and had him arrested. However, as former colleagues and fellow Europeans, they explained to her, that they did not really want the full vent of anger unleashed against him, which they said the Malaysians were capable of carrying out in Bangkok. They impressed upon her that the Malaysians wanted Xavier dead, but that PetroSaudi, in particular Mahony, was anxious, in spite of all the trouble he had caused them, to protect his former friend from such an unpleasant end. As long as he got the company off the hook and played ball sufficiently to convince Najib that Xavier would now work for them, PetroSaudi were keen for him to be freed as soon as possible, no hard feelings. It was a story that sort of made sense. Mahony was "cunning", as a former colleague told me – he had come up with a sufficiently credible narrative for a desperate man behind bars to cling on to in the circumstances.

"They put him in the worst part of the jail for the first week and then they moved him to the best VIP area, which was where Mahony came to see him. Mahony then explained he had the power to keep him in the nicer place or send him back to the bad part for nine years. Xavier knew he could not survive nine years in that part of the jail and anyway, as Patrick said, the Malaysians could easily get to him and kill him there," Laura said.

Finnegan was left by Mahony to manage the day to day situation and to stay with Laura and arrange matters with the authorities – visits, liaison with the local lawyer, etc. He was also given the job of taking down Xavier's confession, which he did over a number of days in Xavier's jail cell, alone, with no lawyer present. He continued to pose as a policeman to the couple, until evolving into an 'ex-policeman'.

All Xavier had to do was to confess and cooperate with Mahony's operative Paul Finnegan and his problems would fairly soon be over. What choice did Xavier have, since his accuser was clearly controlling the manner of his arrest and all his conditions behind bars? Yet, to have cooked up such a wild and outrageous plot and to take it so far...

How had the Thai authorities allowed such an extraordinary situation to develop I asked? A foreigner, with no official status in Thailand, to take her husband's statement? Laura told me that

Mahony had explained to her they had everyone in their pocket, right up to the highest generals – and certainly the managers of the prison. Later I had learnt that, unsurprisingly, the people who had helped Mahony make all the right connections in Bangkok were Jho's contacts from one of Thailand's richest families. Laura had cooperated and for a while hoped that the very friendly and sympathetic team who were spending days shaking down her husband for his confession, were what they said they were.

By the time Laura and Xavier realised that Finnegan was certainly not a Scotland Yard detective sent over from the UK and was in fact a phony working for Mahony, they had been sucked into the whole deception. For months Xavier continued to put his hopes in the promises that this subterfuge dreamed up by his former friend would get him out of jail, once the 1MDB story had been squashed.

"I had to do what my husband told me," Laura said. "He was screaming to do as they said. And for many months they were all so nice. They appeared to be taking care of me, paying for some of my flights, but really that Paul was spying on me, not protecting me. The promise was that if we did what they said, then they would get Xavier out. We had to destroy your name and we had to excuse PetroSaudi and Najib. Then we would be set free."

She paused "It's been like living through a movie," she said again. "Unbelievable, I kept having to pinch myself that these people were really doing all this."

That game of cat and mouse, Laura explained, was behind the strange telephone call she had made to me in August a year earlier just before Xavier's sentencing. She was playing along, because Mahony had explained that the trial was just a formality and they just needed to solve a couple of issues and then Xavier would be out on a technicality. Because I didn't say anything that could be twisted to incriminate me in the phone call, he told Laura he needed her to call me up again and lure me back to her parents' place in Geneva once more. This time the plan was to set up a raft of secret cameras and microphones. She then had to find a way to push me into saying things that they could edit to discredit and destroy me once and for all.

The plan was for a video to be snuck out anonymously along with all the rest of the material on the websites defaming me. "They kept trying to persuade me to do this film while I was over here. To call you and get you to come and lure you to be destroyed like this. It was so hard.

"But I had also been recording everything. Writing a secret diary every day. Taking copies of all their messages and emails, keeping all the receipts and notes and photographing everything I could. Because, I didn't trust them. I had been working both ways for months. I needed to have an alternative strategy if cooperation with these men who were keeping me hostage and manipulating Xavier did not work. I have it all."

"Wow," was all I could think to say. What idiots they had been. Laura had played the beautiful dumb creature to perfection, whilst working like a tigress to protect her husband and her child.

"I have phone conversations with Patrick, where he explains everything was being controlled by the prime minister and that Xavier had to win the prime minister's trust and favour if he wanted to get out of jail. I have their emails. I have the lawyer's emails showing he is working for PetroSaudi and not Xavier."

"What about that video?" I asked. "You never called."

"I knew I needed to protect you. I knew you were not the enemy really, but I had to pretend that I accepted Patrick's argument that it was all your fault that my husband was in jail, not his."

"Well, you needed me as a fallback plan," I acknowledged pragmatically. "No point making me an enemy if you might want to call on me later for Plan B."

"Exactly," she admitted. "But, actually you know I also appreciated you were trying to do the right thing and these men were the criminals not you. Except, they told me you had broken the law by publishing private information and all these powerful people and the British police were also after you for that, so it would only be a matter of time before you were arrested just like Xavier."

I nodded my head in wonder. A young person lost in this

bewildering nightmare, she had played it both ways, just in case, and had brilliantly hoisted them on their own petard.

"I told them I did not want to do the recording, because I believed that could also be illegal and get me into trouble. They tried so hard to force and bully me to do it. Next they sent me the link for the video they'd made with the earlier telephone conversation. Here," she clicked a link on her computer. "It is still up there. They wanted to publish it and I refused permission. It was a horrible, horrible attack on you and they had edited it so carefully to make you seem as terrible as possible. I said I was afraid that I would get in trouble and if they put it up without my permission I would go public and say they were behind it. That scared them, so they didn't. But look at all the texts and emails that September," she said, passing me pages of them, all handily transcribed and also screen-saved, "They were trying so hard to persuade me to release the video. They also wanted me to do newspaper interviews here in Switzerland attacking you. If I did this, Patrick told me, then the prime minister would be satisfied and would let Xavier go, even though he was fearful he could not trust what he would say once he was free."

Laura and I were on to coffee by this stage. While she popped out for a quick cigarette I reflected on what she had told me. The situation was very clear. Najib had thrown his weight and money behind PetroSaudi's antics in Bangkok. Jho was helping with all the contacts. Xavier had allowed himself to be framed. The courts had spoken. It was going to be very hard to get him out.

"Then they dropped me," Laura said, rounding off her tale when she returned. "Just before Christmas they were trying again to make me do these things. I have that phone call with Patrick explaining how we had to make Najib trust us by damaging you. Then, because I would not take that step, they suddenly stopped pretending they were helping us."

The lawyers had ceased being paid, not just in Switzerland but also a team in Singapore that had been hired in Xavier's name to go for Tong and me to force us to return our copies of the PetroSaudi data (illogically, as it was, of course, never his but PetroSaudi's.) Then in January Paul Finnegan had been dispatched on one last visit to Laura at her parent's home in Geneva. For months the team had told her that their sole priority was to help her husband and to work the system to get him out of jail. But Finnegan had come to tell her that, from now on, she was on her own. Bad luck, sorry, you got played.

But Laura, having made precautions, went back to Thailand and squared the situation with her husband, sharing secret handwritten messages across the grille of the prison visiting room. With his approval, she had rung me up to put Plan B into operation.

My journalist's eyes slid greedily in the direction of her briefcase. "So, all that documentation, is it in there?" I asked.

"Yes. It is also on computer, but I have everything printed out. In sections. I wrote my story, I have secret notes from Xavier copied out, emails copied, texts. I even have the details of this ridiculous plan. They said that if Xavier got out of jail he would have to be spirited out of danger in a special operation, because the Malaysians would try to kill him before he could get out of Thailand. Look, they have all these diagrams and an operation plan which we were supposed to learn. Of course, Xavier was never going to be let free.

"Here. You can keep that copy of all my stuff," said Laura, having rather cautiously at last opened her briefcase to let me flick through her dossier. "In fact there is more. I can send it."

Before I flew to Geneva, we had mooted the idea of Laura possibly coming to London later, getting the whole story down on camera and making a film to put her case. But that was before I knew how our meeting would go. Now she had told me so much, unrestrainedly, I felt there was a trust between us and we were on the same page. So I ventured: "Look, I know it's 10pm on a Saturday night, but, if I can find a film crew available tomorrow, shall we just sit down and do an interview? I believe in striking while the iron is hot. We are both here and I am going to be worried and sleepless until we have this all on record and I know they will be banged to rights. There is nothing they won't stoop to if they find out about us meeting and decide to halt what we are going to do."

"Ok," said Laura. "I will call you in the morning."

That night in my box hotel room I first scoured the web and found a Geneva-based film crew who didn't mind being asked at 11.30 at night to film the next morning on a Sunday – as long as I paid them handsomely to do it. I then rustled up my brother who was eight hours ahead in the Philippines to get him to lend me his Swiss flat – and badger a friend with a key to let me in. Then I put aside much of the remainder of the night to wading through Laura's amazing trove of evidence and preparing my questions, before catching a bit of sleep and messaging her that we were ready to go for 10am.

By the time I flew out of Geneva that Sunday night, with the recording of Laura Justo's heart-rending story and all that damning evidence, I knew we had turned the tables on Patrick Mahony.

◆ ◆ ◆

My first call on Monday was to Randeep Ramesh of the *Guardian*. I had spoken to numerous journalists from all around the world who had picked up on 1MDB and in most cases I had become somewhat jaded, as they shied away from covering the story. The PetroSaudi angle and Xavier's plight had been particularly hard to get anyone to touch, because the company's vigilant lawyers had been effective in scaring off most news organisations. Even the *Wall Street Journal*, which had done a good job keeping on the 1MDB story, had doggedly ignored the PetroSaudi side (in their case possibly because that would have meant acknowledging my role in the story!)

Ramesh was one of the few journalists who had not been deterred by the sheer volume of the 1MDB story and the ferocity of PetroSaudi's lawyers. That was the pleasure of working for the *Guardian*, he explained, it is one of the few publications left with the financial muscle and commitment to stand up to legal bullying. And 1MDB, he reckoned, was a very important story. He just needed a UK angle and something big and new to persuade his editors to run it. Randeep had already been working at the story since February, hounded every step of the way by PetroSaudi's lawyers.

Now as he fitted Laura's tale, which I shared with him, into the jigsaw and prepared the story, the *Guardian* was subject to an intense onslaught from those lawyers, who overplayed their hand with such extreme audacity, in their insistence, for example, that PetroSaudi owned Good Star, that even the *Guardian's* lawyers appeared to wonder if they really could be lying quite so blatantly. But the evidence was incontrovertible. Then PetroSaudi changed its lawyers, who then set about the whole process all over again. Finally, the *Guardian*, having noted that the company's grounds for complaint had altered one way and then another just too many times, lost patience and called their bluff, giving the green light to publication.

◆ ◆ ◆

As Laura and I waited out the tension of those weeks before publication we were aware that each and every day Xavier was sweating it out in diminished conditions since the PetroSaudi minders had evaporated. "They have made a harsher regime under the new regulations," Laura told me. "It is 40 to 45 degrees and they are only allowed one bottle of water a day. They are not allowed to eat after 3pm until the next morning. They have no books allowed." To enjoy one's own moments of pleasure and relaxation knowing that someone you loved, as Laura did, or felt friendship and responsibility for, as I did, was suffering, felt churlish and the failure to get on and act weighed heavily on us. We had to keep the whole project secret until the story was ready to go. Every day I tried to keep in touch and cheer her up. But I too feared Xavier might never get out.

Yet I also felt strangely buoyant. Some around me wondered why. The reason was that I had survived and no one could say that I was wrong. Given what I had faced over previous months, that felt fantastic. What's more, I had a huge, supportive online crowd of active and intelligent people who were there to cheer me on at every step. Each time I stuck my neck out with a risky story, these wonderful people had risen to validate my words. Yes, there was fear and doubt, but I represented something that many others also felt and I was having an effect, as part of this movement to change things for the better. People were even starting to say, "where's the movie, where's the book?"

Others were saying, "What have you achieved? He is still there." But, in the back of my mind was the secret, morale-boosting knowledge that the US investigators were on the case. Compared to those lonely moments in earlier days, I felt I had back up. If I had ever shown any genuine personal courage it had been way back in 2009 when I had decided to do something, because it had to be better than nothing and started up my blog. For now it seemed comparatively easy to just keep on going.

32. BOOM

20th July 2016, Washington DC

L ORETTA Lynch, the 83rd Attorney General of the United States, is not a woman to be trifled with. It is said that her interest in the law came from watching her grandfather, a pastor, helping black residents in North Carolina move north to escape persecution from the racist Jim Crow laws at the time. On the 20th July 2016, flanked by four of her senior colleagues at the Department of Justice's headquarters in Pennsylvania Avenue, Washington, Lynch let rip. In her sights were the perpetrators of the 1MDB affair.

The private conversations I had been having with FBI investigators now bore their fruit – and some. All the threats I had received, all the lonely hours spent poring over documents, all the effort of the last six years trying to bring the appalling criminals of the 1MDB affair to book were about to be validated by the most powerful prosecutor in America.

I had started the day at my favoured corner of the local coffee shop where I liked to work. A story in that morning's *New York Times* had already given an indication of what was about to happen. I decided to write a blog to make some heartfelt points on the nature of journalism and the abuse honest reporters receive:

Sarawak Report would like to put in a small reminder in favour of media freedom, for voices great and small…

It is the core job of a free media to alert the people to abuses of power. If any journalist muddles their facts or gets the story wrong then there are myriad ways to deal with them and to shame them with the truth.

When a powerful government fails to take that path and instead initiates clampdowns, blackouts and arrest warrants then all can guess that far from lying, those journalists have exposed unpalatable facts.

Then, from across the Atlantic, I watched online as Lynch began. This was a flagship case for the DOJ's joint initiative with the FBI called the Kleptocracy Asset Recovery Unit, which was still in its early days. It aimed to target the proceeds of big-scale kleptocracy in developing countries funnelled through the global financial system into advanced economies. The two agencies had put together a 136-page court filing which, with characteristic American flair for a headline, they had entitled 'The United States v The Wolf of Wall Street'. It was a civil lawsuit against the makers of the film, alleging that the cash it had relied upon was gained from stolen 1MDB cash. In a milestone speech in the history of fighting money laundering, Lynch then declared that billions had been "laundered through American institutions in violation of US law." The US would be seeking to recover $1 billion of it.

Najib was not named directly in the speech – he was instead referred to obliquely as "Malaysian Official 1". Lynch declared

Unfortunately, a number of corrupt 1MDB officials treated this public trust as a personal bank account... Our complaint alleges that from 2009 through 2015, these officials and their associates conspired to misappropriate and launder billions of dollars from 1MDB... The co-conspirators laundered their stolen funds through a complex web of opaque transactions and fraudulent shell companies with bank accounts in countries around the world, including Switzerland, Singapore and the United States. The funds were then used to purchase a range of assets for the conspirators and their relatives and associates, including high-end real estate in New York and Los Angeles, artworks by Vincent Van Gogh and Claude Monet and a jet aircraft.

Lynch ended with a statement that left no doubt of her view of the significance of the case:

> This case, and the Kleptocracy Initiative as a whole, should serve as a sign of our firm commitment to fighting international corruption. It should send a signal that the Department of Justice is determined to prevent the American financial system from being used as a conduit for corruption. And it should make clear to corrupt officials around the world that we will be relentless in our efforts to deny them the proceeds of their crimes.

Andrew McCabe, the deputy director of the FBI, then articulated some of the lessons that especially resonated to me after my years of tracing corruption across the globe. "The Malaysian people were defrauded on an enormous scale," he began:

> So, why does a corruption case halfway around the World matter so much to us here today? Well, I'll tell you for a few reasons. First, because some of the profits of these schemes were invested in the United States and when corrupt officials bring their ill-gotten gains to the United States, they also bring with them their corrupt practices and disregard for the Rule of Law and that presents a threat to our economy, it impacts trade and investment. The fuels of the growth of criminal enterprises and undermines our fair democratic processes.
>
> Second, because the stable, healthy democracies around the World are the cornerstone of global security. The more we can do to help our international partners establish and maintain stable governments, accountable to the Rule of Law, the more we do to ensure U.S. National security.
>
> We hope this investigation will send a message to corrupt officials around the world that no person, no company, no organisation is too big, too powerful, or too prominent. No one is above or beyond the Law.

Richard Weber, Chief of Criminal Investigations at the Internal Revenue Service echoed that admonishment on the vast deceit of the past year and a half emanating from 1MDB, Najib Razak and their band of conspirators:

> Let me emphasise that we will not allow the massive, brazen and blatant diversion of billions of dollars from 1MDB and the alleged laundering of those funds through U.S. Financial Institutions to continue. This case represents a model for International Cooperation in significant cross border money laundering matters and sends a message that criminals cannot evade law enforcement authorities simply by laundering money through multiple jurisdictions and through a web of Shell Corporations.

The two agencies meticulously laid out their findings in full: dispassionately, it set out the scale of what had been going on.

They identified three principal phases of criminal conduct. The first was the one I had uncovered with the help of Xavier: the PetroSaudi scam ('the Good Star phase'). As I had reported, $1.03 billion had been taken, the initial $700 million and then a further $330 million, all of which went straight to Jho's Good Star account. The DOJ concluded that, of this cash, $24.5 million had been transferred to Prince Turki. $20 million made its way to "Malaysian Official 1", aka Prime Minister Najib Razak. After this, there was then 'the Aabar BVI phase', in 2012. This was where, together, Jho and al-Qubaisi had concocted the idea of stealing funds from the two bonds organised by Goldman Sachs. In total, a further $1.37 billion had disappeared into the offshore accounts they set up. The majority of this – $1.01 billion – was sent to the "Blackstone" account. The owner of this account was one Eric Tan (this mysterious figure popped up occasionally in the 1MDB files; it is now clear it was effectively an alias for Jho to help conceal his identity.) Jho then distributed $473 million into a Luxembourg account held by al-Qubaisi, $66 million to al-Husseiny (the CEO of Aabar) and $30 million to Najib.

A further $5 million was sent to someone identified in the report as '1MDB Officer 3', who turned out to be 1MDB's general counsel and executive director of group strategy. And $238 million was handed straight to Rosmah's son Riza Aziz, to fund his movie plans. A year later, in 'the Tanore phase', the gang used the same technique: 1MDB issued another $3 billion worth of bonds, of which $1.26 billion was siphoned off. Of this, $825 million was sent to a British Virgin Islands company called Tanore Finance Corp (also held in the name of Tan), from where $681 million was sent direct to Najib. Tens of millions more was used to purchase art for Jho.

The crazy looting had begun almost the moment the cash had landed in Jho's accounts – and the American suit laid it out in full. From the very start, Jho and his friends used the money "to purchase assets and invest in business interests for their personal benefit." These included, but were not limited to "luxury real estate, a Beverly Hills hotel, a private jet and a major Hollywood motion picture."

In addition, the suit continued, it helped to fund Jho's gargantuan appetite for pleasure and excess. For instance, the filing found, "between on or about October 30 2009 and June 18 2010, a period of less than eight months, more than $85 million in funds traceable to the Good Star account was wired… to Las Vegas casinos, luxury yacht companies, business jet rental vendors, a London interior decorator, and associates and family members of Low." The filing set it out in detail: more than $12 million to Caesars Palace, $13.4 million to the owners of the Venetian Las Vegas, $3.08 million to Rose Trading, a Hong Kong jeweller, $2.3 million to Argent Design, a London-based interior designer.

On it went. In early 2010, funds traceable to 1MDB were used to buy L'Ermitage, a luxury hotel in Beverly Hills, for $44.8 million. In May 2010, 1MDB money was then used to buy 912 North Hillcrest, a luxury home in LA for $17.5 million. Ownership was subsequently transferred to Riza. The same pot of cash was used to buy a Park Laurel condominium in New York for $23.9 million – a purchase which came less than 30 days after the $700 million had been wired from 1MDB to Good Star.

In March 2010, Jho then spent $35.3 million on a Bombardier Global 5000 private jet. In March 2011, he bought a Time Warner Penthouse in LA for $30.5 million, and the following year spent $38 million on the Oriole mansion in Beverly Hills (Hollywood's most expensive mansion until al-Qubaisi outspent him with the proceeds of his loot from 1MDB) and then, in 2015, a $13 million condominium in New York.

He lavished $106 million on buying a stake in the EMI music publishing business. He was careful: the filing concluded that the purchase was carried out in a manner intended to "conceal the origin, source and ownership of criminal proceeds" with the exact same amount of money "funnelled through no fewer than six different bank accounts at the same financial institution on or about the same day." The filing also found that Jho and his brother Szen invested in another hotel group, Park Lane partnership, entirely for their own benefit and claimed to be investing "personal family funds", not stolen cash from 1MDB. Asked where the money was coming from, Jho emailed at one stage "Low Family capital built from our grandparents down to the third generation now."

And, of course, tens of millions of dollars were diverted to Red Granite Pictures to help make *The Wolf of Wall Street*.

Come 2013, the conspirators had moved on to using the cash to buy artwork. The filing showed how, in May 2013, "Eric Tan" had opened an account at Christie's auction house in the name of the Tanore Finance Corporation. Between 13th and 15th May, Tanore then bought five works of art together worth $58 million. Most of it went on the $48 million they spent on Michel Basquiat's *Dustheads*. A month later, Tanore was back, buying *Concetto Spaziale, Attese* by Lucio Fontana and *Untitled (Yellow and Blue)* by Mark Rothko for a combined $79 million. Later, in October of that year, "Tan" requested that Christie's reserve a specific 'skybox' for twelve guests at upcoming auctions – a private room where guests are able to bid without having to sit in the public auction area itself. A Christie's employee emailed a colleague: "It better look like Ceasar [sic] Palace in there... box is almost more important for the client than the art." While Jho made significant attempts to keep himself at arm's length from all these purchases, the American filing concluded that "Tan" was purely Jho's nominee for purchasing art in order to obscure the fact he was doing so. "Tan" simply gifted the work to Jho immediately after purchase, more than $100 million worth. Nicely laundered cash, in other words. Indeed, Jho viewed fine art purchases as an increasingly handy way to launder cash, spending a further $35 million on Monet's *Saint-Georges Majeur*, $33 million on his *Nymphéas avec Reflets de Hauntes Herbes*, plus a Van Gogh for $5.4 million.

And Jho's chums had got in on the act too. Funds traceable to the Aabar bond deal had been used to bag al-Qubaisi a $50 million penthouse in the Walker Tower in New York, two mansions in Beverly Hills worth $15 million and $50 million respectively. While Riza bought a townhouse in Belgravia, London for £23 million.

Watching via computer link in London, I felt elated, stunned, numb. Around me, in the coffee shop in Victoria, London was going about its business entirely unaware of this remarkable story. But now, after all the lies, here was the ultimate vindication.

Plus, it was clear the investigation was ongoing. The seizures were merely a start-up action to prevent criminals from selling off the proceeds of their crime in advance of being found guilty. Next step would be criminal charges. It was really fantastic stuff. However, I tried to stay professional. Not only was I having to try and absorb the sheer immensity and significance of this unprecedented move by the US Department of Justice against the leadership of a political ally on the other side of the world, but I was having to write it all up and explain it as quickly as I could.

All I could do was try and plough through the documents and relay to readers in Malaysia the details as simply and accurately as possible. The wider media would be following the story too, at last, but the international press would go broad brush, so there was a job for me in digging through the finer points, which my readership in Malaysia, who had been following the story for two years, would be interested in, and in a position to grasp. It was already late afternoon in London by the time I got going – most would have gone to bed in Malaysia. I had the night to give them something fresh in the morning.

And while there was so much detail on the looting involved, the most significant development of all had to be that the prime minister was squarely identified as thief. To be sure, he wasn't named, as he was not officially registered as an owner of the US assets in question, however, he was referred to as an actor in the crime that generated the money laundered in the United States. There could be not a hint of a doubt but that the person referred to throughout the indictment as 'Malaysian Official 1' was Najib. Malaysian Official 1 was described as "a high-ranking official in the Malaysian government who also held a position of authority with 1MDB" and was a relative of Riza Aziz. There were 33 references to MO1, as he soon became known, all of them confirming the identity was that of Najib and that he was the prime orchestrator of the theft.

In any country with a free media, a prime minister thus identified would have been removed amidst popular fury within hours. However, I knew the mentality of UMNO, whose remaining leadership were all complicit, and that Najib's propagandists would abuse their control of the media to try to gull uninformed people into thinking that the indictment cleared Najib because his name did not appear in it. My counter-blast was to get the simple message across that the United States Department of Justice had just identified the Prime Minister of Malaysia as one of the world's worst ever thieves. Christian was soon at work re-designing our Facebook site with a new banner at the top. Over a picture of Najib was written "Malaysian Official Number One (in case you were wondering)".

However much I already knew of the appalling corruption of Najib and his cronies, the detail of the plethora of money transfers, of often hundreds of millions of dollars at a time, was jaw-dropping. Yet it was some of the relatively smaller ones that tended to reveal more about the character of the criminals.

The indictment ripped apart all attempts by Jho to pretend the purchaser of artwork was not he but "Eric Tan", despite endless subterfuge recorded in emails to disguise his role. Christies apparently tolerated the deceit and kept his identity secret, although Joey McFarland's presence at the auctions had already led me to put two and two together. The indictment described a fascinating touch: these paintings were then each formally 'gifted' by 'Tan' to Jho and McFarland in emails with the identical subject line: "RE: GIFT OF ART-WORK(S) AS STATED BELOW IN CONSIDERATION OF YOUR FRIENDSHIP, YOUR CHARITABLE CONTRIBUTION TO THE WORLD, AND PASSION IN PROMOTING THE UNDERSTANDING AND APPRECIATION OF ART-WORKS"

The main text of the emails, identical except that each referenced a different artwork, was:

> I wish to gift you ALL of the art-work(s) mentioned in this gift letter in consideration of the followings [sic]:
> – all the generosity, support and trust that you have shared with me over the course of our friendship, especially during the difficult periods of my life; and
> – your continuous generosity in providing charitable contributions to advance the well-being and development of our global communities; and
> – your passion in promoting the understanding and appreciation of art-works.
>
> …
>
> All the art-work(s) gifted to you should not in any event be construed as an act of corruption since this is against the Company and/or my principles and I personally do not encourage such practices in any manner whatsoever.

The childish and preposterous style, suspiciously reminiscent of letters sent to AmBank by the supposed Saudi sheikh to justify money transfers to Najib, immediately betrayed the authorship of the Jho, whose cartoonish idea of foolproof deceptions I was becoming familiar with. For once I kicked myself on having been over-cautious in pulling an article in which I had posed some leading questions to a number of those large auction houses who had processed Jho's purchases. They had been every bit as negligent as I had supposed.

And no wonder Riza he could afford to make lavish films at a time few could. When the heat was on, owing to tax related questions from wealth manager Debra's bosses at NKFSB, Riza claimed that this money was a gift from Aabar, as it was owned by a 'family friend'. He had clearly learnt from his stepfather. If a Saudi royal could donate almost a billion to Najib, why not? Mohamed al-Husseiny did the honours by sending a letter confirming his gift to Riza.

This was all small beer though compared to the vast proportion of the stolen money that was laundered back to Malaysia, straight into Najib's account.

The indictment was highly critical of Goldman Sachs and its preparation of the bond issues for 1MDB, stating of each bond, "The offering circular contained misleading statements and omitted material facts necessary to make its representations not misleading."

I wrote a long piece on *Sarawak Report* detailing all of this and concluded as follows:

Najib has been proven a thief and a liar and to be bad at both. He has taken from his own people and abused their trust and he has shamed Malaysia by proving to be not only the greediest and most excessive kleptocrat ever recorded, but also the most inept.

Caught red-handed, Najib has no choice. He has to go.

I amused myself over the following days by writing a series of sardonic 'open letters' to many institutions and individuals who had ignored voluble warnings, buried their heads in the sand and willingly cooperated with the kleptocrats in exchange for investments or donations. People like Lord Marland, President of the British Malaysian Chamber of Commerce, who had ceaselessly promoted trade with Najib; David Greenaway, the Vice-Chancellor of Nottingham University, who had sanctioned the installation of a prominent six-foot high portrait of their former student Najib on their campus; Rick Haythornthwaite, chairman of Global Mastercard, whose involvement had provided a fig leaf to the PetroSaudi dealings; Kathy Calvin, President and CEO of the UN Foundation that had hosted a joint fundraiser with Jho on his hired yacht; Ed Morse, Citibank's Head of Commodities, whose shoddy valuation had facilitated the PetroSaudi heist; Graham Hodges, Deputy Chief Executive of ANZ Bank, whose Malaysian subsidiary AmBank processed all Najib's ill-gotten gains; and Lord MacLaurin, Head of Governors of Malvern College, which named their Science Centre after the Malaysian prime minister.

And, I felt, Mr DiCaprio and Alicia Keys, and the rest of Jho's chums deserved a letter too. This gives a taste of my ebullient mood:

Dear Leo, Alicia and all the Fun Party Team,

We have been warning you for months and months that your favourite party host, charity auction donator, gambling chip provider, Vegas bubbly buyer, yacht and jet supplier was a fake.

You definitely weren't interested in listening or maybe the party music was just too loud?...

Will Leo be returning his fee for Wolf of Wall Street, which we and many others had warned was paid from stolen money from Malaysia's development fund?

We will continue our letter-writing at less busy time.

Yours sincerely,

Sarawak Report

33. FREEDOM

Autumn 2016, London and Geneva

THE world's biggest financial scam had finally been exposed. Najib, Jho, Rosmah and the rest had been outed for the petty thieves they really were. For my tiny team at *Sarawak Report* it was an incredible feeling. Thanks to PetroSaudi's lawyers and the Malaysian government's bullying tactics, there had, until now, been minimal coverage internationally of this mammoth story. The DOJ's indictment changed the calculus.

$700 million dollars *had* been siphoned out to Good Star; Good Star *did* belong to Jho and not PetroSaudi; the later purchase of UBG by PetroSaudi *had* been a front for Jho, who *had* used money taken from 1MDB and channelled through PetroSaudi and there *had* been massive backhanders. The directors of PetroSaudi were now desperately trying to portray themselves to investigators as unwitting bystanders, but had irretrievably compromised themselves through their involvement, as the indictment made clear. And, what's more, the scam had spread into Abu Dhabi and now reached the door of Goldman Sachs, the firm which had helped stitch it all together.

For me, however, there was unfinished business in Malaysia to attend to. Najib was still in power, still brazening it out, insisting he was the victim of a conspiracy. And, more pressingly, I still had a source in jail. The 1MDB affair couldn't end for me until I saw justice served for both of them.

Randeep's major 7,000-word story on the 1MDB heist and PetroSaudi was published in the last week of July. Unsurprisingly, despite their threatening behaviour up to the moment of going to press, Mahony and Tarek did precisely nothing once the story was published, except to moan that the *Guardian* had not warned them that their source of the story was Laura Justo. Laura had rightly been terrified that, had they known she had spoken to the *Guardian,* she would come under intolerable pressure if not worse: an intermediary had already warned her that her life would be in danger if she spoke out. "You will be safer once you've done it," I advised.

And with the DOJ report still reverberating, Laura and I decided to raise publicity in Switzerland by holding a press conference. On the day the *Guardian* story came out, I flew to a low key hotel at Geneva Airport, where I met Laura and another Swiss citizen caught up in the affair, Pascal Najadi, the son of the murdered banker Hussain Najadi.

Pascal and his fiancée Anna were a welcome addition to our team and they helped round up local media, which they had been in touch with during their own campaign to highlight the cover-up of his father's case. A very respectable number of journalists turned up to our press conference – including from papers which, earlier in the story, had been taken in by PetroSaudi's lies and now wanted to set the record straight. The plight of Xavier Justo was about to become front page news in Switzerland.

My own filmed interview with Laura had been edited the weekend I got back – a functional one-hour documentary produced in only three days. Now that the *Guardian* story was out, I uploaded it on YouTube and within a few hours it had received nearly 200,000 views in Europe and in Asia. There were many comments from Malaysia. "Laura i apologize on behalf of my government for the ill treatment of your family. What a nightmare for you and your family [at] the end of the day justice will prevail," was one that spoke for all of them. Laura was in tears. For so many months, she said, even her closest friends had imagined the worst about this case and her husband's character. They had been vilified and criminalised, now at last she was receiving sympathy and understanding and she felt a huge burden had been lifted.

It was time to up the pressure – and expose the PetroSaudi mob properly. I uploaded some of the recorded calls, emails and messages Laura had collected between Mahony, his co-conspirators and herself to reveal the sinister charade they had played to silence Xavier. They included the following recorded exchange in which

Mahony tried to persuade Laura to publicly attack me.

Mahony: "I told you who is controlling this… It is his [Najib's] ultimate nightmare that Xavier could turn on him if he gets out. This is his position at the moment."

Laura: So what do I say to Xavier about getting out – you told me December ?

Mahony: "This guy [Najib] is still stressed it's his political career on the line, he's in deep shit and that's all he thinks about."

Laura: "So what do I say?"

Mahony: "The only way I can show him [Najib] you are on his side, a team player, is if you are ready to put yourself in the media – you must denounce all the people that are making conspiracies against him.. we are all in deep shit. I told you the other day. I am in deep shit and a prime minister of a country is in deep shit because of this … He [Xavier] didn't have to do that [leak the PetroSaudi data]."

But, as we have seen, Laura refused to comply or to condone the release of the attack video against me and, as a result, PetroSaudi eventually ceased pretending to support Xavier's attempts to get out of jail.

I pushed Laura to make formal complaints against PetroSaudi both in the UK and Switzerland. Also culpable were of course those within the Thai authorities who had played ball; according to Mahony, he had paid them. But Laura was confident the Swiss authorities would act. On 5th August, it appeared she was about to be proven right. The Embassy had been in discussions with the Thai government and had arrived at an understanding that Xavier would be transferred back home to Switzerland at the end of the month. The papers just needed to be finalised at a formal meeting, scheduled for the 31st August. Meanwhile, Laura's new lawyers, two high profile Swiss legal practitioners, who had generously taken up the case, and the Swiss diplomats had advised her to keep quiet to avoid upsetting the Thais with any more accusations so as to ensure the whole matter proceeded smoothly. A few days later, Laura was told Xavier received a royal pardon, meaning he would be out by June the following year no matter what – and in the meantime would be allowed to serve the remainder of the sentence back in Switzerland, he would be transferred in a matter of days.

I was still uneasy, however. I had heard that Tarek had gone to China where Jho was now hiding out. Then it emerged that Najib was due to make a state visit to Bangkok early the following month. I felt a pang of nervousness. It was a dangerous situation, I thought. I knew Najib's game, and I was worried he would use his influence while in Thailand to keep Xavier locked up in Bangkok. He was a prime minister of a neighbouring country, with which the Thais had major issues – they had been demanding more Malaysian cooperation to stop terrorists who had been crossing over the border and bombing Buddhist temples and other places. They were also interested in the construction of a high speed rail link to Singapore. It all gave Najib clout, quite apart from all his money and the other normal diplomatic issues.

As the days passed and the promised transfer of Xavier to Switzerland failed to take place, I decided to revert to my usual Plan A: throw a rock via my website. I ran a piece entitled 'Laura Justo Suspects Malaysian Interference Over "Abnormal Denial" Of Husband's Right To Transfer Back To Switzerland' in which Laura voiced her fears that Xavier would be made a bargaining chip in political negotiations. It was good to let the Thais and Malaysians know that no one was under any illusions about what was going on, we reckoned.

Najib's trip to Thailand began on 9th September. He was due to stay there for a week. Each day we awaited the meeting at which, Laura had been assured, the Thai authorities would rubberstamp Xavier's immediate transfer to Switzerland. On the 16th, I woke to a text message from Laura: "The fucking, fucking Thais. It was refused!!!!!!!!!! Call when you can". It was a heart-breaking day. Laura was distraught. The explanation had been given that, thanks to the earlier spontaneous royal pardon, Xavier's remaining prison sentence had been reduced to less than a year and that under these circumstances the Thai authorities had said the rules meant he had to serve his sentence there.

Xavier was incredibly depressed by the turn of events, a friend reported back. He had been full of hope. I smelt a big fat Malaysian rat. I later learnt through sources that Najib had been blatant about his demands to keep Xavier in jail. Jho, inevitably, had been in Bangkok for the duration of the visit. The issue of Xavier had been placed at the very top of the agenda during prime ministerial talks. The man was shameless. The Malaysians had demanded Xavier be extradited to face charges in KL, something he and his inspector general of police had been loudly demanding for months. Their problem was that they simply had no jurisdiction relevant to the alleged crimes for which Xavier had been convicted. The supposed blackmail had not taken place in Malaysia, nor was there any evidence Xavier had distorted or forged any of the contents of the database or had in some way undertaken an enterprise against the Malaysian state. Najib had no legal grounds to stand on and it was clear he wanted Xavier merely for propaganda purposes.

Given the Swiss were, on the contrary, pressing to have their national back, the Thais tried to keep in with both foreign powers by what they judged to be a compromise. They would keep him safe enough in Thailand and refuse the extradition to Malaysia, but they would also try to appease Najib by not returning him to Switzerland.

I often cry over spilt milk and I was livid that we hadn't been across every media outlet going over the previous few weeks, demanding Xavier's return. Finally Laura agreed. "I will find every fucking penny they have stowed away and expose every one of them! Make their lives as miserable as ours!" she spat down the line.

There was one consolation, which was that now we felt like we were doing something, instead of sitting back in tortuous waiting. We badgered everyone, bombarded the media and I started writing articles to tell the world what had been going on. I particularly hoped to cajole and shame the Swiss authorities into doing their part – they would know they had a dangerously undiplomatic loudmouth ready to sound off again if they let the matter slide.

October came with Xavier still in jail. The old and ailing Thai monarch died. It made for a time of uncertainty and, as the administration went into semi-suspension for a while, getting news or progress on his case became harder than ever. Laura and I were sick with worry that we would lose the initiative and excuses would be found to keep him in jail even beyond next June. We no longer held out a shred of hope of seeing him before that date.

The lawyers had also come round to our way of thinking – there was no point treading softly anymore. Then the message came through that there was a big prison amnesty planned for December to mark the ascension of the new king. People in the jail were telling Xavier he could be on the list. Laura and I snorted – we were sure there was no way he would be included.

But our cynicism was proven wrong. In early December I was attending an anti-corruption conference in Oslo. While there, I got a couple of missed calls from Laura. She had left a message. Xavier had been granted an amnesty by the new king, along with 30,000 other prisoners. He looked set to be out before Christmas.

It was wonderful news, completely unexpected. But after so many months of false hopes, during which we had become hardened against any anticipation of a straightforward release, caution immediately kicked in and we knew we must not to get too excited. She had been told that the foreign prisoners would get dealt with last, meaning that the process could take several more days before his papers were signed and he was out. Anything could happen in a few days, especially with the Malaysians doing their best to keep him inside. "Let's keep this under the radar to minimise sabotage," I suggested and Laura agreed.

However, despite our desire to keep quiet, by the very next day the news was everywhere. Stupidly, Xavier's lawyer had spoken to none other than *Bernama*, the Malaysian news agency which was controlled by Najib's governing coalition. He must have been detailed to call them with any news. It could not have been a more dangerous or damaging move. I kept silent and watched along with

Laura for what would happen next. Again the stages were mapped out, then delays started to occur, but word came back that the papers had indeed been drawn up and delivered to the prison, they just needed a final signature or two, the Swiss Embassy reassured Laura. It was nail-biting.

And it was clear that Xavier was in danger. The disappearance of Kevin Morais had shown us already just how brutal the authorities could be with troublesome opponents. As I took a coach journey out of Oslo for a dinner on the final evening of the conference, I began to get messages from my Malaysian contacts telling me to warn Xavier's people that he might end up dead.

The Malaysian government did not want him to leave Thailand. The fear was that they would use their close contacts within the escorting police to prevent that happening when he left the jail. In other words, there was a price on Xavier's head. The sources were extremely credible. One told me: "Either an accident or a hit man, there are Malaysian related entities with far-reaching contacts in Thailand and there is evidence that the instruction has gone out."

Trapped on a coach in the dark heading up a hillside in Norway, I felt momentarily powerless. Within a few moments I collected my thoughts and realised what I had to do. I messaged Laura: "tell your Swiss lawyers and get them to tell the Swiss Embassy". I also knew that going public was the best possible protection. That night on my return from the Oslo Christmas celebration I wrote about the threats, challenging the Swiss to protect their national, warning the Thais to protect a high profile whistle-blower and letting Malaysia know that they had been rumbled. The Swiss media took it up the following day, meaning the Embassy and Thai police faced a publicity nightmare should anything happen to this awkward prisoner on his release.

On 20th December, Xavier emerged from jail. He was escorted out in the manner in which he had come in – surrounded by commandos and with the cameras rolling.

Afterwards I was to learn just how dangerous that moment had been. After Xavier had been escorted out of jail, the top security had evaporated once he had reached the main emigration detention centre to sort out his final papers on the way to the airport. Instead of the large, heavily armed, masked protection squad (as later pictured in all the papers), for this second leg of his journey he was put in an open truck with several Nigerian drug runners, which rattled through the streets vulnerable to pot shots all the way to the airport.

Then the status he was accorded reversed again, he said. At the airport, he was escorted to the VIP lounge and met by the Swiss Ambassador, who had come to see him off. In a kind gesture that she hugely appreciated, the Ambassador then rang Laura from the airport to assure her that the plane was now in the sky with her husband on it.

I reported the news of his release on *Sarawak Report*: 'FREE AND HOME FOR CHRISTMAS!' It was a great story to be able to write.

On Boxing Day I made my own way to Geneva to catch up with the couple. A lot of water had gone under the bridge between Xavier and I since we had first met two and half years earlier in Bangkok. The last time I had seen him was at the dinner in Singapore with Tong and Kay Tat. He still hadn't received the $2 million that he'd asked for back then. Instead, he'd been branded a criminal, left in a Thai jail, and been put under intense pressure to sign a series of false statements in the hope he might get out. But for all that, he still had what the rest of the PetroSaudi mob had given up years before: his honour.

He looked astonishingly well and relaxed, given his ordeal of the past few months. We sat down and listened as he recounted the details of his arrival back in Switzerland. "When I arrived in Zurich I was escorted off by an armed official and placed on the connecting flight," Xavier told me as we celebrated. "There was a guy to meet me also in Geneva – and then they showed us out of the back exit to the airport and that was it, goodbye." It took a few more days for Xavier to feel quite safe back home, but now they were getting used to it. He was completely free.

After their little boy, whom Xavier had only seen once in jail since his arrest, sank into an early night's sleep, exhausted by the excitement of the new presence in his family, we sat and enjoyed a proper supper. I had brought champagne from duty free and Laura had laid on every single luxurious titbit she could find in her local deli to make up for the months of mouldy rice that Xavier had lived off and somehow survived. We could not have had a better time.

Xavier's stories of the inside of Bangkok jail were a book waiting to be written. Laura and I listened open-mouthed. "You realise it is not just a physical challenge to survive, it is mental," he said. Laura's steadfastness and his determination to reach justice had kept him going. As the Justos mapped out their plans and options it became clear that what they needed was not to answer the million and one media requests that were flooding in, but to speak to the authorities and to organise their legal case.

Because, in answer to my question to them that day, yes, they were determined to go after all those who had conspired to put him in jail and then bully and blackmail him into signing a confession that could have kept him there for years. There was no question of letting bygones be bygones. How could there be after what had happened? For the following months Xavier kept himself busy as he compiled his case.

"I was actually expecting to see Patrick [Mahony] at the airport when I arrived, ready to bribe me with a couple of million to keep quiet," Xavier had said. "But, he knows better. He knows that even if I was minded to take that money, which I am not, I would never trust him with any deal he tried to offer me. He would as soon record me accepting his deal and then use it against me."

When you are bitten by a venomous snake you learn your lesson.

34. "YOU WOULDN'T BE THE FIRST PERSON TO BE DROPPED IN THE ANDAMAN SEA"

Early 2017

HERE'S the thing: to expose criminals with the deep pockets and the ruthlessness of the 1MDB mob, requires almost reckless courage and extraordinary determination from those sources who, at great risk to their personal safety, are prepared to get information into the public domain. Without them, we journalists have no stories.

Xavier had paid for that with his liberty. Kevin Morais paid for it with his life. Others – like the poorly paid staff at the Malaysian Anti-Corruption Commission – toiled away in the knowledge that they were risking everything. There is no knowing who may come knocking.

Take one of the people connected to the sources who had given me information about the Aabar link to 1MDB. I have written already about how he was nearly carjacked in Paris. Now, in late 2016, I met him again for the first time since. He recalled what had happened.

"I was driving just near the Champs Elysées one Sunday morning when a car screeched in front of me forcing me to stop just as a motorbike drew up alongside me. I immediately realised they were going to try to kill me."

"How?" I was horrified.

"I was ready for it. I have seen bad days in my country and I used to be in the military. You are always looking behind you and this was a classic manoeuvre. Before they could corner me completely I managed to turn left across the central reservation and drive into other traffic."

It was hard to believe but, thanks to a French journalist who had also been looking into it, it had been corroborated. A source told that journalist that contacts hired by al-Qubaisi had introduced him to a Belgian mafia hitman who had been given orders to kill my source. The price on his head had been a million dollars.

He was yet another person drawn into the 1MDB story who had started to find his life resembled a dangerous part in a movie. Only now – with Khadem al-Qubaisi locked up in jail in Abu Dhabi – had he dared to resume his life. He was elated and passionate. The real people in charge in Abu Dhabi were good people, he insisted. It was just a few bad apples who had been caught up in this web of debauchery and turned dangerous. Strikingly the same trick of using fake policemen had been played on his own wife, just as Laura Justo had been bullied by Paul Finnegan. A 'policeman' had attempted to interrogate her on the whereabouts of her husband, but she had been warned.

◆ ◆ ◆

Instead, it was the big spenders who were now beginning to feel a chill wind. And it was becoming clear they were getting worried that the long arm of the law might reach them.

As regards Jho, "spot the yacht" had become something of an international past-time for 1MDB watchers. *Equanimity* and its entourage spent a lot of time off Phuket, making little excursions now and again around the Andaman Sea and Malacca Straits. Sometimes it would go off radar for a day or so, prompting speculation. Jho was seen elsewhere. Thailand, Taiwan, China, London, KL itself, Turkey… but it was evident he wasn't staying anywhere long.

And Najib's stepson Riza was also getting worried. It was well-known by now that a team from the FBI had set itself up on the West Coast and was asking questions about 1MDB, Red Granite and *The Wolf of Wall Street*. Riza was getting worried. Meanwhile, the authorities in Abu Dhabi were also demanding he be brought in. Publicly, he continued to brazen it out, donating $2.1 million to the Los Angeles County Museum of Art, of which DiCaprio was a board member. Riza's injection of cash allowed the museum to purchase a huge collection of rare movie posters from long-time collector Mike Kaplan, it was explained. I also discovered he was trying to diversify, at one point picking up investment ideas from strangers met at London's Ronnie Scott's Jazz club. And still they partied: Riza, Joey McFarland and the crowd at Red Granite continued to rub shoulders with pals like Leo DiCaprio and Swizz Beatz. It was becoming harder by the day to use ignorance as an excuse, yet these two were still apparently enjoying the dirty money being splashed around town. "There is no expense spared when it comes to chauffeured limos, the best restaurants, parties at the top clubs, tickets costing thousands of dollars for celebrity events and of course, designer luxuries and business class travel," I was told.

But by the end of 2016, it appeared Riza had decided to return home to KL, not just on a fleeting visit, but to stay put it seemed. Rosmah had reportedly expressed concern that her son was not safe over in the United States. Indeed, my enquiries suggested that there was in fact quite a list of 1MDB associated characters who had initially fled KL, but were now back in town, because being in KL was safer than being at the mercy of international law enforcers who had started asking questions and freezing accounts – and who knew what would happen next?

A few months later, when the 1MDB bubble had well and truly burst, it would fall to none other than Jordan Belfort, the former fraudster on whose life story *The Wolf of Wall Street* was based, to say it as it was. He, more than anyone, could spot a con. In an interview in 2017, he declared:

The movie's a huge success, and then it turns out the guys who financed it were criminals. Leo [Leonardo DiCaprio] got sucked in. Leo's an honest guy. But I met these guys... these guys are fucking criminals ... They flew me to Cannes four or five months after they bought the movie and they wanted to announce it in Cannes. It hadn't even gone into production yet, and they threw a launch party. They must have spent $3 million on a launch party. They flew in Kayne West, and I said ... this is a fucking scam, anybody who does this has stolen money. You wouldn't spend money you worked for like that.

In that interview, Belfort also confirmed stories I had heard two years before, that Riza and Jho were offering $500,000 to those of their Hollywood pals, who were prepared to come to Vegas and party with them. DiCaprio took them up, I had heard. Scorsese turned them down and so did jailbird Belfort:

> They offered me money and everything to go to Vegas. A lot of money. Like $500,000, which I really could've used. I was like, 'I can't do it.' Leo went, Margot [Margot Robbie, Leo's *The Wolf of Wall Street* co-star] went. I refused to go. And because of that I'm not mentioned in the articles. I've learnt my lesson. I was like, 'I don't need these fucking people.' I knew it, it was so obvious.

While Jho and Riza were showing signs they were worried, Najib was simply doubling down. And, as 2017 continued, it became clear that, far from accepting the game was up, a wounded Najib had decided to tighten his grip on power still further. He and Rosmah would have known by then that they now were in a fight for survival: win the next elections due in 2018, and they would be able to repress their enemies and continue their kleptocratic regime; lose, and they faced ignominy and, possibly, long prison sentences.

And so, this peaceful, law-abiding, beautiful country witnessed a wave of repression from its appalling government. ISIS-evoking death threats were being made online against the women leaders of the pro-democracy Bersih group. Its chairman, Maria Chin Abdullah (a widow from a mixed marriage and a Muslim convert) was sent altered photographs of herself and her four sons being beheaded. It was a chilling indication of the mentality of the pro-Najib 'Redshirts' now menacing the streets, so named because of the red t-shirts they wore to contrast themselves to Bersih's distinctive yellow outfits, who played up Malay and Muslim supremacy as their rallying cry. Meanwhile Najib, the self-styled moderate Muslim leader, sought to stoke religious tension in order to rally his "Malay base".

As the unpleasant backdrop of intimidation mounted, I started to receive warning of genuine threats against myself. Earlier in the year I had agreed to speak in Singapore at an anti-corruption conference, but I received feedback that Najib had been notified and was looking for ways either to extradite me under the fast-track special arrangements between the states (a false charge was being apparently mooted) or simply to kidnap me. A Malaysian military jet had been detailed to Singapore's Seletar Airport during the planned period of my visit, went one of the tip-offs I received: "You would not be the first person to have disappeared that way and been dropped into the Andaman Sea," the informant messaged. I pulled out of the trip rather than walk into unnecessary problems.

On the eve of another major Bersih march, which had not been given official permission, Najib struck hard. Police swooped on the offices of Bersih and arrested Maria and five of her co-workers. They also confiscated papers and computers, presumably with the primary intention of disrupting coordination the following day. Buses coming into town were simultaneously halted across the country – everything that could be done to keep down the numbers of the crowd was attempted with the usual threats against government workers and students who were told they would lose their jobs if caught on the march.

When the day dawned photographs emerged of a truck which had pulled up in front of UMNO's own headquarters, where it dumped great plastic sacks full of Redshirt logo-emblazoned t-shirts to hand out to the march-fodder and supporters being bussed in for the planned counter-demonstration by pro-Najib bovver boys. It was no surprise. I had already printed a story exposing how UMNO divisions had been instructed to round up, organise and pay Redshirt marchers, who ostensibly had nothing to do with BN. The shirts were not the only thing on the truck. A huge pile of heavy bamboo sticks were also offloaded – this politically backed group was looking for trouble and violence.

But in the event, Najib's powers were limited and the lack of enthusiasm for his tactics also manifest. In a heartening display that the rule of law had not entirely disintegrated, the police immediately removed the sticks and contained the Redshirts with professionalism. The police aggression manifested against the Yellow Shirts at protests in earlier years had also evaporated – officers treated them with courtesy, the marchers later said. There was another encouraging feature of the 2016 march: yes, it was smaller given all the fear and crackdowns, but it still swelled in the course of the day to tens of thousands of people and this time Malay faces were more prominent than before. Najib could not just blame opposition to his rule on Chinese and other minorities. Those people had been very brave to turn up. At the end of the day the peaceful march dispersed without trouble. The Redshirts, with all their UMNO support, mustered far fewer, approximately 4,000.

Yet Maria was kept in solitary confinement for ten days after the march, her colleagues having eventually been let out. Najib attempted to use his new anti-terrorism laws against Maria, accusing her of attacking the safety of the state. It was the law he had forced through whilst assuring opposition MPs that it would never be used against civil rights activists or political opponents. The incarceration caused international outrage, the courts threw out the case and Maria was freed. Again, it encouragingly showed that Najib was still subject to some democratic constraints and meanwhile his personal standing continued to plummet. It did not cause him to hold back though: next Zunar, the cartoonist, already facing charges of sedition that carried a potential sentence of 43 years' imprisonment, was re-arrested, after an exhibition of his cartoons was attacked by violent UMNO protestors -- who were not detained.

In an attempt to bolster a dwindling sense of power, the annual UMNO Party rally at the end of the month was staged as an almost hysterical display of personal adulation. Party officials gathered daily in the enormous stadium all in matching blue or red outfits, depending on the day, chanting and clapping for their leader, the saviour of the Muslim Malays against foreign interferers. Najib obviously loved it – such are the powers of self-deception. He issued blood-curdling Jihadist-like threats against political opponents and minority communities, as if they were an opposing army instead of neighbours with democratic rights, and spoke of "cleansing the party of traitors".

I was at the Panama Transparency International Conference at the time, observing the North Korean-style choreography coming out of KL, only to find that I myself had become a prime target of the whole affair. Zahid Hamidi, Najib's by now thoroughly compromised deputy, accused me in his speech of receiving "foreign funding to topple the government" and announced the launching of a 'special task force' to investigate me. It was the same ludicrous charge levied at me previously by Taib Mahmud, again in a central political arena.

Meanwhile in Malaysia the opposition to Najib continued to consolidate. On 10th February 2017 Mahathir was reported to have contrived a second meeting with Anwar, who was fighting his latest in a string of ongoing cases. It was widely reported after a behind-the-scenes meeting of 45 minutes that they had agreed Najib had to go, and if necessary to achieve that they would re-unite.

I learnt something more beyond what had been then published. In their private meeting the old man had confirmed to his former protégé turned former sworn enemy that he was now utterly reconciled and committed to supporting him to become the next prime minister, a rapprochement people in both camps had never believed would happen. It was a sensational development I realised, because it would signal a combination that could capture the imagination of both Malay nationalists and reformers. It would give Najib and BN a serious run despite their money.

"The clock is now ticking for Najib," I texted.

◆ ◆ ◆

By April 2017 events seemed in suspended animation. Yet it felt as busy as ever managing the information flying in from all over. Investigations were underway in Switzerland, the US, and Singapore, and the judgement in a legal case between IPIC and 1MDB over the missing money would soon come in, and was likely to put heavy financial pressure on Malaysia.

My life felt utterly surreal. On one side of the world, I was being castigated by an authoritarian kleptocrat, and being warned that secret service operatives were planning attempts on my life. On the other, back home in London, I was trying to keep on top of family meal times, mundane appointments, and the dog needed walking. My younger son was home from university and my retired husband was floating around, but I was hopeless company for either of them. Never mind, I told myself, we touched base as stomachs brought the menfolk into the kitchen at various intervals.

One evening I had been struggling to download something that was important and was at the end of my tether and unwilling to discuss supper being an hour late.

"So what's the issue Mum?" my son had eventually asked.

I glanced up at him. "Oh, it's just to do with these people who were trying to kill my sources and it's on the web and I can't download the leaked documents – ex-Mossad head in Tel Aviv and that secret service boss from France."

"They were working together targeting us and trying to hunt down the guy who was in hiding."

My son nodded.

"Please, just pass over the sausages behind you, I need to get them into the oven," I added.

Not for the first time, my son looked at me somewhat askance. "That's a fairly unusual sequence of subject matters, Mum," he declared.

There was no deceiving myself: I had become distant from my family as I had thrown myself body and soul into exposing the 1MDB story. It had been six years and a mad adventure, but at that point I realised what I really needed was to go away and have a break. However, much as I might want to put it all behind me, the tentacles of this story had now enveloped me.

Xavier was back with his family: I could tick that off. Now there was the small matter of Najib.

35. NAJIB GOES TO WASHINGTON

Summer and autumn 2017

FOR the remainder of 2017, there was every reason to fear the worst. Cash, as Najib once put it, was still king, and he was able to use his enormous powers of patronage to reward his political network. He had replaced all those who had been investigating him at the MACC, Central Bank, the Attorney General's and Auditor General's Offices. It meant that, after eight years in charge he had his loyal placemen in all the key positions governing Malaysia's supposed independently run funds such as the Employee Provident Fund, FELDA, FELCRA, KWAP, Tabung Haji and so forth – all of which were therefore ripe for plundering. It was beginning to leak out that huge sums of money had been disappearing. FELDA had gone from riches to ruin and Tabung Haji was struggling too. But Najib and Rosmah still seemed confident they could sweep it all under the carpet.

The question as the election wound ever closer was whether any credible alternative might step forward. It had become clear to observers like myself that the only man of real stature who remained outside jail to confront Najib was Mahathir himself. And notwithstanding his advanced years, he had the appetite for it too. Mahathir had gone on the stump and drew crowds wherever he went. The message was simple, Najib had turned out to be a crook and was ruining the country, so he had to be turfed out.

But it was also clear that there was a deadlock between the pro- and anti-Mahathir factions of the opposition and the hope of a unified front against Najib was in question. Then in July, I learnt from two sources that both Mahathir and Nurul Izzah, the daughter of Anwar Ibrahim, and a leading politician in her own right, were due in London on separate visits. It seemed too good an opportunity to miss. Tipping off press contacts who might be interested in interviewing them I also suggested that perhaps they should meet as part of the round of interviews I had organised. I managed to catch up with Nurul just beforehand and travelled with her by cab to the location where journalists were arriving to speak to Mahathir and then herself.

I was able to pass her an assurance I had received through a third party that Mahathir was ready to agree to support Anwar's immediate release and pardon and succession as leader and sign up fully to the reformist agenda.

"If he commits to that, ought you not accept that he is your best figurehead for now and make him the temporary leader of the opposition movement?" I ventured. We swerved round Hyde Park, me facing backwards and feeling sick.

Nurul's response was so immediate and forthright that it was shocking: "Absolutely I am for it. If he will pledge himself to my father's freedom and succession on the record now, then I will support that he becomes the leader of the coalition for the election. This is not about any feelings I might have or my family, it is about rescuing the future for all Malaysians."

I got to stay for a brief moment as parties were introduced, before taking my leave. Nurul introduced me to Mrs Mahathir, with whom she had plainly maintained a cordial relationship, despite all the traumas over the years. Indeed, Siti Hasmah is about as opposite to Najib's wife Rosmah as it is possible to be. For twenty years Malaysians had admired her for her practised grace and modest manner whilst in office. When she came to London she would shop at Primark, I had been told.

"This is Clare Brown," Nurul had told the older lady, who cocked her ear a little puzzled. "The one who is the nuisance blogger," Nurul helpfully added.

"Ah!" Siti's face lit up with understanding, "*that* Clare Brown."

After their separate returns to KL, it was confirmed that Mahathir would indeed lead them as the prime ministerial candidate into the next election, with Nurul's mother Wan Azizah standing in for her husband as the deputy leader, with a pledge that the party would hand over leadership as soon as possible to the jailed Anwar.

A ray of light had emerged.

◆ ◆ ◆

And handily, just as it did, yet more evidence emerged of Najib and Rosmah's staggering excesses. As before, they had simply failed to factor in the procedures of foreign investigators and their inability to keep things under wraps outside of Malaysia jurisdiction. And once again, it was US prosecutors who bore their teeth.

In June, the DOJ's Kleptocracy Unit issued a further joint announcement. Their court filing was now being expanded from 136 pages to 251 pages. And they were now doubling their list of asset seizures from the previous year. They were also increasing their estimate for how much had been pilfered to $4.5 billion. Now it was undeniable: this was their biggest ever seizure, making it the largest ever kleptocracy action in US history.

Top of the list was Jho's super-yacht, *Equanimity*. The Feds had now traced how the vessel had been paid for. Shockingly, the final $140 million or so payment had been filched by Jho straight from an emergency loan raised from Deutsche Bank in 2014 in order (supposedly) to bail out 1MDB's spiralling debts.

The DOJ now added to their previous three phases of the scam – 'the Good Star Phase', 'the Aabar BVI Phase', and 'the Tanore Phase', with a fourth, the 'Options Buy-Out Phase' – referring to further massive-scale shenanigans in 2014, which I had also revealed.

The DOJ revealed Jho's splurge on supermodel Miranda Kerr. Given she was so beautiful and he was so pudgy, writers speculated what she had seen in him? Miranda had just wed the billionaire Snapchat owner Evan Spiegel and she hastily announced she would be handing in the diamonds Jho had given her. However, a custom made see-through baby grand piano on which she had sprawled for glamour photographs, and which Jho had given her as yet another present, was not seized. Kerr was apparently happy for it to be taken away, but it stayed put because it was too damn big to lug away.

Following suit was Leo DiCaprio, cited by his own name for the first time in this updated document, not only for receiving entertainment in Las Vegas gambling dens as a guest of Riza and Jho, courtesy of money stolen from 1MDB, but also as the recipient of a string of valuable gifts, which he appeared to have orchestrated for himself, including a Picasso painting and movie poster memorabilia. The deposition declared that DiCaprio introduced Riza to the owner of a company called Cinema Archives, who in turn put him in touch with Jho. Buying up rare and hugely expensive movie posters became an obsession, the deposition revealed. Riza and McFarland emailed each other, discussing how badly they wanted to own them. Copying in the owner of Cinema Archive, McFarland stated: "I have decided – I have to own these. It's a must. Not to mention a 1000 others… Can't sleep – obsessing." Riza replied: "Hahaha now you feel my pain!! Mwahahahaha – $$$$." McFarland replied in part: "I'm obsessing over posters… we are such neurotic obsessive creatures… WE HAVE TO OWN THEM ALL."

Meanwhile, Jho organised for purchases of paintings for DiCaprio, including in January 2014 a $3,280,000 painting *Nature Morte au Crane de Taureau* by Picasso. The painting was gifted to DiCaprio with a handwritten note in the name of Jho's proxy/alias Eric Tan "Dear Leonardo DiCaprio, Happy belated Birthday! This gift is for you."

The DOJ also demanded a photograph gifted in November 2013, *Boy with the Toy Hand Grenade* by Diane Arbus, purchased from Cinema Archives in New Jersey for $750,000, and a Basquiat oil painting, *Redman One* purchased for $9,191,040 from the Helly Nahmad Gallery in New York. All of these had been bought with money stolen from 1MDB, of course. DiCaprio handed them in.

But these gifts paled into comparison next to the staggering revelations the DOJ deposition had on Rosmah. The expense of the gifts provided for her dwarfed the money spent on the likes of DiCaprio, Jho's mum, sister and even Miranda Kerr.

After the 2013 election, the indictment confirmed, the remaining money in Najib's account, $620 million was passed back to Tanore, where it was then spent by Jho. It was from this money that the

$27.3 million Schwartz necklace mentioned earlier in this book was bought for Rosmah.

It was just the start, explained the DOJ, as it carried on describing the money trail through which such purchases were arranged:

This was far from the only time that TAN and LOW used the Blackstone Account to pay for jewelry purchases for themselves and their associates. Between April 2013 and September 2014, the Blackstone Account was used to purchase a total of approximately $200 million in jewelry from firms located around the world, using funds traceable to the 2013 bonds and the 2014 Deutsche Bank loans.

The next major haul for Rosmah was arranged the following Christmas, when Rosmah visited her son in Hollywood (while I too was there). During this stay Schwartz was again flown over to show pieces to the PM's wife. She chose no fewer than 27 different 18-carat gold necklaces and bracelets at a total cost of $1,300,000.

What on earth would Team Najib say to defend this, I wondered? Their answer was to declare that no criminal charges had been brought, so that meant no crime had taken place.

And then the prime minister made perhaps his most desperate and pathetic gambit yet: he decided to suck up to the new US President Donald Trump in the hope that the Donald might call the whole thing off.

On 13th September Najib and Rosmah, with a large entourage of Malaysians, all checked into the Trump Hotel in Washington (running up a bill into the millions of dollars according to local journalists who later contacted me) and made it known there would be an official meeting with Donald Trump. With the White House agreeing to it, Najib's spin machine went into overdrive, declaring that the Najib-Trump meeting was evidence that their man had no case to answer. What surer sign could there be that Najib was safe than the fact the US President was prepared to see him face to face?

The argument had traction in Malaysia, as critics listened dismally to the line that the all-powerful Najib had tamed his overseas enemies. Except the entire plan promptly fell to pieces. As Najib and Trump met in a White House meeting room, the cameras kept on rolling. They depicted a clearly nervous Najib seated opposite an impassive Trump, looking for all the world like a big bully-boy auditioning the latest candidate for a college 'frat'.

Then, on camera, Najib declared that the Malaysian Employee Provident Fund, a body which was supposed to be investing funds for people back home, "have got quite a big sum of capital to be exported… they intend to invest three to four additional billion dollars to support your infrastructure redevelopment in the United States." It was obvious to everybody what he was offering to Trump: if only he could get the Feds off his back, billions of dollars' worth of Malaysian investment in jets and on the stock market, all from funds like EPF and the sovereign oil fund Khazanah, would be forthcoming.

'Najib Promises To Pour Out Cash-Strapped Malaysia's Wealth Reserves 'To Help Strengthen US Economy'!' I wrote on my blog the following day. Najib's carefully constructed PR blitz collapsed. The US media made sure that anyone who wasn't aware of Trump's new chum was informed of his kleptocratic tendencies. The opposition in Malaysia was also having a field day. *Newsweek*, meanwhile, concluded that it was a meeting the White House should have avoided. "Even a photo op with Kim Jong-un would be better," it declared.

On his way back to Malaysia, Najib stopped off in London for a meeting with Theresa May. This time, he went in and out for the photo-op, with no statements, and nothing was released until he was back on the plane. During the visit, I had for the first time in months received the strange sense of being followed again and spied on as I met my colleague Christian at a coffee shop. We walked out frustrated, only to receive a text: "Najib just left Downing Street." They must have feared I would get wind and disrupt the event.

After Najib's return to Malaysia that summer, I got to work. An anonymous source had sent me the full breakdown of the expenditures from Najib's 1MDB- and SRC-funded accounts – it was the list of names which I had longed to receive back in 2015 and for some weeks I combed stories out from the pages of data. They proved that the prime minister had shelled out hundreds of millions of ringgit to his UMNO party machine to fight the 2013 election – some of it plainly designed to be disbursed at the back of election booths. Much would have seeped into the pockets of key conduits, thereby keeping them happy and loyal to Najib personally, as president of their political vice ring. There were also vast payments made out to Najib's political allies. Indeed, one former chairman of the Malaysia Chinese Association – a key component of Najib's ruling coalition – admitted he had never seen so much cash being handed out.

This was where the $681 million wired to Najib's personal bank account had ended up – it was spent on buying him an election. Hundreds of millions of Malaysian dollars had found their way to the crucial state of Sarawak. Najib's henchmen had literally flown the cash in by private plane, I was told. Yet more millions of stolen public money had gone to pay for Najib's PR operation and media support. And $3 million had gone to Najib's personal legal fixer, Shafee Abdullah, who, in 2014, had masterminded the legal strategy to overturn the High Court acquittal of the case against Anwar Ibrahim and to drive him into jail anyway. Payments to Shafee had been made just a fortnight before the Court of Appeal overturned Anwar's acquittal. Shafee, it would appear, had been handsomely paid by the prime minister who had a direct political interest in seeing his opponent jailed. And he was paying him with money stolen from the public purse.

I guess I had a personal reason for wanting to expose as much as possible. For some time I had faced a raft of legal actions. Under the notorious UK libel laws, the cost of defending such actions can be bankrupting and it has become a favourite tool for the wealthy to put pressure on British journalists to remain silent. Even with my own good-hearted lawyers willing to defer their costs, I had the problem that even in the event of winning a case in the UK, I felt hugely uncertain I would be able to enforce a court order in KL to repay my costs were Najib to remain in office. There was no way I was going to settle; it would have given a massive boost to Najib and his army of cyber warriors. But I was in no doubt: given the evidence of his influence over the judiciary, my chances of enforcing payment seemed virtually nil if he triumphed in the election. I stood to lose my home.

36. A MALAYSIAN REVOLUTION

Election day, 9th May 2018, London

I WAS in London, nervous as hell and utterly, infuriatingly powerless. I had barely slept the night before. Now, awake, I felt sick. My father, the old Sarawakian hand, was a lone voice of optimism. "When the electorate turns, it really turns," he reassured me. "What people quite rightly loathe is blatant corruption and it doesn't matter who they are or where they are." I too held out some hope that the people I had met across Malaysia – from rural Sarawak to urban KL – would recognise the folly of putting a proven thief back into power. And yet, and yet…

I went for a coffee with an old friend, a Russian-born confidante who was quick to remind me that elections were entirely hopeless, given how they could always be rigged by the ruling authorities. Stirring my coffee, I concurred. I prepared for the worst. I went home. For once, I couldn't even bear to open my laptop and see what was going on. Long experience watching sport or any kind of competition has convinced me that I only have to root for one side to ensure that the other team wins. There was nothing for it: I opened up my cleaning cupboard and started attacking a series of jobs that had been neglected over the previous few months. I scrubbed furiously away at every surface going. Wisely, my husband kept his silence. Meanwhile, in Malaysia – seven hours ahead – they continued to count.

◆ ◆ ◆

My pessimism arose for good reason. For the few months leading up to the election, Najib had thrown overboard all pretence of a fair and free system of governance and his ruling coalition had taken ever more shameless measures to try to make it impossible to defeat.

On various pretexts, the Register of Societies (ROS) announced a

30-day suspension of Bersatu, the Malay-based party that Mahathir now headed. The Election Commission also banned the Harapan coalition, which had represented the now solid alliance of opposition parties (PKR, DAP, Bersatu). The opposition parties retaliated by agreeing to go into the election under the one PKR banner. Najib simply hit back with more abuse of power. Thanks to a tame Speaker in the Malaysian Parliament, he bulldozed through the shocking re-delineation of constituency boundaries: it was gerrymandering gone crazy; after his changes went through, it was calculated that he could win a majority with just 16.5 percent of the votes.

Likewise, a so-called 'Anti-Fake News Law' was steamrolled through the Parliament in a matter of hours, supposedly to tackle the problem of 'misleading information' from news outlets, online media and even social media users. The new law allowed government to arrest anyone who it deemed to have spread 'lies' – and bang them up in jail for up to ten years, or fine them 100,000 ringgit.

It was a draconian attempt at open intimidation of government critics and indeed the entire population. It also reinforced the widespread assumption that an election was on its way. Ramadan was due to begin on 15th May and an election would not be held during that month of fasting. But Anwar was due to be released in June, and Najib would not wish to risk an election without him under lock and key.

A fatalist mood settled over the country. Frustratingly for me, it turned out that the hardest people to persuade that the opposition could win this upcoming election were the opposition themselves and worse, civil society campaigners, who had dedicated their lives to championing reform. Educated, passionate and unstinting in their work, practically every single one of these marvellous people would, every time I met them, start within seconds lecturing me as to why their cause could never win. It drove me nuts. I told them it drove me nuts. How could they win if they thought it could never happen? These people had experienced disappointment so many times, they were protecting themselves from the bitterness of failure by accepting it in advance. This time it is different, I told them.

People don't want corrupt leaders who lie and cheat and persecute their opponents. They will vote him out. And there was the Malay factor. The entire gerrymander was based on moving Malay votes around on the assumption that Malays who had voted for BN in the past would continue to vote for them no matter what. I argued they would not.

None of them believed me... and in the dark hours as the election got ever nearer, I doubted it myself.

On 7th April Najib finally called the election. The moment the campaign was launched there was another slew of measures to hamper the opposition further. Just eleven days were to be given for the campaign (making it impossible for postal votes to reach foreign parts, where the voters were overwhelmingly opposition supporters, in time) and, unprecedentedly, the election was fixed for a weekday, to make it hard for working people to reach the polling stations, which closed at 5pm.

"Don't bother to come back to vote," Nur Jazlan, now deputy home minister, told Malaysians in Singapore, who were considered pivotal opposition voters. But the bullying seemed to be having an opposite effect to the one intended, making voters all the more determined to cast their votes. In the end, the government was forced to allow a bank holiday for them to do so as employers in Malaysia and Singapore started to give their workers leave in a gesture of solidarity anyway.

When the budget airline Air Asia announced more and cheaper flights for returning voters. Najib forced it to cancel the flights and then to take part in a ghastly publicity stunt where they had to paint an aircraft Barisan Nasional blue to ferry Najib on his campaigning in Sabah to support the hated chief minister, Musa Aman.

Najib even managed to get the Election Commission to announce that Mahathir's face must not appear on opposition posters since his official party had now been banned. Malaysians were treated to the bizarre spectacle of men on ladders ordered to cut the face of the widely revered elder statesman out of posters up and down the country, whilst the smug and pudgy features of his kleptocratic opponent continued to smirk down on them.

By now, no Malaysian news media dared reproduce my stories. But they spread anyway, on private WhatsApp groups. Scenes of huge crowds gathering across the country to attend opposition rallies night after night started to be uploaded, together with contrasting images of deserted events held by BN. Khairuddin Hassan was one prolific and enthusiastic uploader of such material. "Is it true NO ONE turned up?!" I asked of one typical BN event, where money had plainly been lavished on marquees, prize draws and food, but only a handful of people could be seen in the enormous space. "Nobody!" Khairuddin replied cheerfully.

What a contrast to the unsheltered gatherings, where people came to listen to Mahathir and his top team. These vast crowds could be seen patiently waiting for hours, sometimes in pouring rain and sitting on the wet ground. No food, except for thought, for which they were plainly hungry. Was something happening? There were promising signs: the head of the navy and then the new head of the police issued instructions to their staff that every man had the right to vote according to his conscience. It was an unprecedented announcement. Voting for the ruling party had been treated as an obligation for such groups in previous elections.

Yet in the hours before polling, the tide seemed to turn and again hearts started to sink. The prime minister had retaliated with raw power. First, the causeway over from Singapore was blocked, just as hundreds of thousands of Malaysians started to queue in cars and buses to get across the night before the election. Sudden roadworks, it was announced. Desperately, stranded Malaysians sought other ways to get home: one contact told me that they had taken 19 hours to perform the one-hour trip, but they had not given up and instead taken a flight. That was just one story of many, dubbed "the Amazing Race". Malaysians scattered all over the world had in the final days built an incredible organic grassroots movement, coordinating via social media, to ensure that postal votes were signed, brought home and delivered to polling stations. Many travelled thousands of miles to do so.

On the eve of the election, Najib lashed out one last time. In an astonishing speech, broadcast across national television, he offered bribes to the entire nation. He was sweating noticeably, and stumbling in his speech. Those under 25-years-old would receive back their annual taxes if he won, he suddenly declared. There were other off-the-cuff sweeteners, including a national holiday after the election, which had already been promised by the opposition.

Here was money politics reduced to the theatre of the absurd.

◆ ◆ ◆

As the day wore on, I convinced myself that he would succeed. This was Malaysia: a country where Najib's UMNO party had ruled without break since independence 50 years before. We were naïve to think that the cash Najib had at his disposal wouldn't have a defining impact. We were daft to assume it could be any other way. I was still scrubbing. Dimly I became aware that my husband had entered the kitchen. "Clare," he said, "Come and look at this. Najib's losing."

In a flash, I was on the computer and ringing up my contacts. The situation by 5pm UK time – midnight in Malaysia – was that the parties were neck and neck on around 70 seats each. Yet something seemed to be stalling events: results would normally have been announced by this time. The reason, as would become clear, was that Najib's party wasn't losing, it was being massacred.

The PM and his coterie were in a blind panic trying to work out what the hell to do. The Malaysian online news portal *Malaysiakini* had unofficial results showing that several of the PM's allies had already lost. The service was pulled down by the providers for about an hour, but by that time WhatsApp messages were circulating mobile phone footage of people of every community out on the streets, waving the opposition Harapan flags, hugging and jumping together, cheering into the night. Try as he might to suppress the flow of news, Najib could not stop it.

Back in London my phone went into meltdown. Malaysian friends started arriving at my door, clutching food and even champagne. By 7pm UK time, from phone calls and other communications, we knew what was going on.

The results had all returned to the Election Commission, Najib had apparently gone into shock. Rosmah was crying like a baby and wouldn't stop (according to one visitor I spoke to later) and the Election Commission had frozen the announcement process to try and hold back the 'bad news'.

The National Security Council was going to be called, we heard, and Najib would make an announcement. I would later learn the details of the last desperate moments of his regime. Firstly, he rang Anwar Ibrahim in his jail cell, twice, to see if he could persuade him to form a coalition. When that failed, Najib's second gambit was escape. Tarek Tarek's brother, Nawaf, was pressed into action over in Saudi Arabia to despatch two jets, which duly arrived in the early hours, according to a source. They weren't alone; many of his key aides had smelled the coffee several hours before and had slipped out of the country via the airport as polling started.

But the couple were trapped. The airport refused landing rights and the planes were forced to return after a few hours on the ground (although not before certain officials were allegedly able to board, custodians, it is believed by some, of Rosmah's most valuable jewellery, including that notorious pink diamond worth $27 million bought from money stolen by Jho from 1MDB.)

Meanwhile, it was rumoured that opposition politicians who had won were being called up by Najib's allies and offered millions of Malaysian dollars each to cross over and back him.

There was a fear that, even then, the election could be stolen. He may have been in his 90s, but the redoubtable Mahathir realised he need to move quickly. Shortly after midnight, he announced to waiting cameras in the Sheraton Hotel that he was claiming the election, because the unofficial results confirmed he had over 112 seats, the number required to win an overall majority.

Faced with paralysis from Najib, the election commissioners started to publish the rest of the results. Once we reached that magic 112, I allowed myself to open a very chilled bottle of Bollinger, in order to ceremoniously take a symbolic gulp of celebratory bubbly.

And why not celebrate? Not a drop of blood had been spilt and a united population was dancing in the streets.

The following 48 hours would sum up the moral cowardice of Najib and Rosmah in full. Having failed to escape on the night of the election, they tried a different route, this time on another private jet owned by their business partner Peter Sondakh in Indonesia. But news of the flight manifest and its controversial guests leaked out and hundreds of angry citizens rushed to the airport to prevent what the couple later claimed had been plans for "a short holiday". The couple's passports were removed and Mahathir, who had by then finally established himself in office, despite the dallying of a clearly shocked and reluctant Agong, announced they were banned from leaving the country pending investigations into 1MDB and other crimes.

At the same time, they tried desperately to hide the ill-gotten gains they had piled up from years of corruption in high office. Hundreds of boxes were spotted being transported from their home to other properties they owned around the country. Again, however, they failed to get away with it. Acting on a complaint that a government vehicle had been used to transport the boxes to one particular KL apartment block where Najib's relatives had been staying, around 20 officers entered the marble-floored lobby of the Pavilion Residences. An array of orange boxes was carted out. When the count was done, the loot amounted to $274 million worth of items. The seizure included 12,000 pieces of jewellery, 567 handbags, 423 watches and $28 million in cash.

Two months later, on 3rd July , Najib appeared in court in KL to face charges of abuse of power and three counts of criminal breach of trust – with each charge carrying a prison term of up to 20 years. He maintained the aura of the political aristocrat, dressed in the dock in a dark blue suit. And, indeed, over the coming months, the pretence continued. But it didn't take much to puncture the façade. In October, during another PR exercise which would go disastrously wrong, Najib walked out of an interview with Al Jazeera, after reporter Mary Ann Jolley confronted him over the

1MDB money and the murders of Altantuya Shaaribuu, Hussain Najadi and Kevin Morais. "That's it, I'm done," he snapped. "Come on, you are not being fair to me… Look I've done my part and I'm not going to stand anymore for this." Najib's defence appeared to be that he too had been deceived by the dastardly Jho Low. And as for the $680 million that had landed in his personal bank account, he was still maintaining that he thought it was a "donation". The $27 million pink diamond? That too was a gift from the UAE's Sheikh Mansour, though Rosmah, he insisted, had never received it. "It's a matter of dispute what happened to the pink diamond," he declared unconvincingly. "So let's not jump to conclusions."

37. GUILTY GOLDMAN

IT'S a cliché to say it but no less true, that if a fiction writer had come up with the cast of characters involved in the 1MDB affair, they would have been dismissed as being too fantastical. Only in real life could something as demented as this scandal have occurred.

At the time of writing, Najib is on trial. He is facing 38 charges ranging from abuse of power and criminal abuse of trust. Rosmah is facing nineteen charges, including soliciting and receiving bribes of $45 million from a company pitching for a government contract. She has pleaded not guilty. On 5th July 2019, Rosmah's son Riza appeared in a Malaysian court charged with laundering $248 million from 1MDB into Red Granite. Like his mother, he too has pleaded not guilty. Joey McFarland still seems to be hanging around Hollywood, a survivor to his core. Malaysia has also filed arrest warrants for Jho Low's associates, whom he put in place in 1MDB, such as Casey Tang. In Abu Dhabi, al-Qubaisi and al-Husseiny have fallen. They were kicked out of their jobs following an investigation ordered by the Crown Prince, Sheikh Mohammed bin Zayed al-Nahyan. In June 2019, the *Wall Street Journal* reported that the two men had been found guilty of financial crimes, with al-Qubaisi sent down for fifteen years and al-Husseiny given ten. The *WSJ* also reported that the men were ordered to repay over $336 million to IPIC.

Xavier and Laura Justo are now living in Switzerland having finally received the payment that he was promised in Singapore. Meanwhile, Mahathir – now 94 years old – is still serving as prime minister. Many Malaysians who campaigned to remove Najib are expressing impatience in their desire for further reform, and an end to the corruption at the top. It's a healthy sign of how Malaysia's democratic traditions are slowly growing strength.

Jho, meanwhile, is still at large. Right up to the end, this bizarre enigmatic character was still partying – in 2017, he hired celebrities such as Nicole Scherzinger to perform at a party in Phuket, Thailand, to mark his brother's birthday. Najib's defeat in 2018, however, deprived him of his last remaining hope of political cover. As of now, and with warrants out for his arrest across the world, Jho is hiding in China – a diplomatic pawn in an extradition game where evidence from this key witness could prove embarrassing to his hosts, to say the very least. After all, it was a Chinese state company that quietly agreed to inflate the costs of a railway project by 100 percent to hide debt repayments 1MDB couldn't pay because of all the stolen money. It was China that had advanced a soft loan to bail Najib out and started to exert a swathe of disadvantageous deals on Malaysia once it appeared they had the prime minister neatly in their pocket.

But there is one final player I've left till the end. It's tempting to dismiss the 1MDB affair as a one-off: a bizarre story which only happened thanks to coming together of Najib's corruption, Rosmah's greed and Jho's brass neck. Tempting but wrong. Because none of it could have happened without the support and complicity of an array of bankers and lawyers who were keen to dip their fingers into Najib and Jho's stolen pot of cash. They were the midwives of this scandal. And, if lessons are to be learnt from the 1MDB affair, they must focus on reforming the behaviour of these masters of the universe who, twelve years on from the financial crash, are still recklessly borrowing and issuing billions with little thought of the consequences for real people.

And none more than Goldman Sachs and their star Asian banker, a man called Tim Leissner. At the time Jho and Najib hatched their plan to steal Malaysia's billions, Leissner was head of investment banking at Goldman Sachs. A tall, flamboyant German, he had already gained a reputation in Southeast Asia as an instinctive networker; a man who positively loved wining and dining clients, who could charm officials, politicians and royalty at whim. He was a party lover, like Jho, who went on to marry supermodel Kimora Lee Simonds. The flipside to this was a cavalier attitude to procedure.

But Leissner was given a long leash. With the financial crash having hit Goldman hard, there was pressure on the bank's executives across the world to find new markets with ready cash. Asia was top of the list. And Leissner was to be their star man.

He had first done business with Jho in 2009. Leissner then assiduously courted his new Malaysian friend. He would travel all over the world to meet him. In 2012, his networking paid off when Jho brought Leissner in on his new plan. He invited Leissner to Abu Dhabi for a meeting with none other than Sheikh Mansour bin Zayed, the man behind Manchester City Football Club, currently worth an estimated £40 billion. Jho and Mansour's aide Khadem al-Qubaisi were plotting their second big heist – siphoning off half of the $3.5 billion bond they wanted 1MDB to buy. They suggested Goldman organise the bond. Leissner's proposal was for Abu Dhabi to guarantee the issue of the bond, which became the mechanism for siphoning out billions in bogus payments for that favour.

It was an unusual arrangement to say the least, and red flags immediately were raised. Why couldn't Malaysia guarantee the cash, given 1MDB was its fund? Who was this Jho Low character, and what role exactly did he have in all of this? But these concerns were swatted aside by Leissner, and he was backed by his bosses. Indeed, it was disclosed afterward, by the *New York Times*, that, in 2012, Jho had been invited into Goldman's for a meeting with its long-time chairman and chief executive Lloyd Blankfein.

In other words, despite the all too pungent smell surrounding the 1MDB deal, the top executives at the mighty Goldman Sachs willingly sanctioned Leissner to press ahead with arranging billions in bonds to be given to Jho. Their price was the kind of fee that would make a loan shark proud: Goldman earned a staggering $590 million. To get an idea of how egregious this is, I learnt that its cut on the first $1.75 billion of the $6.5 billion bonds issued was eleven percent – more than 40 times the typical commission. Leissner would later admit to paying bribes and kickbacks to Jho and others – helping at one point pay millions to a jeweller for more diamonds for Rosmah.

At the time of writing, Goldman Sachs is desperately trying to limit the damage to its reputation from this shameful episode, depicting Leissner as a rogue banker. "For Leissner's role in that fraud, we apologize to the Malaysian people," David M. Solomon, the bank's new chief executive, told analysts in January 2019. "As you would expect, we have looked back and continue to look back to see if there is anything that we as a firm could have done better."

It isn't washing. While Leissner pleaded guilty to charges of money laundering and conspiring to corrupt foreign officials (and returned $43 million as part of his plea), he also told a judge that his hiding his actions from Goldman's compliance department was "very much in line" with what was expected of him. Meanwhile, it has emerged that Blankfein had praised his efforts at a presentation in 2014. "Look at what Tim and Andrea [Vella, Leissner's immediate boss at Goldman] did in Malaysia," Blankfein is reported to have said. "We need to do more of that."

Leissner is now facing up to 10 years in jail, but Goldman is on the hook. Following the election, Malaysia's government is now seeking redress. Just before Christmas 2018, prosecutors in Malaysia filed criminal charges against the bank, accusing it of defrauding investors. "We have suffered extremely large losses, and you were the financial adviser," said Lim Guan Eng, the Finance Minister of Malaysia, speaking directly to Goldman Sachs. "Now how do you account for that? And don't tell me you don't know where the money went."

Potentially more damaging still is the possibility of criminal charges in the United States. If Goldman decides to settle, it could be stung for billions of pounds. Investors have noticed, with its share price markedly lower compared to last year. It is facing one of the most serious crises in its 149-year history.

Good. The role of global banks in facilitating all the corrupt practices that has been recorded in a place like Malaysia, driving the misery and destruction that corruption brings, is at the heart of this story. More than anything, it is their behaviour that has been behind my determination to bring the whole matter to light. These billions of pounds which were spirited away from the people of Malaysia are not just numbers on a spreadsheet. The thieving has a consequence and it is paid by the poor people of that country and its degraded environment. And for 'Malaysia', read 'right across the world', because there is no doubt that, the world over, kleptocrats are being assisted in just the same way by bankers turning a blind eye.

1MDB wasn't a one-off. It is, sadly, merely an example. Just one of many cases which demonstrates what is going on in our global financial system. Bank compliance is being ignored, stolen money is being taken offshore, dark money is being hidden around the world. We are being cheated.

1MDB was the story I uncovered.

But what other scams are still to be exposed?

EPILOGUE: UNFINISHED BUSINESS

IT seems to be a fact of life (mine at least) that the moment you have a big job out of the way others loom undone.

The 1MDB affair had taken me away from where I had started – Sarawak, the Borneo state where I was born. With Najib facing trial and the US investigation rolling onwards, I have in recent months returned to the unfinished business.

In the neighbouring Borneo state of Sabah, the former chief minister Musa Aman and his UMNO henchmen had been kicked out in the same election tidal wave that accounted for Najib. He now faced a mass of charges relating to timber kickbacks I had exposed back in 2012. But my old friend Governor Taib and the entire Sarawak administration remained untouched – their own elections are not due till 2021.

Even so, the once 'safe deposit' had lost a swathe of 'rock solid' federal seats in the Parliament – a clear sign of future trouble. Taib acted swiftly to recalibrate the situation. Mahathir was an old ally. He flew over to see his colleague the day after he took office to offer an extraordinary deal. The ruling Barisan Nasional alliance was dissolved in the state and all the constituent parties joined a new coalition called GPS – which Taib promptly announced would switch sides and support the new government in the Federal Parliament. In other words, business as usual in return for being left alone to run his fiefdom as before.

It was not acceptable. After all these years the people of Sarawak also deserved to get rid of their marauding kleptocrats. To see their right to justice once again pushed aside to suit the government of the day soon sparked angry talk of independence. Ironically, that played right into the hands of Taib and his political allies who immediately postured as the 'pro-autonomy' defenders of the state against 'interference from KL.'

There was very little cogent argument in the local media to counter that canny strategy and with the federal government almost immediately distracted by internal squabbling and other issues I realised *Sarawak Report* would have to start focusing on Sarawak matters once again. I would also have to challenge the so called reforming federal government to live up to their duties and investigate the gross corruption in the state, despite evident reluctance to open that particular can of worms any time soon.

And there was another tantalising issue that had to be grasped as vigorously as possible – the opportunity to change policy on deforestation. For me, the hard work I'd put in on 1MDB would only be worthwhile if I could count the result in tree trunks – and nothing else. Above everything I shared the passionate desire of so many of Sarawak's natives peoples to try to save at least a portion of their desecrated Borneo jungle and nurture it back to its former glory.

Neither of these targets were going to be easy or welcome. Indeed, Sarawak has proved the biggest barrier to Malaysia making progress over sustainable palm oil. Whereas the rest of the country agreed to freeze further oil palm encroachments on forest lands, the state of Sarawak solidly refused to suspend another million or so hectares concessioned out for yet more deforestation.

The minister responsible bottled immediately by agreeing to revise the cap on logging. Anyone who criticised that policy (like me) was shouted down as 'unpatriotic' or 'outside interference' – there was talk of prosecutions for utterances against the national interest. It felt just like the good old days in fact.

I was left to point out the corruption behind the story of Sarawak's palm oil all over again. For example, a large chunk of the land earmarked for this new deforestation had been originally handed out (for free) to none other than Governor Taib's own son Abu Bekir. Now Abu Bekir was cashing the concessions in, selling them on to loggers for a vast profit, presumably before any awkward change of government could stop the destruction.

So I got back on the case of Taib with the benefit of a whole new national readership, people who had taken up reading *Sarawak Report* thanks to 1MDB. And it seemed to work as story after story I exposed a multi-billion dollar kleptocracy. The Taibs had even secretly taken control of a joint venture to exploit Sarawak's remaining oil and I worked with local politicians to show how half of the state budget was being siphoned off each year to service the debt on at least five billion dollars' worth of offshore loans. No one knew anything about the cash or where the money had gone to. And there were so many more such stories of theft from top to bottom.

The popular cry of outrage started to get traction, demanding the authorities investigate. I lobbied and got a grant to re-start the shortwave radio station with a view to once again giving voice to the natives of Sarawak.

And I started up a new campaign called Forest South East Asia. I started badgering the new West Malaysian political leaders, the EU and British government (and anyone else I could get my hands on) to raise global capital to fund a major regeneration project for the Borneo rainforest – money that could support the rural communities as they took up jobs replanting the jungle and developing alternative economies around more sustainable crops, tourism and local industries.

This was the future to campaign for, along with a clean and fair election for the people of Sarawak. It wasn't going to be an easy target, but there was now a much better chance of making it happen, thanks to the exposure of 1MDB.

Exposing the multi-billion dollar 1MDB heist may end up being the biggest scoop of my life and I hope it will have a global impact in tightening up the rules of a game that allowed billions of stolen money to flash across the world at the press of a button. But the sad truth is that, where there is money to be me made, corruption will continue. It means that the need for campaigning, independent journalism is more necessary now than ever if we are to have any chance of stopping well-connected powerful figures at the top of the tree continuing to steal billions from their own people.

For myself I intend to keep going. As I write this in July 2019, I'm preparing to head to Papua New Guinea to witness and report on further evidence that Malaysian timber companies are destroying thousands more acres of virgin rainforest in some of the most untouched parts of our planet. Forests that have stood for thousands of years look set to be sacrificed in the pursuit of a quick buck. There is always more to report on and expose. The scandal of 1MDB is now out of my hands. The fight to expose corruption and protect our environment continues.

AFTERWORD

IT'S being called the theft of the century – billions of the Malaysian people's money gone missing during a ten-year binge. And the scale of the wrongdoing, and how it happened, is exposed in meticulous and dramatic detail in this book by Clare Rewcastle Brown.

At great personal cost, including risks to her safety, and out of a love of Sarawak, where she was born, Clare has spent a decade investigating what's been going wrong at the highest level in Malaysia – from wanton environmental damage through the destruction of the country's forests to the unaccounted-for billions of the Malaysian people's savings. In doing so, Clare has uncovered the truth of how an elite at the top of a now discredited government authorised and benefited from downright immoral acts.

Clare, who is also my sister-in-law, charts something more than rottenness at the core of one disreputable regime: in a way no other account has successfully done, she reveals the loopholes in our modern global economy and the flaws in our global financial and legal architecture that allow wrongdoing to flourish unchecked at the highest level and for years go unprosecuted.

When she fled the country, Imelda Marcos, the then First Lady of the Philippines, left behind 2,700 pairs of shoes at the presidential palace in Manila. When, in June 2018, the home of the 'First Lady of Malaysia', Rosmah Mansor, was raided, investigators found what her daughter described as "steel safes full of jewels, precious stones and cash". The treasure trove included 567 Hermès, Prada and Chanel handbags, among them a $200,000 Hermès Birkin version; 423 watches, mostly made by Rolex; 234 brand-name sunglasses; and other luxury items that between them were estimated to be worth $274 million – on top of the $28 million cash found lying around in 26 different currencies. And this example of personal avarice is just the tip of an iceberg of greed, extravagance and waste. In total, billions have gone missing from one fund, 1MDB (1Malaysia Development Berhad) – losses on a scale few African dictators have yet been able to match and perhaps today rivalled only by Russian oligarchs.

This is not just a morality tale about corruption in high places. It is a morality tale about how what has become the economic jungle of modern globalisation costs ordinary citizens billions in lost income, lost services and lost savings when the transactions of a ruling clique are not subject to cross-border rules governing proper behaviour.

Globalisation has come to mean the free and unrestricted flows of capital that render borders porous and allow for money to be moved unsupervised and unchecked from state to state. Clare charts how the wealth of the Malaysian people – accumulated in the fund 1MDB and personally under the control of Prime Minister Najib Razak – was sent out of Malaysia and round the world, flowing into shell companies in Curacao, the British Virgin Islands, the Seychelles, the Cayman Islands and many other tax shelters and havens, the sole purpose being to disguise what is alleged in indictments by US prosecutors to be the plundering of the nation's wealth.

In recent years there have been two notorious cases of wrongdoing at the highest level: Malaysia's 1MDB and Brazil's Petrobras. Both expose the loopholes in the way we manage globalisation. But the Malaysian 1MDB theft – with its global scope and scale, and its geopolitical fall out – has reached even deeper than the oil company scandal that has engulfed Brazil.

What happened at 1MDB reflects the way modern globalisation can work to aid, rather than prevent, wrongdoing – not only enabling money to be sent at speed, at the flick of a switch, from place to place and to any and all corners of the world, but also enriching secretive tax havens operating questionable practices to hide assets and so disguise the real patterns of ownership and all too often to hide criminal acts. The money of the Malaysian people landed up in British Virgin Islands and Seychelles-based companies with accounts in Singapore through a bank owned by the United Arab Emirates. Ironically, at a time when our ability to connect and communicate instantaneously should enable us through forensic accounting to track suspicious transactions and ensure there is no hiding place for them, things have got worse, not better. As long as national legal systems are limited in their ability to monitor and supervise extra-territorial transactions, and as long as international cooperation remains ineffective and deficient, then sending money offshore will continue to deprive national treasuries of the revenues they need, leaving domestic populations worse off and in many cases impoverished.

What's more, the global economy is only as strong as its weakest link. Islands, small states and territories today advertise themselves as offshore financial markets, flags of convenience, economic free zones and tax havens – and many specialise in laundering money with laws that are so lax and easy to manipulate that no one can begin to discover who are the true beneficiaries of the wealth that is being stashed away. It is estimated that today seven trillion dollars' worth of the world's wealth is hidden away offshore, mainly to escape taxation. As long as we fail to ensure compliance from those havens and shelters, and let wrongdoers hide behind a veil of secrecy, billions that could finance decent public services will continue to be lost.

But corruption flourishes not just because these shelters, shell companies, offshore bank accounts, and dubious trusts are located in far-flung overseas territories, and often in rogue or 'bandit' states, but because they are supported by apparently respectable firms at the heart of some of the world's biggest and most advanced cities. As capital has gone global, a sufficiently significant corps of our professions, from lawyers to bankers to accountants to consultants, have facilitated these practices, excusing themselves from taking moral responsibility for activities that take place outside their own countries' jurisdictions. Despite there being world famous names involved, too many institutions have compliance departments that lack real teeth, and too often they have made the calculation that they will not suffer any reputational damage even if they fail to discharge their legal and moral obligation to report suspicious transactions. It makes it essential that legislators increase the penalties and sanctions against these intermediaries, including revoking the licences of offending firms.

Geopolitical rivalries also allow disreputable regimes to continue their wrongdoing by exploiting big power rivalries and attempting to play off one set of competing interests against another. Indeed, for a time, as Clare charts in some detail, the then Malaysian prime minister's influence reached right into the heart of the citadels of power in the United States of America. The support he then had from the USA led him to believe that his powerful contacts made him immune from exposure. And when America's justice officials woke up to the wrongdoing, for a time the Malaysian government believed they could escape scot-free by turning to China for loans that could bail them out and hide their losses.

But at last, thanks to Clare's detailed research, the truth is coming out. The story she has uncovered, which takes us from country to country, offshore shelter to offshore shelter, shell company to shell company, and from one dubious financial practice to another, will surely prompt a more rigorous scrutiny of offshore centres, tax havens and the rules that govern transnational financial transactions. At the minimum, we need, as the Panama and Paradise papers have shown, non-compliant tax havens to be blacklisted and fully sanctioned; the international exchange of tax information agreed by all countries; and the opening up of secretive trusts to public scrutiny, accompanied by wide-ranging reforms in legal, accounting and banking practices. The Malaysian people, who have had to suffer a decade of wrongdoing, deserve nothing less.

The Right Honourable Gordon Brown, FRSE
Former Prime Minister of the United Kingdom